Working with Young People

Legal responsibility and liability

The last edition of *Working with Young People* was published in 2002. Since then there have been a number of significant changes in the law relating to children. In particular, the *Adoption and Children Act 2002* and, following on from the Climbié enquiry and the Soham murders, the *Children Act 2004*. Some chapters of this book have been significantly amended to take account of these changes. New chapters have also been added reflecting current concerns. The new chapters deal with refugee and asylum seeking children, children who work, children estranged from their families, advocacy and vulnerable witnesses.

Under the *Children Act 2004*, responsibility for children's services will no longer lie with social services departments, but with Children Services Authorities. These authorities will also be responsible for much of the work currently undertaken by local education authorities. As yet, there is no date by which local authorities must effect this change. However, it is likely to take place in the near future. As a result *Working with Young People: Legal responsibility and liability* now uses the term 'local authority' in place of 'social services department' in most places in this publication. This is in line with Statutory Guidance on making arrangements to safeguard and promote the welfare of children under s.11 *Children Act 2004*. It will be important for organisations and individuals to discover whether local services are being provided by a Children's Services Authority or a social services department and to respond accordingly.

The Children's Legal Centre no longer runs a general advice line for the public, but does have a website, which provides answers to many of the questions that children and those caring and working with them raise. The website can be found at www.childrenslegalcentre.com. For those who are not able to find the answers they seek, the Centre would recommend phoning Parentline, who are able to refer callers to our advice service.

The Centre has expanded significantly since the last edition of *Working with Young People* was published. It is now able, as a result of Legal Services Contracts, to provide legal advice and representation to children from anywhere in England and Wales on all issues of law, other than criminal law and immigration. The Centre specialises in assisting advocates with legal advice for their clients, and in issues of local authority duties and human rights. Those wishing to make use of this service should telephone 01206 873873.

The Centre also operates the National Education Law Line for Legal Services Direct. Everyone is entitled to half-an-hour of legal advice on issues relating to education and to further legal advice and representation if they meet the criteria of the Legal Services Commission. This telephone number for this service is 0845 456 6811.

I would like to thank all those who helped in the writing of this new edition, in particular: Alison Fiddy for her general help with updating the text; Elaine Laken and her team for revising the police chapter; Rachel Yates for her invaluable work on anti-social behaviour and her permission to use part of her dissertation; Adrian Matthews for the refugee and asylum seeking chapter; Douglas Hiscock for his assistance with the advocacy chapter and Christine Daly for keeping everyone up to date on law and policy on a very regular basis. Last but not least my thanks to Becky Dobson, who updated the chapter on running away and has edited this book assiduously and efficiently.

Carolyn Hamilton

Director of the Children's Legal Centre
Professor of Law, University of Essex
Barrister, 1 King's Bench Walk, Temple, London

i

Contents

contents

General responsibilities and duties

Youth workers, teachers and others who have control and care of a young person for a period of time are sometimes described as being *in loco parentis*. This pre-*Children Act 1989* concept was never clearly defined in law, but was interpreted as giving teachers the delegated authority to act as a wise and responsible parent would. In terms of the duties and responsibilities of youth workers, the concept of *in loco parentis* is not particularly helpful. The law in this area is complex and it is doubtful, post-*Children Act 1989*, whether it is really applicable to youth workers.

The rights, responsibilities and duties of youth workers are best described in terms of the *Children Act 1989*. Under this Act, parents cannot transfer or surrender any of their parental responsibilities, although they can arrange for some or all of them to be met by one or more persons acting on their behalf. Although it could be argued that parents have delegated their parental responsibility, or part of it, to the youth club or project for the duration of the session attended by the young person, this gives no legal rights to youth workers, only responsibilities and duties.

The responsibility of youth workers for young people who attend their projects, clubs or activities is best defined by s.3(5) *Children Act 1989*. This section provides that an individual shall do what is reasonable for the purposes of safeguarding or promoting a child's welfare while the child is in his or her care[1]. The duties owed to children by staff of a youth club or project derive from the general law relating to negligence, assault, contract or specific statutory requirements which might arise if certain events occur.

THE DUTY OF CARE

While youth leaders or other professionals will not have parental responsibility for young people who take part in the activities run by their organisation, or attend their clubs or projects, nevertheless each youth worker will owe a legal duty of care towards those young people. This has been interpreted in case law as the duty (as opposed to the authority) to act as a careful parent would. If a member of staff causes injury or loss to a young person, by failing to carry out his or her responsibilities in a reasonable and careful way, that staff member could be held liable in negligence to the young person.

The responsibilities of a careful parent are not defined in legislation, but the courts have generally interpreted them as a duty to exercise adequate supervision. Whether a staff member is judged to have exercised the appropriate level of supervision will depend on the age and the relative maturity of the young person involved, whether the young person is affected by any disability and on the circumstances of the case.

Supervision can mean giving adequate advice and instructions, rather than constantly watching a child or young person, unless there is an obvious danger. Some activities, such as activity holidays, require greater supervision on the part of the staff (see chapter 6).

HOW FAR DOES THE DUTY EXTEND?

Sometimes children or young people attending an activity run by a youth organisation may want to leave early. This can cause a certain amount of anxiety for youth workers who may worry that they are responsible for the young person during the time of the project or youth club session, and that the young person does not have parental permission to leave. It is the duty of those running a youth project or club to take all reasonable and proper care for the safety of the children and young people attending. Where there are young children attending for a fixed session of time, there is a high duty of care to ensure that they are supervised and do not leave without the permission of their parents or at least without the knowledge of the youth workers. Where the club is a drop-in centre and the expectation is that children and young people will come and go as they please, the duty of care is much lower. The responsibility remains with the parents to make arrangements with the child. As children get older, the responsibility of the youth club for their safety changes according to their maturity. The keynote is '*reasonableness*': youth workers must do what is reasonable in the circumstances to safeguard children in their care.

Youth workers may need to take extra care in supervising learning disabled children to ensure that they do not put themselves and other young people at risk. The organiser of the youth project should ensure that there are safety measures to cover all the young people in the project or club. This may mean making special arrangements for some young people with special medical needs.

> If a young person contributes to an accident by his or her own behaviour, this does not totally negate a youth worker's liability, but it could reduce the amount of damages involved *(Fowles v Bedfordshire County Council [1996] ELR 51).*
>
> Where admission to a club is by membership only, the duty of care nevertheless extends to any other child or young person who attends with the permission of the youth organisation, whether or not he or she is a member.

The duty of care also applies to property. Thus, if a staff member agrees to look after the personal possessions of a young person, liability can arise if the property is lost or damaged, though not if the property is stolen by a third party. This applies equally to confiscated property. It is, therefore, important to have somewhere that is secure in which to keep young people's belongings.

PROTECTING CHILDREN AT YOUTH CLUBS AND PROJECTS

The *Children and Young Persons Act 1933* specifically protects young people under the age of 16 from cruel treatment, as s.1 of the Act begins:

> '*If any person who has attained the age of sixteen years and has responsibility for any child or young person under that age, wilfully assaults, ill-treats, neglects, abandons, or exposes him*' or causes or enables any of these things to happen '*in a manner likely to cause him unnecessary suffering or injury to health that person shall be guilty of [an offence].*'

Under s.11 *Children and Young Persons Act 1933*, it is an offence to expose a child under the age of 12 to the risk of being burned or scalded.

A person can only be convicted if it can be shown that the act which caused the suffering or injury was done '*wilfully*'. This has been interpreted as '*deliberately or intentionally*', rather than accidentally.

The general law on assault applies to adults, children and

CASE STUDY

The Children's Legal Centre received a telephone call from a youth organisation that had arranged a special disco during half-term for 13- to 17-year-olds. The disco was held from 8.00pm until 11.30pm on a Thursday night in the centre of town at one of the new, very fashionable night clubs. Susie, aged 14, arrived at 8.30pm. Susie told Mike, one of the youth leaders, that her parents had agreed to pick her up at 11.30pm. At 10.00pm, Susie told Mike that she was having a horrible time and wanted to go home. Mike, knowing that Susie lived some three miles away, was not happy with her travelling back on her own, and was reluctant to let her leave. Susie was adamant that she was going to leave. Mike felt he had done all that he reasonably could to prevent her leaving. When Susie's parents arrived to collect her at 11.30pm, they were very angry that Susie had been allowed to leave.

This can be a difficult situation for youth leaders: Mike was worried both about Susie's safety and the extent of his power to control her movements. He had requested that Susie ring her parents to see if she could be picked up early, or at least get her parents' consent to her leaving. Susie refused. Mike could do little in this situation other than ask Susie to stay until her parents arrived. While under s.3(5) Children Act 1989 he could take action to safeguard and promote her welfare, this does not extend to physically restraining Susie from leaving the disco. Indeed, Mike would have run the risk of being prosecuted for assault had he attempted to do so. In addition, it would not be feasible for the youth club to have a policy of locking the club and refusing to allow people to leave, as such a policy could amount to unlawful imprisonment of a child. A parent can be guilty of false imprisonment if he or she forcibly detains a child against his or her will (R v Rahman [1985] 81 Cr App Rep 349) and there is little doubt that a youth worker seeking to do the same could face a similar charge. Parents retain parental responsibility for their children even when they are at youth clubs (see D v D [1991] 2 All ER 648), in this case the parents must take responsibility for their daughter's refusal to stay at the disco, or to telephone them.

As a matter of good practice, parents should be informed of the nature of the activity offered and whether young people are expected to stay for the session or whether they may come and go at will. It is recommended that youth clubs draft a policy on the acceptability of young people leaving events early and without their parents' knowledge, and ensure that this is given to both parents and young people.

young people: anyone assaulting or even threatening to assault another may be criminally liable and/or be subject to civil proceedings.

Although corporal punishment is not specifically forbidden by statute in youth organisations – as it is in schools – its use could, and probably would, amount to assault. Under s.58 *Children Act 2004* the law on physical punishment was amended by removing the defence of reasonable chastisement in any proceedings for an offence of assault occasioning actual bodily harm, unlawfully inflicting grievous bodily harm, causing grievous bodily harm with intent, or cruelty to a child under the age of 16. This means that no assault on a child can be justified as constituting reasonable punishment and as s.58 *Children Act 2004* applies to parents it most definitely applies to those who exercise no parental role, such as youth workers.

As a matter of policy, any form of physical punishment of children should be forbidden in youth organisations. This includes smacking, slapping, pushing, pulling or shaking. It is permissible, in an emergency, to take necessary physical action to prevent physical injury either to the child or to another child or adult or, possibly even, serious damage to property. Physical action such as grabbing or restraining the child should only be used as a last resort. Physical force may lawfully be used to eject a trespasser, to prevent an accident or in defence but, only as much force as it is reasonable to use in the circumstances. In all cases where physical force is used, the circumstances of its use should be recorded in the incident book kept at the premises.

RESPONSIBILITY FOR PREMISES

Under s.2 *Occupiers' Liability Act 1957*, the 'occupier' of premises is under a duty to:
> '… *take such care as in all the circumstances of the case is reasonable to see that the visitor will be reasonably safe in using the premises for the purposes for which he is invited, or permitted by the occupier to be there.*'

An employer, and any employee who has control over the premises, may be deemed to be an 'occupier'. The term 'visitor' includes any young person who uses a club or project or has the permission of a youth worker to use it. Under s.2(3)(a) the Act also provides that people responsible for children and young people must be prepared for them to be less careful than adults.

Youth workers should be aware that they may also have certain limited duties towards trespassers. The *Occupiers' Liability Act 1984* creates a limited duty of care to trespassers. This is enforced under s.1(3)(a) provided that the occupier knows, or ought to know of the existence of the danger; under s.1(3)(b) provided that the trespasser is in the vicinity of the danger; and under s.1(3)(c) provided that:
> '…*the risk is one against which, in all the circumstances of the case, he may reasonably be expected to offer some protection.*'

Under these circumstances the occupier will owe a duty of care to the trespasser. Once again, an occupier must take greater care for the safety of children and young people.

> It should be remembered that under s.2(1) *Unfair Contract Terms Act 1977*, a project or agency cannot avoid legal liability for death or personal injury caused by negligence simply by displaying a disclaimer notice on the premises.

Responsible youth workers and employers are under a duty to take reasonable measures to ensure that accidents or injuries are prevented on the premises under their control. There are also regulations and local byelaws relating to health and safety (see p.6), and to the making of adequate arrangements for fire prevention and precautions in the event of fire. Organisations and projects should ensure they are aware of and comply with these, insofar as they relate to their particular premises. To obtain information, organisations should contact the local environmental health service and fire authority.

> Any organisation or project planning an indoor entertainment that is likely to be attended by more than 100 children should be aware of their obligations under s.12 *Children and Young Persons Act 1933* to provide sufficient attendants and take other safety precautions.

WHO HAS LIABILITY?

Where a child or parent brings a civil action for negligence, the individual youth worker whose negligent act caused the child's accident or injury may be sued and may be held personally liable for damages. However, employers can also be held '*vicariously liable*' for the actions or omissions of an employee, if that worker was negligent in the course of his or her employment (*Aldred v Nacano [1987] IRLR 292*). An employer may be held '*vicariously liable*' and sued for damages even if the worker disobeys a direct order about the way he or she should carry out the work. The correct question is not whether the employee's conduct is wrongful conduct outside the scope of employment, but whether the employee's actions are so closely connected with his or her employment that it would be fair and just to hold the employers '*vicariously liable*' for them (*Lister and others v Hesley Hall Ltd [2001] 2 FLR 307*). In practice, it will often be the employer who is sued, since the plaintiff is more likely to obtain prompt payment of damages from an employer than an employee. The principle of '*vicarious liability*' may apply in the case of those working on a voluntary (unpaid) basis (see *Mason v Essex County Council (unreported) 29 March 1988*). It is, therefore, important for agencies and projects using volunteers to make sure that their insurance policies cover them.

If a young person commits a negligent act which leads to an accident or injury whilst under a youth worker's control and supervision, that youth worker can be held liable for the

> **Lister and others v Hesley Hall Ltd [2001] 2 FLR 307**
> Between the ages of 12 and 15, the claimants had lived in the boarding annex of a school for children with emotional and behavioural difficulties. During this time, they were sexually abused by the warden. The school and boarding annex were owned and managed as a commercial enterprise by Hesley Hall Ltd. The claimants sought damages from the employer on the grounds of vicarious liability. The House of Lords held that the sexual abuse was inextricably interwoven with the carrying out by the warden of his duties. The fact that he performed those duties in a way which was an abuse of his position and an abnegation of his duty, did not sever the connection with his employment.

> **Mason v Essex County Council (unreported) 29 March 1988**
> A 16-year-old boy worked as a volunteer at a youth camp owned and managed by Essex County Council. He and a female employee were asked by the warden of the camp to load some mattresses into the back of a minibus for delivery to another youth camp. They loaded the mattresses, after which the boy was left on his own. The warden had left the minibus keys in the ignition, and the boy took it upon himself to drive the minibus to the warden's house. During the journey, he knocked down and injured an 11-year-old girl who was staying at the youth camp. The court held that, although the boy was a volunteer, he was a servant of Essex County Council, having been engaged by the warden. The Council was, therefore, 'vicariously liable' for his negligent act.

negligence. The older and more mature young people are, the more responsible they are expected to be for their own actions in the eyes of the law. Therefore, the likelihood of a youth worker being liable decreases.

The position in criminal law is somewhat different. An employer will not, as a general rule, be held liable for injury caused to a child by the criminal acts of a young person under a youth worker's control and/or supervision.

BEHAVIOUR POLICY

All youth projects and clubs should have a behaviour policy, preferably drafted with the help of, and as a result of consultation with, the young people involved. The policy should be made known to both young people and their parents. It should spell out what constitutes unacceptable behaviour, and sanctions which will be applied. Young people who breach this behaviour policy should be taken aside, and a member of staff should explain to them, calmly and clearly, why their behaviour is unacceptable. Any sanctions which are applied by the staff, such as a refusal to allow participation in a particular activity, should:
- take account of the age and stage of development of the child;

- be given at the time;
- be relevant to the actions; and
- be fair.

If a young person is causing distress and harm to other young people in the club or project, and is unable to modify his or her behaviour, youth workers should inform the parents, especially if the young person is under 16 years old. If the issue cannot be resolved, the youth organisation would generally be justified in asking that young person not to attend the club or project, but only as a last resort, after all other avenues have been explored.

MEDICAL TREATMENT

The imposition of medical or dental treatment can constitute an assault unless a valid consent to the treatment has been obtained. Young people aged 16 and over are given the right under s.8(1) *Family Law Reform Act 1969* to consent to or refuse medical treatment. Children and young people under the age of 16 may provide consent to their own medical treatment if they are deemed by the doctor to have the '*understanding and intelligence*' necessary to understand the nature and consequences of the medical treatment in question (see *Gillick v West Norfolk and Wisbech Area Health Authority and the Department of Health and Social Security [1985] 3 ALL ER 402*, and see also chapter 5).

When a child is not deemed capable of consenting to treatment, the consent of a parent or someone with parental responsibility is considered necessary.

Youth workers are not in a position to provide consent to medical treatment for a child. However, in emergencies, where immediate medical treatment is required, a doctor may go ahead with the treatment, even in the absence of consent. In rare cases where a parent objects to medical treatment that is deemed necessary by a doctor, an application may be made for a Specific Issue Order or, in exceptional circumstances, a child may be made a ward of court and the court may authorise medical treatment. Where youth clubs or projects are involved in activities which carry a risk of injury, or where young people are taking part in a trip away from their parents, youth organisations should, as a matter of good practice, ask the parents to sign a consent form agreeing to necessary medical treatment in the event that they cannot be contacted (see chapter 6).

YOUNG PEOPLE WITH DISABILITIES

DISCRIMINATION
The law relating to the provision of services for young people with disabilities is complex. It is governed by the *Children Act 1989*, the special educational needs provisions in the *Education Act 1996* and the *Disability Discrimination Act 1995* (DDA). The DDA is the most significant of these, as it extends the anti-discrimination principle to disabled people

and seeks to ensure that they have equal access to services as non-disabled people.

Definition of disability

Under s.1(1), a person has a disability for the purposes of the *DDA* if:

> *'... he has a physical or mental impairment which has a substantial and long-term adverse effect on his ability to carry out normal day-to-day activities.'*

Disabilities covered by the *DDA* include:

- sensory impairments, for example impaired vision or hearing;
- learning disabilities;
- diabetes;
- epilepsy;
- mobility impairments;
- severe disfigurements; and
- progressive conditions, such as HIV and Multiple Sclerosis.

This list is by no means exhaustive. However, the *DDA* excludes some conditions from the definition of disability, including:

- addictions, including nicotine, drugs and alcohol, unless as a result of provision through a prescription;
- seasonal allergies, such as hayfever, unless it aggravates another condition;
- a tendency to start fires or steal;
- a tendency to sexually or physically abuse others;
- exhibitionism; and
- voyeurism.

Definition of discrimination

A claim under the *DDA* may be based either on less favourable treatment or on a failure to make reasonable adjustments. Under s.20, a service provider discriminates against a disabled person if it:

- for a reason which relates to a disabled person's disability, treats him or her less favourably than it treats or would treat others; or
- has a practice, policy or procedure which makes it impossible or unreasonably difficult for disabled people to make use of a service which it provides, or is prepared to provide, to other members of the public.

The *DDA* states that it is unlawful for a service provider to discriminate against a disabled person by:

- refusing to provide (or deliberately not providing) any service which it offers or provides to members of the public;
- providing service of a lower standard or in a worse manner;
- providing service on worse terms; or
- failing to comply with a duty to make reasonable adjustments (under s.21 *DDA*) if that failure has the effect of making it impossible or unreasonably difficult for the disabled person to make use of any such service.

The duty to make reasonable adjustments

Under s.21 *DDA* the duty to make reasonable adjustments comprises a series of duties falling into three main areas:

- changing practices, policies and procedures;
- providing auxiliary aids and services;
- overcoming a physical feature by:
  - removing the feature;
  - altering it so that it no longer has that effect;
  - providing a reasonable means of avoiding the feature; or
  - providing a reasonable alternative method of making the service available to disabled people.

A service provider's duty to make reasonable adjustments is a duty owed to disabled people at large. It is not simply a duty that is weighed up in relation to each individual disabled person who wants to access a service provider's services. The duty to make reasonable adjustments is a continuing duty and not something that needs simply to be considered once and then forgotten.

What is a reasonable step for a particular service provider to have to take depends on all the circumstances of the case. It will vary according to:

- the type of services being provided;
- the nature of the service provider and its size and resources; and
- the effect of the disability on the individual disabled person.

It is more likely to be reasonable for a service provider with substantial financial resources to have to make an adjustment with a significant cost than for a service provider with fewer resources.

Justified discrimination

Under s.20 *DDA* discrimination on the grounds of disability is potentially justifiable if, in the opinion of the provider of the services (and that opinion must be reasonable), one or more of the following conditions is satisfied:

- the treatment is necessary in order to avoid endangering the health and safety of any person (which may include that of the disabled person);
- the disabled person is incapable of entering into an enforceable agreement, or of giving informed consent;
- where the case relates to a refusal to provide a service, the treatment is necessary because the provider of the services would otherwise be unable to provide the service to members of the public;
- where the case relates to the standard or manner of the service or the terms on which it is provided, the treatment is necessary in order for the provider to be able to provide the service to the disabled person or to other members of the public; or
- where the case relates to different terms of service, the difference in the terms on which the service is provided to the disabled person and those on which it is provided to other members of the public, reflects the greater cost

to the provider in providing the service to the disabled person.

Both statutory and voluntary youth services are covered by the *DDA* and so they both need to be aware of actions that could constitute discrimination.

HEALTH AND SAFETY

There are no health and safety regulations applying specifically to youth organisations. However, employers are under a duty to provide a healthy and safe workplace for employees. The duties of the employer are laid out in the *Health and Safety at Work Act 1974* and a number of statutory instruments, including the *Management of Health and Safety at Work Regulations 1999*. There is also guidance from the DfES, *Health and Safety: Responsibility and Powers* (DfES 0803/2001). Although this applies primarily to schools and to statutory youth groups, non-statutory youth groups will also find the guidance useful.

The statutory Regulations cover duties towards employees, but also require that each employer shall make a suitable and sufficient assessment of '*the risks to the health and safety of persons not in his employment arising out of or in connection with the conduct by him of his undertaking*' for the purposes of identifying the measures that need to be taken to meet their statutory obligations. This would cover youth clubs and the activities of other voluntary organisations. Thus, youth organisations, and all other organisations working with children, should carry out a general assessment of the risks to health and safety faced by their users.

If an organisation employs young people under the age of 18, it will owe duties over and above that which it owes to adult employees. The organisation must also take account, in assessing risk, of the lack of experience and awareness of risks, and the immaturity of young people. If the organisation employs a child, defined in the Regulations as a person under the age of 16, it must not only carry out an assessment of risk, but must also provide a parent with information on the risks to that child's health and safety.

The need for schools to address the health and safety of their pupils, both in school and on educational trips, is covered by DfES Circular 14/96 and DfES Guidance, *Health and Safety: Responsibility and Powers* (DfES 0803/2001). This Circular places a duty on the local education authority to ensure the health and safety of both their employees (the teachers etc.) and pupils.

RISK ASSESSMENT

It may be worth undertaking a risk assessment, which is nothing more than a careful examination of potential hazards in buildings and in activities. Possible hazards are dealt with by taking adequate precautions in order to minimise the risk of harm.

A hazard is something which can cause harm (e.g. high

stacks of chairs, uneven floors, unsafe electrical equipment, blocked fire exits, lack of fire escape signs, missing light bulbs, overfilled cupboards, high shelves, loose carpets etc.).

A risk is the chance, great or small, that someone will be harmed by the hazard.

It is not necessary to write risk assessments for venues that have already gone through this procedure (e.g. a hotel or youth hostel).

The procedure for carrying out a risk assessment should consist of the following stages:

Stage 1 – Identify hazards
- Walk around the premises, looking out for things that could reasonably be expected to cause harm.
- Consult other people about what they consider could cause harm.
- Consult accident reports to identify previous hazards.

Stage 2 – Consider who might be harmed and how this could happen
- young children;
- visitors;
- members of the public; and
- parents.

Stage 3 – Establish risks and take action to eliminate or minimise them
- How likely is it that the hazard could cause harm?
- Can more be done to reduce the risk?
- Assess the significance of each risk – high, medium or low – both before and after you have taken action to reduce the risk.

Stage 4 – Record findings and action taken
- The record should show that a proper check was carried out.
- The hazard should be recorded, and an assessment of the risk recorded as high, medium or low.
- The action taken should be recorded showing the date and the name of the person carrying out the remedial action.
- The level of risk that the hazard presents after action is taken should be low.

For more detailed information about conducting a risk assessment, contact the Health and Safety Executive (telephone: 08701 545500, website: www.hse.gov.uk).

FIRST AID

The *Health and Safety (First Aid) Regulations 1981* (SI 1981/917) and the approved Code of Practice, *First Aid at Work* (1997 HSE Books), which gives practical guidance with respect to the Regulations, set out the essential aspects of first aid that employers have to address. The Regulations do not oblige employers to provide first aid for anyone other than their own employees. Indeed, Regulations requiring first aid provision for members of the public cannot be made under the *Health and Safety at Work Act 1974*. However, many organisations, such as schools and youth clubs, provide a service for others, and employers may wish to include them in their assessment of needs and make provision for them – the Health and Safety Executive strongly recommends that they do so. Employers should be aware that the compulsory element of employers' liability insurance (see p.8) does not cover litigation resulting from first aid to non-employees. However, many public insurance policies do cover this aspect, and employers may wish to check their public liability insurance policy on this point.

Each employer should make an assessment of first aid needs, taking into account the activities carried on at the premises. Regulation 3 *Health and Safety (First Aid) Regulations 1981* provides that first aid provision needs to be adequate and appropriate in the circumstances. However, Regulation 3(4)*Health and Safety (First Aid) Regulations 1981* states that where the assessment of needs indicates that the activities taking place on the premises are such that a qualified first-aider is not necessary, the minimum requirement on an employer and, by analogy, on a youth organisation, is to appoint a person to take charge of the first aid arrangements, including looking after the equipment and facilities, and calling the emergency services when required. It is recommended that, as a matter of good practice, at least one person with a relevant first aid qualification should be present at any youth activity. Failing that, there should always be an appointed person with responsibility for first aid, although that person need not hold a relevant qualification in first aid. A failure to provide first aid to young people when they are injured during an activity could lead to a claim for damages for negligence if the young person suffers damage as a result.

What first aid should you give?

Before taking up first aid duties, a first-aider must hold a valid certificate of competence in first aid at work, issued by an organisation whose training and qualifications are approved by the Health and Safety Executive[2]. First aid at work certificates are only valid for the length of time the Health and Safety Executive decides (currently three years), and employers need to arrange refresher training with re-testing of competence before a certificate expires. First aid is defined as follows:

- in cases where a person will need help from a medical practitioner or nurse, treatment for the purpose of preserving life and minimising the consequences of injury and illness until such help is obtained; and
- treatment of minor injuries which would otherwise receive no treatment or which do not need treatment by a medical practitioner or nurse (Reg. 2(1) *Health and Safety (First Aid) Regulations 1981*).

First-aiders should not step beyond the definition of first aid, or seek to provide treatment beyond their competence.

It is essential to provide the first-aider with a book in which to record incidents and injuries. While there is a duty to report accidents suffered by employees under the *Reporting of Injuries, Diseases and Dangerous Occurrences Regulations 1995*,

these regulations do not apply to volunteers or to the young people themselves. However, there may be a duty to report an accident to the Health and Safety Executive, to the Environmental Health Department or the local authority. The organisation may also be faced with potential liability under the *Occupiers' Liability Act 1984* (see p.8) if the organisation owns the premises.

If a young person attending a youth club or project suffers from an illness or disability, it may be useful to look at the guidance in *Supporting Pupils with Medical Needs in School* (DfES Circular 14/96), and *Managing Medicines in Schools and Early Years Settings* (DfES Circular 1448/2005) on caring for the young person within the youth organisation. The Guidance recommends that in the case of some young people it may be helpful to draw up individual procedures, in the form of a health care plan, to ensure their safety.

For further information, contact the Health and Safety Executive (Infoline: 08701 545500; website: www.hse.gov.uk).

INSURANCE

It is very important for projects and agencies working with young people to ensure that they are properly covered by insurance. When seeking to obtain appropriate insurance, it is worth approaching an insurance broker. The British Insurance Brokers Association (BIBA House, 14 Bevis Marks, London EC3A 7NT. Telephone 0870 950 1790) will supply details of local member firms. Alternatively, an independent approach may be made to a number of insurance companies to assess what kinds of cover are on offer and to compare costs, although a broker will also do this. For information on insurance companies, contact can be made with their trade association – the Association of British Insurers (51 Gresham Street, London EC2V 7HQ. Telephone 020 7600 3333).

Insurance policies can be tailored to meet the needs of individual projects. They should always be thoroughly checked to ensure that they do cover all the eventualities a project may be faced with. The following forms of insurance should be considered.

PROFESSIONAL INDEMNITY

A professional indemnity policy can cover the damages, costs and expenses involved in claims for breach of professional duty by reason of negligence, error or omission. Projects and agencies that offer advice to young people should consider taking out a professional indemnity policy. Standard policies do not normally cover claims brought about by libel or slander, by dishonest or criminal acts or omissions, or by loss of documents, but they can be extended to provide this cover. Professional indemnity insurance can apply to the errors and omissions of employees and also to errors or omissions in carrying out work under the supervision of employees (e.g. by volunteers).

PUBLIC LIABILITY

This covers claims against an employee or employer by third parties (i.e. those who are neither employees nor employers). If accidental injury is caused, or someone's property is lost or damaged as a result of an employee's or employer's negligence, they could be sued for damages. As explained earlier, liability for personal injury caused by negligence cannot be avoided simply by displaying a disclaimer notice. Public liability insurance is, therefore, essential for any project or agency working with young people. The insurers should be informed in detail of the activities involved to ensure that the cover is comprehensive. Public liability insurance policies may also be extended to provide an indemnity in respect of liability arising out of defective products.

A number of insurance companies now make it a requirement of cover that agencies and projects working with children have in place a policy to deal with the vetting of youth workers and volunteers to try and screen out those who might abuse children. Many insurance companies have drawn up guidelines for such policies (see chapter 2).

EMPLOYERS' LIABILITY

If a worker becomes ill or is injured as a result of negligence or breach of a statutory duty by an employer or fellow employee, that worker may sue the employer. If an agency or project employs a worker under a contract of employment, the *Employers' Liability (Compulsory Insurance) Act 1969* provides that the employer must insure against such liability. If youth workers are paid by an outside body and seconded to a project or agency, the responsibility for employee liability insurance normally remains with the outside body, but this should be verified. The project managers or agency will, of course, be responsible for extending their own public liability insurance.

Volunteers are not necessarily covered under employers' liability insurance; it is important to check their position and arrange special cover if necessary.

PERSONAL ACCIDENT

If youth workers are injured in the course of their work, but the employer is not held responsible for that injury, the injured youth worker might not receive any compensation. Personal accident insurance can cover compensation for injury, as defined in the policy, when a youth worker has an injury that would, in the absence of negligence, not otherwise be covered.

Personal accident insurance can also be extended to cover sickness (for instance, to insure against extra costs involved if a youth worker is taken ill whilst on holiday with a group of young people).

PROPERTY

Fire insurance is essential. Where a youth organisation owns the building or premises, it will be responsible for the insurance. Where the premises are rented or leased, the youth organisation will often be responsible under the terms of the tenancy or lease for maintenance and/or insurance. Cover for contents is also essential. A public liability policy will normally cover liability for damage by fire to neighbouring houses or premises. Insurance of property can also cover storm, flood, riot, burst pipes, malicious damage and other eventualities. Theft insurance can cover loss or damage where the thief uses force to break into, or out of, the premises. Commercial policies do not normally cover theft where the thief is legally on the premises.

It may be possible to get 'all risks' insurance to cover loss or damage to property on or off the premises. It is important to check an 'all risks' policy to ensure that it does cover all the situations envisaged. (It may also be useful to draw the attention of young people involved in projects to the possible existence of cover in respect of their personal belongings as part of their family's household comprehensive contents insurance.)

YOUNG CARERS

This group of young people will not always be identified either by their school or by the local authority. The young people concerned may be of almost any age - children as young as seven and eight have been known to provide help and support within families where a member is sick or disabled. It is not known how many young people provide family members, most usually parents or siblings, with significant amounts of practical care and support. This help may include managing medication, lifting and helping family members to the toilet. Young people will provide support not only to parents who are physically disabled, but also to those who are mentally ill and drug or alcohol abusers. The consequences can be disruption of their school life, loss of social contacts through leisure and risk of significant harm.

In the majority of situations, parents who are ill or disabled are entirely capable of exercising parental responsibility and should be supported in doing so. A report produced by the Social Services Inspectorate about services to disabled parents, *A Jigsaw of Services*[3], comments that parents who were reluctant to seek help were:

> '... scared that the children would be taken away; and/or they were concerned that there would be difference of view about what was an appropriate level of caring to be provided by the children.'

The Report also notes that in some cases young carers were constrained to use such facilities as school clubs to carry out their work because of '*lack of assistance in getting to school*' and '*lack of help in the evenings to give them time to do their homework*'[4]. It suggests that:

> '*Young Carers*' schemes should consider very carefully when plugging gaps in statutory services as responsibility may be shifted from a mainstream universal service with more secure funding to a targeted service often with less secure funding.'

Youth workers are particularly well placed to support young

people who are fearful of seeking help, but may be in significant need of assistance.

The importance of ensuring that young carers do receive appropriate support is now recognised in both education and local authority provisions.

EDUCATION

Social Inclusion: Pupil Support (DfES Guidance, Circular 10/99) suggests that schools should recognise the needs of young carers, allowing leave of absence where appropriate and providing work to be done at home. The Circular also suggests that schools should consider designating a member of staff to take responsibility for the needs of young carers and contribute to schemes that help them, working with local authorities and voluntary agencies[5].

LOCAL AUTHORITIES

Young carers may be entitled to support as a child in need under s.17 *Children Act 1989*. In such a case, the local authority should carry out an assessment under the *Framework for the Assessment of Children in Need and their Families*[6] to make sure that all the relevant services are provided. The Framework states that young people should not be expected to carry out inappropriate levels of caring that have an adverse effect on their development and life chances, and also draws attention to the role of health authorities in supporting the family.[7] Services may include:

- advice, guidance or counselling;
- occupational, social or cultural activities;
- home help (which may include laundry facilities); and
- assistance to allow the child concerned or the family to have a holiday.

As well as confirming that the needs of the young carer are met, local authorities should also ensure that they have carried out the appropriate assessment for the parent. Support for a disabled parent under the *National Health Service and Community Care Act 1990* and the *Chronically Sick and Disabled Persons Act 1970* can include:

- adaptations to the family home suggested by an occupational therapist;
- help with bathing and personal care;
- home help; and
- access to support groups and outside activities.

Young people who are providing care to adults are likely to be entitled to an assessment under:

- the *Carers (Recognition and Services) Act 1995*, which permits people providing care to others under the terms of the *National Health Service and Community Care Act 1990* to ask for an assessment of their own needs; or
- the *Carers and Disabled Children Act 2000*, which allows local authorities to offer support to carers who are 16 and over, even if the person for whom they are providing care has refused an assessment for, or the provision of, community care services.

YOUNG CARERS AND THEIR SIBLINGS

Young people frequently provide support to a brother or sister who is disabled in some way. The *Children Act 1989* recognises that the presence of a child in need, such as a disabled child, may have an impact on the lives of siblings by giving powers to local authorities to provide a service to them under s.17. It is not certain that a carer's assessment would be offered to a child in a setting where they were looking after a brother or sister if a parent was present and also provided care.

FINDING OUT ABOUT WHAT IS AVAILABLE

Local authorities have a duty to publish information about the services they provide to children, young people and adults, and this information should be available on request.

Young carers can face substantial difficulties in getting the help they need because several organisations, such as schools, health and local authority services for children and adults, may have to work together to provide the right package. Youth workers can play an important role in helping the young people find their way through what can be a daunting process.

CONNEXIONS

The Connexions Service is the Government's support service for young people aged 13 to 19 in England. It aims to provide advice and guidance to assist them in making the transition to adulthood and working life. The particular focus of the service is providing support in the areas of education and employment, although it can also provide help and advice on others issues, such as drug abuse, sexual health and housing.

The Connexions Service has brought together existing agencies in the public, private and voluntary sectors to provide support. The Service is delivered through 47 local Partnerships working to national planning guidance (See www.connexions.gov.uk).

PERSONAL ADVISERS

A fundamental tenet of Connexions is to make Personal Advisers (PAs) available to all young people between the ages of 13 and 19. PAs work in a range of settings, including schools, colleges and one-stop shops. They are able to provide information, advice and practical help with any problems or issues that affect young people in school, college, work or personal life.

HOW DOES A YOUNG PERSON FIND A PERSONAL ADVISER?

Each school should have a Personal Adviser available in the school for a minimum of one day per week, but Connexions also run outreach and drop-in centres. A young person can access the service by a variety of routes:

- Self-referral – for example, in school or college, at Connexions centres, through the Youth Service, over the telephone or via the internet.

- Parental or carer referral.
- Professional referral. Where a child is in either the formal or informal education sector, he or she can be referred by the school, college, training provider or a youth worker. Where a child is not in school, he or she should be considered a priority client and may be referred by any agency in contact with the young person.

CONNEXIONS DIRECT

This is the helpline section of the Connexions Service, which can be accessed via telephone, email, text message or live online chatrooms. Advisers at Connexions Direct provide advice and signpost young people on to other sources of help if appropriate. If an adviser and a young person agree that face-to-face support is required, Connexions Direct will refer the young person to the local Connexions Partnership for one-to-one support from a Connexions Personal Adviser.

COMPLAINTS

There is no national formal complaints procedure for making a complaint about the Connexions Service, but local Connexions Partnerships should have some kind of policy and procedure for making a complaint.

FOOTNOTES:

1. s.175 *Education Act 2002* imposes a more specific duty on local education authorities and the governing bodies of maintained schools and further education colleges to make arrangements for ensuring that their functions are exercised with a view to safeguarding and promoting the welfare of children.

2. Code of Practice para 48.

3. *A Jigsaw of Services: Inspection of services to support disabled adults in their parenting role.* 2000. Department of Health.

4. Ibid. para 4.12.

5. *Social Inclusion: Pupil support.* DfES Guidance, Circular 10/99. para 3.10-3.12.

6. *Framework for the Assessment of Children in Need and their families.* 2000. Department of Health.

7. Ibid. para 3.62-3.63.

Recruitment:

Appointing staff and volunteers to work with children and young people

It is important that youth organisations involved in the recruitment of staff and volunteers to work with children understand the importance of vetting applicants and how to do it appropriately.

Organisations working with children and young people need to give considerable thought to the ways in which they select their staff and volunteers. As the Soham murders proved, dangerous people can slip through even apparently safe systems with devastating consequences for children. It is also well known that many abusers actively seek out situations that provide access to children and young people. It is frightening to consider that:

'*Most people have never knowingly met or seen a child abuser. This may lead us to imagine that anyone capable of such appalling acts must appear and behave very differently from the rest of society. We may persuade ourselves that no one we know could ever abuse a child. Yet it is likely that most of us will know or meet at least one abuser during our lives, probably without being aware of it*'.[1]

Although in the vast majority of cases checks on potential staff and volunteers will prove negative or show only the most trivial of offences, in the context of the danger a minority of people may pose, it has become essential to undertake thorough checks.

This Chapter does not deal with the processes involved in the management of crèches and day nurseries, or with services subject to registration and inspection by the Commission for Social Care Inspection, namely fostering, adoption and residential care. These services are subject to strict regulatory requirements developed as a result of the *Care Standards Act 2000*.

WHAT DOES THE LAW REQUIRE?

The law in this area is detailed and often confusing due to the piecemeal amendments of legislation at different times and for various reasons. However, although the law does not explicitly state the range of people working with children who must be checked, it does make clear who is disqualified from working with them.

The starting point is Part II *Criminal Justice and Court Services Act 2002*. This Act states that it is an offence for an employer to permit a disqualified person from working in a '*regulated*' position with children. Individuals disqualified from working with children include:

- people on a list kept under s.1 *Protection of Children Act 1999* (individuals considered unsuitable to work with children);
- people subject to direction under s.142 *Education Act 2002* (prohibition of teaching etc); or
- people subject to a disqualification order under the *Criminal Justice and Court Services Act 2000* (having committed a sexual offence or an offence of violence against

a child or having been involved in the supply of drugs to a child).

WHAT IS A REGULATED POSITION?

These are positions which involve regular, close contact with children, or where the person concerned is in a position of trust in an organisation working with children and young people, such as a school governor or the trustee of a children's charity.

'*Regulated*' positions include:

- work in institutions such as detention centres, hospitals, children's homes, schools or colleges;
- work on day care premises;
- caring for, training, supervising or being in sole charge of children;
- work involving unsupervised contact with children;
- caring for children under the age of 16 in the course of their employment; and
- supervision or management of people in regulated positions.

Other regulated positions include:
- school governors or governors of further education colleges;
- directors of Children's Services Authorities and chief education officers; and
- charity trustees of a children's charity[2].

WHAT SHOULD YOUTH ORGANISATIONS DO TO MAKE SURE THAT THEY DO NOT EMPLOY DISQUALIFIED PEOPLE?

Youth organisations who employ staff to work in 'regulated' positions need to undertake background checks on prospective staff, whether they are paid staff or volunteers, as well as on management committee members and trustees. The process of checking is usually called 'vetting', but the legal term is 'disclosure'. The check involves confirming that the person concerned does not have a history of abusing or exploiting children, or is unsuitable to work with them for other reasons.

The regulated status of a position should be advertised and should indicate the level of check required. Once an interview has taken place and a decision has been reached an offer of employment should be made conditional on the outcome of an appropriate Disclosure. Disclosures are *complementary* to existing recruitment practice and should only be sought after a candidate has been made a provisional offer of employment. It is not appropriate to make background checks on all the applicants for a post.

CONSIDERATIONS WHEN CARRYING OUT A BACKGROUND CHECK

Once a decision has been made to appoint an employee or to take on a volunteer, a decision needs to be made about whether a Disclosure should be obtained. All regulated positions *must* be subject to Disclosure. There are, however, a number of other positions which do not fall within the definition of regulated, but which an organisation may feel ought to be subject to a Disclosure. For instance, administrative staff who are involved in work giving them access to detailed information about the children supported by the organisation[3]. In law, Disclosures are *not* needed for all staff and volunteers, particularly where access to children is fleeting or irregular. Organisations can make their own judgements as to whether employees should undergo Disclosures. However, it has to be

The Criminal Records Bureau can provide two levels of background information: *Standard* or *Enhanced* Disclosure. There is an additional provision which allows individuals to apply for *Basic* Disclosures. These only hold information about convictions which are '*not spent*' and would not be an alternative to either a *Standard* or an *Enhanced* Disclosure required for a '*restricted*' position. *Basic* Disclosures are not currently available.

Standard Disclosure
This Disclosure will reveal any record of:
- cautions;
- reprimands;
- warnings; or
- convictions (including those spent under *Rehabilitation of Offenders Act 1974*).

It will indicate whether or not an individual has a record. If the applicant will have regular contact with children under 18 years old, it will also check DfES records of people considered unsuitable to work with children within the social care, health and education services. The *Standard* Disclosure will reveal whether the applicant is in any way barred or disqualified from working with children.

Enhanced Disclosure
In addition to the information provided by the *Standard* Disclosure it will provide all non-conviction information from local police records. Non-conviction information is likely to include such material as whether a person has been subject to an investigation for alleged child abuse or is suspected of association with abusive activity. Such information may be highly sensitive and requires extreme discretion in its use.

Enhanced Disclosures are sought for posts which regularly involve training, supervising, caring for, or being in sole charge of children and young people under 18. They are also used for the managers of such staff and the trustees of children's charities.

said that the decision whether or not to check can be difficult and many youth organisations have decided to check all staff working in their projects and services.

If it is felt that this is too burdensome and that not all staff should be subject to vetting, the following guidelines may be helpful in reaching a decision whether or not they should be checked. They should generally be considered as a whole, although there will be situations in which one factor alone will mean that a Disclosure is justified.

Does the position involve one-to-one contact?

Such contact is relevant, especially if it occurs on a regular basis, away from children's homes, or out of sight and hearing of other adults or children.

Is the position unsupervised?

Where no other responsible adult is likely to be present, and the position involves appreciable periods of time with children, this should be taken into account.

Is the situation an isolated one?

There is greater vulnerability where a child is living away from home, in residential care, where the child is far from the parental home or where parental visits are infrequent. A similar situation could arise where there is opportunity to take children away from the family surroundings.

Is there regular contact?

The more regular contact a person has with the same child, or group of children, the greater the risk. This is especially so if the contact is unsupervised or occurs away from other children. Intermittent limited contact would not normally be regarded as constituting substantial access for the purpose of requesting checks. Checks should not be carried out where an individual works at, or visits, establishments where children are present, as part of their duties. However, should those duties bring them into unsupervised direct contact with the same children on a regular basis checks may be appropriate.

Are the children particularly vulnerable?

It may be considered that younger children are more vulnerable and less able to protect themselves than older children, but the nature of the risk involved must also be considered. Younger children may be more at risk of sexual abuse; older children from drugs. More particularly, children with a physical or learning disability, or who have social or behavioural problems, are likely to be more vulnerable than those who are without disability or have a stable home background.

> Organisations should not rely on the fact that a person is known to an existing member of staff or volunteer as evidence that they are not a potential abuser.

HOW DOES A YOUTH ORGANISATION GO ABOUT OBTAINING A DISCLOSURE?

Background checks are carried out by the Criminal Records Bureau (CRB). In order to obtain a check, organisations must first either register with the CRB or use an umbrella body. Most youth organisations and bodies will find it easier to use an umbrella body, especially if they:

- do not have the administrative resources to undertake the documentation necessary;
- are unwilling to pay the registration fee that the CRB requires;
- are unable to comply with the storage and handling provisions of the *CRB Code of Practice*; or
- another organisation has stated that they are willing to countersign applications on their behalf.

The list of umbrella bodies may be obtained from the CRB website[4]. They are generally employment agencies, large voluntary organisations or public sector services, such as local authorities. Organisations which make use of umbrella bodies must agree to comply with the *CRB Code of Practice* and the standards of confidentiality and security which it requires.

> **Criminal Records Bureau**
>
> The Criminal Records Bureau was set up in 1997 as an executive agency of the Home Office to carry out criminal record checks where the law required this. It operates according to a Code of Practice which includes details about use and handling of information disclosed.

> Any person for whom a Disclosure is required must complete a form issued by the CRB, giving details of personal information and history. The form must be countersigned by an approved signatory who must have seen specified documents, such as a passport and a utility bill or bank statement, which give proof of identity and address. The applicant must sign the form and express consent to disclosure as required by the *Data Protection Act 1998*.

POLICE RECORDS

The check against police records is the best known part of the Disclosure process and is made against national and local police records.

National records include details of people who have been convicted of more serious offences, called reportable offences. These are people who have committed crimes for which a term of imprisonment may be given. They also hold records of those for whom a prosecution for such an offence is pending, but who have yet to be found guilty.

Local police authorities exercise discretion about the retention of records, but convictions for minor offences, cautions and reprimands and bind-overs (which may not have involved an admission of guilt) are likely to be available. The police may also hold other factual information arising from an investigation, as a result of an acquittal or a decision not to prosecute, where the circumstances of the case were such that they gave rise to a cause for concern.

In certain cases, information may be disclosed, about which the prospective employee is unaware. For instance, the CRB check may indicate that the employee's partner has been convicted of supplying drugs to a child (an offence which would disqualify the partner from working with children). In such instances, the employer may wish to discuss with the police how this information should be managed and the impact this information is likely to have on the decision to employ.

WHAT IF THE RECORD INDICATES CRIMINAL CONVICTIONS?

If potential employees or volunteers have a conviction for one of the offences that would result in them being disqualified from working with children within the meaning of Schedule 4 *Criminal Justice and Court Services Act 2000*, they are not permitted to work in a regulated position. It does not matter how long ago convictions took place.

IS IT AN OFFENCE TO EMPLOY A PERSON WHO IS DISQUALIFIED FROM WORKING WITH CHILDREN?

When the police record check shows other convictions, the employing body will need to make a judgement as to the suitability of the applicant. The very fact that an employee may have a criminal record will not necessarily mean that he or she is unsuitable. Research has shown that one adult male in three will have a criminal conviction (excluding motoring offences) by the time he is 30 years old. The employing body should only take into account those offences which may be relevant to the particular job or situation in question. A person's suitability should be looked at as a whole in the light of all the information available.

In deciding what action to take if a conviction is disclosed, the following should be considered:
- whether the conviction or other matter revealed is relevant to the position in question;
- the seriousness of any offence revealed;
- the length of time since the offence occurred;
- whether the applicant has a pattern of offending behaviour;
- whether the applicant's circumstances have changed since the offending behaviour; and
- the circumstances surrounding the offence and the explanation offered by the convicted person.

The applicant should receive a copy of the Disclosure sent to the employer. The employer should discuss the content of the Disclosure with the applicant, who may wish to have an opportunity to dispute it.

If a decision is made to employ or to continue to employ a person after the record of convictions has been revealed, it is good practice to write to the employee and state that the employer considers that the conviction does not impact on the employee's capacity or suitability to undertake the work involved in the job.

ARE THERE ANY OTHER STEPS THAT THE YOUTH ORGANISATION MUST TAKE?

Organisations must include a statement in application forms or accompanying material to the effect that a criminal record will not necessarily be a bar to obtaining a position, in order to reassure applicants that the police record check will not be used unfairly. Some umbrella bodies take this further and require organisations to have a written policy on the recruitment of ex-offenders.

Organisations also need to have a written security policy covering the correct handling and safekeeping of Disclosure information and ensure that it is put into practice[5].

Recipients of Disclosure information must ensure that:
- it is not passed onto those who are not authorised to receive it;
- it is only available to those who need to use it in the course of their duties;
- neither Disclosures nor Disclosure documents are retained for longer than is necessary: the *CRB Code of Practice* states that this should generally be no longer than six months after the date on which recruitment decisions have been taken or after the date on which any dispute about the accuracy of the Disclosure has been resolved. If it is considered necessary to hold Disclosures for more than six months advice should be sought from the CRB.

The CRB may refuse to issue a Disclosure if it believes that a registered person, or someone on whose behalf a registered person has acted, has failed to comply with the *CRB Code of Practice*.

Managing the system
Designated staff at an appropriate level in the organisation should be responsible for the operation of the vetting procedures, and in particular for:
- overseeing the operation of the checking procedure within the organisation (including training);
- ensuring that requests for checks fall within the terms of Government guidance;
- ensuring that requests are made at the right time;
- ensuring that information received from the police is released only to those who need to see it; and
- ensuring that records are kept securely and destroyed after use.

DISPUTED INFORMATION

The information in a Disclosure may be subject to challenge, on the grounds of accuracy. The CRB operates a disputes and complaints procedure for managing such situations.

WHAT CHECKS CAN BE MADE ON APPLICANTS FROM ABROAD?

The CRB can only provide its full Disclosure service within the UK. However, the CRB now operates an Overseas Enquiry Line (08700 100 450) for information about records from the following countries, which will provide a fax back service:

EUROPEAN:	NON-EUROPEAN:
Denmark;	Canada;
France;	Jamaica;
Germany;	South Africa;
Republic of Ireland;	Malaysia;
Italy (excluding Vatican City);	Philippines;
Netherlands;	Australia; and
Spain;	New Zealand.
Sweden;	
Poland; and	
Finland.	

Other than in exceptional circumstances, the police cannot make enquiries about the antecedents of people from other countries or establish the details of convictions acquired outside the UK. Some countries require finger prints to be submitted for applications for 'Certificates of Good Conduct': these may be obtained from Belgium, Luxembourg, Greece and Portugal.

Various countries elsewhere in the world also have a system of certificates of good practice, and employing organisations may therefore wish to consider requesting such certificates from applicants who are nationals of these countries. The level of information disclosed varies from country to country: some are complete extracts from the criminal record, others are partial[6]. Certainly, some form of certificate of good conduct may be obtainable from Singapore and Hong Kong in addition to those listed above.

WHAT REFORMS CAN BE EXPECTED IN THE FUTURE?

At the time of writing this edition, a consultation paper, *Making Safeguarding Everybody's Business: a post Bichard vetting scheme* (2005 DoH), has been issued jointly by the Department for Education and Skills and the Department of Health. It deals with the ambiguity and confusion in the present system and recommends that all those who work with children (and not just those who have substantial unsupervised contact) should be subject to checking at the Enhanced level. The Consultation document also reveals that the Government plans to extend the scope of the *Rehabilitation of Offenders (Exceptions) Order*. This would mean that those who

have indirect access to children through telephone help lines and those who manage databases which include sensitive information about children, would have to reveal 'spent' convictions. The intention of the Government is to create a single point of reference to identify all those who are unsuitable to work with children and to streamline the transfer of information.

FOOTNOTES:

1. David R Smith. 1993. *Safe from Harm - A Code of Practice for Safeguarding the Welfare of Children in Voluntary Organisations in England and Wales*. Home Office, London.

2. s. 36 *Criminal Justice and Court Services Act 2000*.

3. *Protection of Children: Disclosure of Criminal Background of those with access to children*. DfES Circular 9/93.

4. www.disclosure.gov.uk

5. Para 2. *CRB Code of Practice*.

6. Dr Judith Unell. *Criminal Record Checks Within the Voluntary Sector. An Evaluation of the Pilot Schemes*. The Volunteer Centre, UK.

USEFUL ADDRESSES:

Home Office
Action Against Crime and Disorder Unit
Criminal Records Section
50 Queen Anne's Gate
London SW1H 9AT
The section of the Home Office which deals with the policy making behind disclosure of criminal backgrounds.

Protection of Children Act List (PoCA)
(previously Department of Health Consultancy Service)
Wellington House
133-155 Waterloo Road
London SE1 8UG
Holds lists against which the names of prospective staff may be checked.

National Centre for Volunteering
(previously The Volunteer Centre UK)
Regents Wharf
8 All Saints Street
London N1 9RL
Provides information, training and support to people who work with volunteers.

Criminal Records Bureau
PO Box 91
Liverpool L69 2HU
Information line: 0870 90 90 811
www.crb.gov.uk
An executive agency of the Home Office which will eventually offer a one-stop service for all organisations wishing to check the background of potential employees or volunteers.

Department for Education and Skills
Teachers Misconduct Team
Ground Floor
Area E
Mowden Hall
Staindrop Road
Darlington DL3 9BG
Provides advice on the misconduct of teachers and workers with children and young persons.

Advocacy services

This chapter explores the role of advocacy services in supporting young people to express their views about matters that affect them. Youth workers need to be aware of the statutory right of looked after children, children in need and young people leaving care to an advocate. They should also be aware that advocacy is also available to children who fall outside these categories. Youth workers may find themselves acting as an informal advocate for young people who may require assistance or support in expressing their views.

WHAT IS ADVOCACY?

Advocacy involves an independent person (an advocate) assisting a young person to make his or her voice heard. In some situations advocates may speak for young people or assist and support them in putting their views across. It is important to remember that advocates are present to put forward the views of young people and should not put forward their own views or the views of others. Advocates are not present to make decisions or to act in what they believe to be the best interests of the young person they are representing: rather they are there to act as a facilitator or bridge-builder.

Advocates may accompany young people to meetings, help them to fill in forms, write letters on their behalf or assist them in instructing a solicitor.

WHO MIGHT NEED AN ADVOCATE?

Advocates can be of help to young people who may be involved in disputes about the provision of services, or who may be unhappy with the way in which they have been treated by a local authority. Advocating on behalf of such young

people may mean complaining to the organisation concerned, for example, a school, a local authority, the National Health Service (NHS), the police, or the Children and Family Court Advisory and Support Service (CAFCASS).

THE STATUTORY RIGHT TO AN ADVOCATE

LOCAL AUTHORITY

Children who are receiving services from a local authority have a right to receive support from an advocate under s.26A *Children Act 1989* if they want to make a complaint or representation. Under this section all local authorities must make and publicise arrangements for the provision of advocacy services to looked after children, children in need and children who are affected by the leaving care provisions of the *Children Act 1989* (relevant children, former relevant children and children qualifying for advice and assistance), to enable young people to make a complaint about the service they have received from the local authority or the way they have been treated.

CASE STUDY

Martin was looked after by the local authority, as were his two younger brothers. He was aware that his brothers were in the process of being adopted, but he knew nothing more about the adoption. Martin's behaviour was deteriorating significantly and he was about to lose his placement. He contacted his local advocacy service who assisted him in writing a letter to his social worker requesting information about his brothers' adoption. This helped put Martin's mind at rest and he settled down again.

CASE STUDY

Anita was an in-patient in a psychiatric unit suffering from anorexia. She had not engaged with the service and wanted to leave the unit. There was an advocacy service in the unit, and Anita asked the service to support her at a review meeting. At the review, Anita asked her advocate to put forward her view that she did not want to eat anymore and that she wanted to leave the unit. This was the first occasion during her time in the unit that Anita had expressed her feelings regarding her eating, and it gave the psychiatric team a starting point to work with Anita. Following the meeting, Anita began to engage with the service and started to improve.

The local authority should not only provide a young person with information about advocacy services but should also offer to assist him or her in obtaining an advocate[1]. Guidance published by the DfES[2] sets out the role of an advocate in the complaints procedure as follows:

- to empower children and young people by enabling them to express their views, wishes or feelings, or by speaking on their behalf;
- to seek the resolution of any problems or concerns identified by children by working in partnership with them and only with their agreement;
- to support children and young people pursuing a complaint through every stage of the complaints procedure and to provide them with information about their rights and options, helping them clarify their complaint and the outcomes they are seeking; and
- to speak for or represent children at any stage of the complaints process, including at the informal stage or at any formal hearing or interviews (Para 3.9).

The Guidance stresses that while the provisions in s.26A *Children Act 1989* are primarily concerned with complaints, the section also covers representations which are not complaints:

> '... *children and young people should be able to secure the support of an advocate in putting forward representations for a change to be made in the service they receive, or the establishment they live in, without this having to be framed first as a specific complaint.*'[3]

An advocate should not prevent a child making a complaint because he or she believes this is not in the child's best interests.

Any advocacy service provided must be independent, therefore, the *Advocacy Services and Representations Procedure (Children) (Amendment) Regulations 2004* specify who may not act as an advocate. These include:

- a person against whom a child wishes to make a complaint;
- the manager of an individual about whom a child wishes to make a complaint;
- the manager responsible for a service about which a child wishes to make a complaint; and
- the person who will consider the complaint on behalf of the local authority[4].

CHILDREN'S HOMES

Standard 16 *National Minimum Standards: Children's Homes Regulations 2002* stipulates that children living in children's homes should know how to complain if they are unhappy with any aspect of living in the home. The Standard also requires that children should be provided with information about how to complain, including how they can secure access to an advocate.

COMPLAINTS ABOUT HEALTH

Advocacy services are also provided for under s.12 *Health*

and Social Care Act 2001 for anyone, including children, wishing to make a complaint about the service they have received from the NHS. These advocacy services are provided by the Independent Complaints Advocacy Service (ICAS). ICAS offers one-to-one contact with an advocate within three weeks of initial contact being made by a complainant. Although the service is not specifically for children and young people, they are entitled to use the service in the same way as any adult complainant.

The relevant ICAS provider for a particular region can be found via the Department of Health website: www.dh.gov.uk.

ADVOCACY SERVICES: NATIONAL STANDARDS

All children and young people are entitled to advocacy services and so it is important to ensure that all providers comply with the *National Standards for the Provision of Children's Advocacy Services*[5]. These Standards set out what young people are entitled to expect from professionals providing advocacy services. Local authorities commissioning independent advocacy services must ensure that these comply with the National Standards.

Core Principles for Advocacy Services
- Advocates should work for children and young people and no one else.
- Advocates should value and respect children and young people as individuals and challenge all types of unlawful discrimination.
- Advocates should work to make sure that children and young people in care can understand what is happening to them, can make their views known and, where possible exercise choice when decisions about them are being made.
- Advocates should help children and young people to raise issues and concerns about things they are unhappy about, including making informal and formal complaints under s.26 *Children Act 1989*.

Standard 1: Advocacy is led by the views and wishes of children and young people
The child or young person should lead the advocacy process. The advocate should act only upon the young person's express permission and instructions, even where these conflict with the views of the advocate or the young person's best interests.

Standard 2: Advocacy champions the rights and needs of children and young people
Where appropriate, advocates should refer children and young people for legal and other specialist advice.

Standard 3: All advocacy services have clear policies to promote equality issues and monitor services to ensure that no young person is discriminated against due to age, gender, race, culture, religion, language, disability or sexual orientation

No young person should be prevented from accessing advocacy services and participating effectively on the grounds of gender, race, religion, culture, age, ethnicity, language, disability or sexuality. This means, for example, where children are unable to visit the advocacy office, arrangements are made for advocates to meet with children in a place of their choice.

Standard 4: Advocacy is well-publicised, accessible and easy to use

Any child who may benefit from the advocacy service should know of its existence, what it can and cannot offer, and the means by which it can be contacted.

Standard 5: Advocacy gives help and advice quickly when they are requested

Delays in responding to children and young people may prejudice their welfare and will reduce trust and confidence in the service.

Standard 6: Advocacy works exclusively for children and young people

Advocacy will only be successful if children and young people are confident that advocates are acting exclusively on their behalf and have no potential or apparent conflicting interests or pressures.

Standard 7: The advocacy service operates to a high level of confidentiality and ensures that children, young people and other agencies are aware of its confidentiality policies

Children and young people need to be assured that their privacy will be respected at all times and that nothing will be disclosed outside the service without their agreement, unless it is necessary to prevent significant harm to the young person or to someone else, or if disclosure is required by a court order.

Standard 8: Advocacy listens to the views and ideas of children and young people in order to improve the service provided

Advocacy services may wish to involve young people in:
- staff recruitment;
- staff induction, training and appraisal;
- management committees;
- the production and promotion of publicity and information materials; and
- evaluating and monitoring the service.

Standard 9: The advocacy service has an effective and easy to use complaints procedure

A well-publicised and accessible complaints procedure is essential if the service is to be credible and accountable to young people.

Standard 10: Advocacy is well managed and gives value for money

Advocacy services should set out their legal constitution, powers, management structure and services.

WHERE CAN A YOUNG PERSON FIND AN ADVOCATE?

There are national organisations that provide formal advocacy for young people such as Voice for the Child in Care, and there are local advocacy groups throughout the country. Informal advocacy may be provided through Connexions personal advisers, adult relatives, teachers or youth workers.

COMPLAINTS AGAINST LOCAL AUTHORITIES

All local authorities and voluntary organisations looking after children on behalf of a local authority are required to establish a procedure for considering complaints about the discharge of their duties in relation to service provision and the manner in which they look after children and young people. The complaints procedure may be used by 'looked after' children and 'children in need' in the community who are not being provided with appropriate services. The complaints procedure cannot be used by those assessed not to be in need. Others may make representations on behalf of children where they are parents, foster parents or other persons considered to have sufficient interest in a young person's welfare.

Stage 1: Informal complaint process

Most local authorities recommend concerns about service provision or delivery should be raised with the local authority staff involved, so as to give the staff an opportunity to put things right. Young people can be helped by youth workers if they feel awkward about making a complaint.

A complaint or representation is not an appeal against a decision made by the local authority. However, it does allow individuals to challenge the way in which a local authority has acted.

Complaints may be about the fact that a local authority has not answered letters, that someone has been rude and that there has been no apology for a mistake made. Also, it would be appropriate to complain if a local authority had failed in its statutory duties, such as failing to hold a review for a looked after young person or failed to help a child to have contact with his or her family.

When a formal complaint is made an investigation will take place. If the complaint is found to be justified the local authority should take action to rectify the wrong. This may include apologising, making arrangements to resolve the matter or in some cases by providing compensation.

Stage 2: Formal complaints process

If the young person is still not happy he or she can make a formal complaint. Each local authority should have a person or department responsible for complaints. This department will arrange for an independent review of the complaint to be carried out by a senior manager from within the local authority and an independent person. The review team have access to files and will interview any relevant staff members, before making recommendations to resolve the complaint.

Stage 3: Issues still outstanding

If the complaint has not been resolved satisfactorily, and it involves the provision or delivery of services or care by the local authority, the young person may ask for the complaint to be sent to an Appeal Panel consisting of an independent person, a senior manager and a county councillor. Full details about the procedural rules are contained in the *Representations Procedure (Children) Regulations 1991*, but each authority is obliged to publish information about its own scheme which should be easily accessible to the public, including young people, and widely distributed. Youth workers should ensure that they have copies of these leaflets for their own information and for distribution to the young people who attend their projects and clubs.

Local authorities must take into account the findings of the Panel and must notify the complainant and anyone else likely to be affected by the decision, of its reasons and proposed action. The panel will only notify a young person who is of sufficient understanding. The local authority is not bound to implement the decision, although failure to do so might constitute grounds for challenge in the courts by way of judicial review or by application to the Local Government Ombudsman.

IF YOU ARE STILL NOT SATISFIED

While the complaints mechanism is satisfactory to deal with many complaints, sometimes this system is simply too slow to meet the child's needs or is inadequate as a mechanism, particularly where there is a failure to provide services. In such cases there may be other more appropriate forms of redress, such as an application to court for judicial review or an order under the *Children Act 1989* or inherent jurisdiction. Alternatively, the young person can refer the matter to the Local Government Ombudsman, who can deal with cases involving maladministration. If in doubt, it is worth consulting the Children's Legal Centre or a solicitor. The child will nearly always be entitled to legal help from the Legal Services Commission.

> Each local authority is obliged to publish information about its own complaints procedures, which should be easily accessible to the public. Youth workers should ensure that they have copies of these leaflets for their own information and for distribution to the young people they work with.

CASE STUDY

Sandra, a 15-year-old living in a children's home, complained to her aunt that she had been sexually assaulted by another resident. The aunt in turn informed the children's home, who then informed the police. The boy was arrested, but released on bail and placed in a small residential unit in another town. However, two weeks later his new accommodation was closed down and in the absence of anywhere else to accommodate him he was placed back into the same children's home as Sandra and began to intimidate her again. Sandra's aunt complained to the Director of the home and to the local authority, but no action was taken to remove the boy from the home.

In such a case, an immediate complaint should be made under s.26 Children Act 1989. However, such a complaint may be insufficient to protect Sandra. Intimidation of a witness is a breach of bail conditions, and the police should be informed. Sandra's aunt should also take Sandra to see a solicitor with a view to taking immediate legal action.

Note: A new complaints procedure for local authorities, involving the Commission for Social Care Inspection (CSCI), was due to be implemented in April 2005 under the **Health and Social Care (Community Health and Standards) Act 2003.** *The Act requires regulations and guidance to be drafted before the new system of complaints can come into force. The relevant regulations together with the supporting guidance describing how the new process will operate in more detail, are currently in the final stages of drafting. However, following feedback to the recent consultation exercise on the draft guidance and regulations, ministers have agreed to delay implementation until 1st October 2005. Until these new complaints procedures are implemented, local authorities will need to continue to operate their existing complaints procedures in accordance with current legislation.*

FOOTNOTES:

1. Reg. 4 *Advocacy Services and Representations Procedure (Children) (Amendment) Regulations 2004.*

2. *Get it Sorted: Providing Effective Advocacy Services for Children and Young People Making a Complaint under the Children Act 1989. 2003. DfES.*

3. Para 1.1, *Get it Sorted: Providing Effective Advocacy Services for Children and Young People Making a Complaint under the Children Act 1989. 2003. DfES.*

4. Reg. 3 *Advocacy Services and Representations Procedure (Children) (Amendment) Regulations 2004.*

5. *National Standards for the Provision of Children's Advocacy Services. 2002.* Department of Health.

USEFUL CONTACTS:

Children's Rights Officers and Advocates (CROA)
94 White Lion Street
Islington
London N1 9PF
Tel: 020 7833 2100
Email: info@croa.org.uk
CROA is a membership organisation for children's rights officers and advocates, children's participation officers and individuals working to promote children's rights and participation in England and Wales.

Voice for the Child in Care (VCC)
Unit 4, Pride Court
80 – 82 White Lion Street
London N1 9PF
Tel: 020 7833 5792
Email: info@vcc-uk.org
VCC provides independent confidential advocacy services to children in need, in care or leaving care.

Parental responsibility and the Children Act 1989

This chapter gives an overview of the 'private law' provisions of the *Children Act 1989* as they relate to young people. A 'private law' dispute consists of legal proceedings between private individuals, such as family members. Public law proceedings are also covered by the *Children Act 1989*, and relate to legal proceedings taken by or against the State, usually by local authorities. Public law proceedings are covered in chapter 10.

Youth workers are unlikely to become directly involved in private law disputes involving young people. However, those working with young people should be aware of the *Children Act 1989* and its main provisions, particularly those relating to parental responsibility. While youth workers should try not to act as a substitute for legal advice they can play a useful role in providing information and assistance to young people seeking to exercise their rights under the *Children Act 1989*. This chapter highlights the main provisions of private law. Where further help is needed, youth workers should consider referring a young person to a solicitor on the Law Society Children Panel, which is a panel of expert solicitors in child law, administered by the Law Society.

PARENTAL RESPONSIBILITY

One of the key principles of the *Children Act 1989* is the concept of '*parental responsibility*'. When the *Children Act 1989* was being drafted, it was decided that the law should no longer talk of '*parental rights*', but of '*responsibilities*' owed by parents to their children. While the primary responsibility for children generally rests with parents, others may also have responsibility at the same time.

Parental responsibility is defined in s.3(1) *Children Act 1989* as:
> '... *all the rights, duties, powers, responsibilities and authority which by law a parent of a child has in relation to the child and his property.*'

In general terms, however, parental responsibility can be regarded as the power to make decisions in relation to a child. There are a number of situations when it is important for a youth worker or other professional to know who has decision-making power. The allocation of parental responsibility is clearly laid out in the *Children Act 1989*.

WHO HAS PARENTAL RESPONSIBILITY?
The mother of a child
Mothers have parental responsibility regardless of whether they are married to their child's father. Mothers may only lose parental responsibility if their children are adopted or if they have acted as a surrogate mother and so made an agreement under s.30 *Human Fertilisation and Embryology Act 1990*.

The married father of a child
Fathers have parental responsibility if they are currently married to a child's mother, were married to her at the time of the child's birth or marry her after the birth (in which case, they would gain parental responsibility from the date of the marriage).

The unmarried father of a child whose birth was registered before 1 December 2003
Unmarried fathers of children registered prior to 1 December 2003, may only acquire parental responsibility if they:

- marry the child's mother;
- make a parental responsibility agreement with the mother under the *Children Act 1989*, which must be registered in court to have legal effect[1];
- apply for a parental responsibility order: fathers will usually be granted a parental responsibility order if they can show both attachment and commitment to the child[2]; or
- obtain a Residence Order for the child (see chapter 11).

The unmarried father of a child whose birth was registered on or after 1 December 2003

Unmarried fathers of children registered on or after 1 December 2003, *automatically* acquire parental responsibility on signing the birth register jointly with the mother[3].

If fathers do not sign the birth register jointly with the child's mother at the time of first registration, they can re-register the child's birth, but again this only applies where the child was first registered on or after 1 December 2003. A request for re-registration must be made by both parents or by one parent with the written consent of the other[4].

Others

Parental responsibility is also acquired automatically by anyone in whose favour a Residence Order is made. A Residence Order is a court order which determines with whom the child is to live[5]. Usually, it is obtained by one parent upon separation from the other parent. However, Residence Orders may also be obtained by grandparents, foster parents or indeed anyone who wishes the child to live with them and who needs the security of a court order. A successful application for a Residence Order will give parental responsibility to the holder of the order for as long as the Residence Order is in force.

The local authority will acquire parental responsibility if it has obtained a Care Order in relation to the child. A Care Order is an order made by the courts which places the child in the care of a designated local authority[6]. It is important to note that when a child is taken into care, the parents still retain parental responsibility for the child. Although, the local authority has the right to determine the extent to which the parents may exercise that responsibility.

A step-parent can acquire parental responsibility by obtaining a Residence Order or by applying for a Parental Responsibility Order. If a step-parent acquires parental responsibility as a result of a Residence Order his or her parental responsibility will terminate automatically if the Residence Order terminates. All private law orders including Residence Orders terminate when a child reaches the age of 16.

A new provision under s.112 *Adoption and Children Act 2002* will allow step-parents to acquire parental responsibility by making a parental responsibility agreement with their spouses and the other parent of the child (if the other parent holds parental responsibility). However, at the time of writing this provision had not yet come into force.

> In December 2005 same-sex couples joined through Civil Partnership will have the same parental rights and responsibilities as married couples. This right has come about under s.75 (2) *Civil Partnership Act 2004*, which provides for the acquisition of parental responsibility in much the same way as step parents acquire responsibility after marriage.

DECISION MAKING WHERE MORE THAN ONE PERSON HOLDS PARENTAL RESPONSIBILITY

Each person with parental responsibility may act alone in meeting that responsibility[7]; consequently in most circumstances a person with parental responsibility can exercise that responsibility without obtaining consent from other parental responsibility holders.

There are two instances where the consent of the other parental responsibility holders is always required.

Where one parent seeks to change the child's surname

If there are two or more persons with parental responsibility the surname of the child may only be changed with the consent of all people with parental responsibility. If consent is not given by one of the parties, then the parent seeking to change the name of the child needs to obtain a court order permitting the change[8]. Where the mother has sole parental responsibility she may lawfully change the surname of her child without the consent of the father (where the father does not have parental responsibility). However, the name change may be open to challenge in court by the father[9]. Where a Residence Order is in force[10] no person may change the child's surname without the written consent of every person with parental responsibility or the leave of the court.

Where children who are *Gillick* competent (see chapter 5), in particular children who have reached the age of 16, wish to change their names, or consent to a change proposed by another, a court order will probably still be required. However, it is highly likely that *Gillick* competent children (see chapter 5) or children over 16 years old will be granted the necessary leave to apply to the court for the relevant order[11].

Schools, doctors and other holders of 'official' or formal records should be satisfied that everyone with parental responsibility and unmarried fathers without parental responsibility have consented to a change of surname or that there is a court order to that effect.

CASE STUDY

Tom, aged 14, wanted to take part in a trip organised by the youth club he had been attending for a year. The plan was to spend a fortnight youth hostelling in the Lake District during the summer holidays. Tom's mother, Ellen, and his father, Jack, are divorced. Ellen was pleased that Tom had been invited on the trip and gave her consent to him participating in the outing. However, when Jack found out he was angry that he had not been asked to consent to the trip. He telephoned the youth leader in charge of the trip and told him that he would not give his consent. Ellen told the youth leader to ignore Jack and that Tom would be able to attend. The youth group felt that Tom would benefit from the experience, but were also concerned that they could face legal action from Jack.

The youth club can take Tom on the trip if they have the consent of one parent with parental responsibility. If Jack does not want Tom to go on the trip he would need to seek a Prohibited Steps Order from the court. However, it is highly unlikely that the court would grant such an order. As a matter of good practice, organisations should try to keep both parents informed of events and activities.

Where one parent seeks to take the child abroad

As a general rule, one parent should not take a child abroad without the consent of other parental responsibility holders. The only exception to this rule is where a parent or carer has a Residence Order. Anyone who has a Residence Order in relation to a child may take that child abroad for a period not exceeding one month[12]. A parent or carer who does not have a Residence Order may not take the young person abroad, or agree to the young person going abroad with a youth group or any other body, without the consent of the Residence Order holder.

Therefore, where a parent or carer does not have a Residence Order, but wishes to take, or send, a child abroad for a short holiday, he or she may only do so provided that the following have consented:

- the mother;
- the father if he has parental responsibility;
- any legal guardian of the child; and
- any person who has a Residence Order in relation to the child.

If a child or young person is removed without the consent of the above an offence is committed both by the person who gave consent and the person travelling with the child, for example, the youth worker running the trip[13]. There are a number of defences available to a person removing the child from the UK without the required consent. These include:

- a belief that the other person has consented or would have consented if he or she were aware of all the circumstances;

- that all reasonable steps have been taken to communicate with the other person, but it has not been possible to do so; or
- that the other person has unreasonably refused his or her consent.

Before taking the child abroad, youth organisations should check with parents that all necessary consent has been obtained. It should be noted that very few such prosecutions have ever been brought and none in relation to trips taken with youth organisations. Further, the consent of the Director of Public Prosecutions is necessary before a prosecution can be brought. However, if youth organisations are aware that one of the people whose consent is required is refusing such consent, the young person should not be allowed to join the trip until such consent is forthcoming.

WHEN DOES PARENTAL RESPONSIBILITY END?

Parental responsibility terminates:

- when a young person reaches the age of 18;
- when a young person between the age of 16 and 18 marries;
- when a child or young person is adopted. When this occurs, the natural parents lose their parental responsibility for the child and all legal links with the child are severed. The adoptive parents automatically assume parental responsibility on adoption; or
- where parental responsibility has been acquired via a Residence Order and the Order is discharged or expires.

Where parental responsibility was obtained by an unmarried father under an agreement or Parental Responsibility Order, parental responsibility may only be terminated in exceptional circumstances, for example, where the father has seriously abused the child or the other parent.

A father who holds parental responsibility by virtue of marriage does not lose parental responsibility on divorce.

WHAT HAPPENS IF A CHILD IS BEING LOOKED AFTER BY SOMEONE WHO DOES NOT HAVE PARENTAL RESPONSIBILITY?

Children and young people may live with people, such as aunts or siblings, who do not have parental responsibility and so do not have the power to make decisions on their behalf.

The *Children Act 1989* does provide for a person who cares for a child, but does not have parental responsibility. Under s.3 *Children Act 1989* they:

> '... may ... do what is reasonable in all the circumstances of the case for the purpose of safeguarding or promoting the child's welfare.'

Therefore, it would be acceptable for youth groups to accept the consent of the person with whom a young person lives for an activity (although if an overseas trip is planned, parental consent should be sought if possible, and may be needed to obtain a passport)[14].

Young people who have reached the age of 16 may be living on their own or in a semi-independent setting. They may have little or no contact with parents and may be regarded as able to provide consent for themselves. However, young people looked after by the local authority should have the consent of the local authority and depending on the circumstances the parents.

DISAGREEMENTS OVER THE EXERCISE OF PARENTAL RESPONSIBILITY

In a situation where parents disagree strongly about decisions made by the other or another parental responsibility holder, they may seek an order from the court.

Disputes may arise over matters such as the school to be attended, medical treatment, taking children abroad, or even the religion to be followed. In such situations, parents may seek a Specific Issue Order, which allows the court to give *'directions for the purpose of determining a specific question which has arisen, or which may arise, in connection with any aspect of parental responsibility for a child'*[15], or a Prohibited Steps Order, which prohibits a step *'which could be taken by a parent in meeting his parental responsibility for a child'*, without the consent of the court[16].

There are two important points to note about these orders:
- They can only be used to determine issues of importance in relation to the exercise of parental responsibility.
- It is unlikely that youth workers would be allowed to make applications for such orders. However, they may advise young people that such orders exist and that it is possible for young people to make such an application themselves.

ACTION BY SEPARATING PARENTS

When parents separate, many of them arrive at an amicable agreement on such issues as where the child should live, with whom, and the amount of contact the child should have with the non-resident parent. However, when an amicable agreement cannot be reached the courts may be needed to resolve their dispute. While youth workers are unlikely to become directly involved in such proceedings themselves, the Children's Legal Centre is frequently contacted by youth workers and counsellors who wish to know the rights of young people on their parents' separation.

Parents who cannot come to an agreement about where their child should reside may seek either a Residence Order or a Contact Order from the court.

When either parents or other relatives apply for Residence or Contact Orders, young people are not party to the proceedings. They are not present in court and so do not have the opportunity to put forward their own views and wishes directly.

> A CONTACT ORDER is defined by s.8 *Children Act 1989* as an order which requires *'the person with whom a child lives, or is to live, to allow the child to visit or stay with the person named in the order, or for that person and the child otherwise to have contact with each other'.*
>
> A RESIDENCE ORDER is an order that determines with whom the child is to live on a day-to-day basis. Residence Orders are usually made in favour of one parent upon separation from the other parent. However, it is possible for more than one person to obtain a Residence Order over the same child[17]. This is known as a Joint Residence Order. Where these people are not living together, the Order may specify the period the child is to spend with each person. Individuals with Residence Orders automatically obtain parental responsibility for the child. Therefore, if a Residence Order is made to a mother and a step-father, the step-father will also have parental responsibility. If a Residence Order is made in favour of a grandmother she will have parental responsibility in addition to the parents.

In many disputed cases of residence and contact, the court will order a Children and Family Reporter from the Children and Family Court Advisory and Support Service (CAFCASS) to prepare a report. The reporter will interview the young person and inform the court of the views expressed. However, many young people feel uncomfortable talking to the reporter and do not feel that their views are being correctly interpreted. In such cases youth workers may contact reporters on the behalf of children to ensure that their views are expressed properly in court. The CAFCASS reporter will make recommendations to the court on the basis of what they determine to be the young person's best interests. The CAFCASS reporter's judgement may not be the same as the young person's views and wishes.

APPLICATIONS BY YOUNG PEOPLE

Young people can make their own application for Residence or Contact Orders. They will become party to the proceedings and have their own representatives in court. The courts do not recommend legal action by young people against their parents; they prefer disputes to be settled through mediation. However, if young people wish to pursue legal action on their own behalf, this may be done in the following two circumstances:

1 If a young person has obtained the leave (permission) of the court for that purpose. The judge will need to be convinced that the young person is of 'sufficient understanding' before granting leave[18]. It is the experience of the Children's Legal Centre that such leave is reluctantly given, and is unlikely to be given to a child below the age of 13, unless the child is part of an older sibling group.

2 Where a solicitor considers that the young person has sufficient understanding to give instructions in relation to the proceedings and agrees to act for the young person.

In the event of a dispute over a child's maturity, the court rather than the solicitor has the power to decide whether the young person is of '*sufficient understanding*' to instruct his or her solicitor. There is no definition of '*sufficient understanding*', but the court will want to know whether the young person understands the nature of the order sought and the implications of it being made. A youth worker may supply a

CASE STUDY

Barry, a 15-year-old boy, has lived with his mother since his parents separated when he was 12. He attends a youth club each week, and spends a lot of time talking to one of the youth workers there about the problems he faces at home. He does not get on well with his step-father, whom his mother married 18 months ago, and is increasingly unhappy at home. After several weeks of discussion, Barry told the youth worker that he wanted to live with his father and older brother. His father had said that this was acceptable to him, and that he would indeed welcome the move. Barry spoke to his mother, but she was adamant that Barry should remain living with her. There have been previous court proceedings and Barry's mother has a Residence Order in respect of him. The father told Barry that he could not afford to go back to court and fight for residence again, and that if Barry wants to move he will have to sort it out himself. Barry wants to know whether it is possible for him to make an application to court that would allow him to live with his father. He feels that this is the only way he will get what he wants.

As a matter of general practice, it is usually better to try to resolve residence disputes without going to court. If this is impossible, Barry needs to make an appointment to see a solicitor to discuss the possibility of making an application for a Residence Order under s.8 *Children Act 1989*, which will allow him to live with his father. The solicitor will only be able to act for Barry if he or she determines that Barry is mature enough to give instructions. Barry will also need the leave of the court before making an application for a Residence Order.

Youth workers should explain that taking legal action can be stressful, that it is likely to affect his relationship with his mother and that the application may not be successful. Where he lives will be decided on the basis of his best interests. It is also worth suggesting that Barry might benefit from discussing his dilemma, and asking if there are any other family members who might mediate between Barry and his mother. It may also help to talk through the implications of a move: for instance, considering whether it will involve a change of school, being far-away from friends or the youth group, so that Barry really understands what a change of residence would involve.

Note: When choosing a solicitor, choose one from the panel of solicitors who are accredited to The Children Panel. A list of such solicitors is available from The Law Society (Telephone: 020 7242 1222).

letter to the court in support of a young person, giving an opinion of the young person's understanding of his or her circumstances.

If a child is deemed not to be sufficiently mature, but wishes to seek a Residence Order, Contact Order, Specific Issues Order or Prohibited Steps Order, action must be taken through a Litigation Friend (an adult) or Children's Guardian (from CAFCASS). In any family proceedings where it appears to the court that the child should be separately represented, the court may appoint the Official Solicitor or some other proper person to the Children's Guardian.

In reaching any decision on the 'private law' orders described above, the court shall have regard to the welfare checklist[19]. These are:
- the ascertainable wishes and feelings of the child concerned (considering age and understanding);
- the child's physical, emotional and educational needs;
- the likely effect on the child of any change in his or her circumstances;
- the child's age, gender, background and any characteristics that the court considers relevant;
- any harm which the child has suffered or is at risk of suffering; and
- how capable each of the parents, and any other person relevant to the child is of meeting the child's needs.

Although the first factor in the checklist is the ascertainable wishes and feelings of the child, no greater weight is to be given to this factor than to any others.

FOOTNOTES:
1. s.4(1)(b) *Children Act 1989*.
2. s.4(1)(c) *Children Act 1989*.
3. s.4(1)(a) *Children Act 1989*.
4. s.4(1A) *Children Act 1989*.
5. s.8 *Children Act 1989*.
6. s.33(1) *Children Act 1989*.
7. s.2(7) *Children Act 1989*.
8. *Re PC (Change of surname) [1997] 2 FLR 730*.
9. *Dawson v Wearmouth House of Lords [1999] 1 FLR 1167*
10. s.13(1)(a) *Children Act 1989*.
11. *Re M, T, P, K and B (care= change of name) [2000] FD 2 FLR 645*.
12. s.13(2) *Children Act 1989*.
13. s.1 *Child Abduction Act 1984*.
14. Generally a parent will need to sign an application form for a passport of a young person aged under 16. However, where the child has a guardian, or a non-parental carer who has parental responsibility that person may sign the form instead.
15. s.8(1) *Children Act 1989*.
16. s.8(1) *Children Act 1989*.
17. s.11(4) *Children Act 1989*.
18. s.10(8) *Children Act 1989*.
19. s.1(3) *Children Act 1989*.

Confidentiality

Building a good working relationship with children and young people often requires an assurance of confidentiality. As a result, services frequently advertise themselves as confidential. However, it is sometimes necessary for information to be passed on to others, so youth workers need to understand what is meant by confidentiality, and when information should be disclosed.

WHEN DOES A CONFIDENTIAL RELATIONSHIP ARISE?

There is no definition in statute law in England and Wales of a confidential relationship. However, some relationships are automatically regarded as confidential: the relationships between doctor and patient, lawyer and client, and counsellor and client. It is also generally accepted that a duty of confidence arises where confidential information comes to the knowledge of a person in circumstances where that person has notice, or has agreed, that the information should be treated as confidential.

ESSENTIAL CONDITIONS FOR CONFIDENTIALITY

There are three principles to be applied in assessing whether information given is to be treated as confidential:

1 The information must be confidential. Once information is in the public domain and is generally accessible to others, it is no longer confidential. Therefore, if a young person has told a number of his or her friends, or all the youth workers in a project, the information will not be regarded as confidential.
2 The information must not be useless or trivial.
3 The information must have been given in circumstances where the confidant would reasonably have understood that what was said was confidential.

INFORMAL CONFIDENTIAL RELATIONSHIPS

Young people often discuss their own problems or pass on information about others without questioning whether what they say will go further. A young person may assume that information, particularly personal information, will be treated as confidential. If the relationship fulfils the essential conditions for confidentiality, the individual receiving the information (the informal confidant) will be in the same position as the professional, formal confidant (e.g. a doctor).

FORMAL CONFIDENTIAL RELATIONSHIPS

Children and young people may ask youth workers to provide information or advice on sensitive issues on a confidential

What impact does the Human Rights Act 1998 have on confidentiality?

Article 8 *European Convention on Human Rights* (which is incorporated into English law by the *Human Rights Act 1998*) recognises a right to respect for private and family life:

8.1 Everyone has the right to respect for his private and family life, his home and his correspondence.
8.2 There shall be no interference by a public authority with the exercise of this right except in accordance with the law and as is necessary in a democratic society in the interests of national security, public safety or the economic well-being of the country, for the prevention of disorder or crime, protection of health or morals or for the protection of the rights and freedoms of others.

Disclosing confidential information may well be a breach of an individual's Article 8 right, the question though is whether such a disclosure would be justified under Article 8.2. If a young person is at serious risk of significant harm, breach of the young person's right would probably be justified as in accordance with the law, and necessary in a democratic society for the protection of the young person's health.

basis. It is the view of the Children's Legal Centre that the law allows youth workers to provide information on a confidential basis, regardless of the age of young people and without the need for prior parental consent. Therefore, children under the age of 16 may be given information or advice on sensitive issues upon request.

However, the situation is different where children or young people are seeking more than just information and advice, such as counselling or medical attention. In such cases, if children are under the age of 16, the youth worker should ask if they are willing to inform their parents and obtain parental consent to the counselling or other services being offered. If children refuse to inform their parents, youth workers must consider whether the service can be provided without express parental consent.

> Counselling or treatment may only be provided to young people under the age of 16, without parental consent or knowledge, if they are sufficiently competent to consent on their own behalf.

COMPETENCE

WHEN IS A CHILD SUFFICIENTLY COMPETENT?

Adults are regarded by the law as being competent to consent to their own medical treatment and counselling. Young people from 16 to 18 years of age are also generally regarded as competent and able to consent to their own medical treatment[1], although it is possible for the court to override their refusal to consent to treatment in certain instances. However, if children under the age of 16 wish to receive counselling or medical treatment without parental consent or knowledge, the counsellor or doctor would need to decide whether or not the individual were competent to make the decision.

The decision as to whether or not a child is competent depends on a number of factors, including the maturity and understanding of the child as to the consequences of his or her actions. This is often referred to as *Gillick* competence.

There is no minimum age at which children can be regarded as competent to consent to medical treatment. However, it is unlikely that many children under the age of 13 would be deemed competent to consent to either medical treatment or counselling without the involvement of their parents. It is also unlikely that children misusing drugs or suffering from intermittent mental illness would be regarded as *Gillick* competent.

It is worth remembering that even if a child is deemed competent to consent to counselling without the parents being informed or providing their consent, that does not mean that the counsellor or youth worker can assume parental responsibility and make decisions about a child that usually fall within the remit of parental responsibility.

WHAT IF A CHILD IS NOT GILLICK COMPETENT?

If a child is not competent, then a person with parental responsibility must consent before the child is provided with counselling or treatment. It is only necessary to obtain the consent of one person with parental responsibility. One parental responsibility holder cannot veto the consent of another parental responsibility holder. The objecting parental responsibility holder could, however, seek a court order to prevent the treatment or counselling. It is possible to provide initial *information and advice* to the young person, prior to treatment or counselling, without parental consent. This can allow time for encouraging, preparing and helping the young person to inform and involve the parent.

SHOULD PARENTS BE INVOLVED IN TREATMENT OR COUNSELLING?

The *Children Act 1989* is clear that parental responsibility and primary responsibility for the welfare of the child will, in most cases, be held by the child's parents. Parental consent and involvement in any form of medical treatment or counselling of a child under the age of 16 is, therefore, regarded as good practice. For any professional adult who wishes to treat or counsel a child, there are several points to note:

- If the child is not competent, parental consent must be sought before treating the child. However, in emergencies, the need to treat quickly may take precedence over the need to obtain parental consent where it is judged by the professional to be of primary importance to that child's welfare.

- If a child under the age of 16 is deemed not to be competent and insufficiently mature to consent to counselling or medical treatment, and refuses to allow the youth worker or counsellor to approach the parent for consent, treatment cannot proceed. However, the youth worker still owes the child a duty of confidentiality. The parent should not be informed that the child has sought advice and treatment unless the child agrees to the release of this information.

- Even if the child or young person is considered competent and can consent to his or her own counselling or treatment, he or she should be actively encouraged to involve his or her parents.

- If the child is competent and refuses to inform his or her parents, then the youth worker, counsellor or medical professional may not breach the child's confidence by informing the parents that the child is seeking advice or treatment.

- Even if a parent consents to a youth club policy, for example, that medical treatment will be provided to a child as necessary, the parent is free to withdraw that consent at any time. The youth club cannot fetter a parent's right to make decisions in relation to his or her child by assuming this parental responsibility. Even where the parent has agreed that medical treatment can be provided as necessary, it is always wise to ensure that the parent is informed and consents to any but the most trivial medical treatment or counselling.

IF A CHILD DEEMED NOT TO BE COMPETENT IS COUNSELLED WITH PARENTAL CONSENT, IS THERE STILL A DUTY TO MAINTAIN CONFIDENCE?

While the parent may need to consent before a young person can receive treatment or counselling, it is not always necessary for the parent to know the content of that treatment. Where the child or young person requests that what is said during counselling or treatment is not relayed to the parent, that request should be respected. Therefore, a parent may consent to a young person receiving counselling for drug misuse or for bullying, but need not be informed of what the young person said during the counselling session.

SEXUAL HEALTH

Some young people may seek contraceptive or sexual health advice from youth workers, and the Government considers it acceptable for youth workers to provide it:

> 'Youth workers ... can and should encourage young people [including under-16s] to seek advice and contraception and direct them to local services if it appears that they are, or are thinking about becoming, sexually active.'[2]

The Government also suggests that it would be appropriate for a youth worker to take a group of young people to a sexual health clinic to find out about local services, and that parental consent would not be required for such a visit. However, the Children's Legal Centre believes youth workers should be wary of doing this. Unless a school or youth organisation has the general consent of the young people's parents to take them on trips, it is difficult to see how specific permission would not be required. Government Guidance also suggests that if a young person requires sexual health advice, but is reluctant to attend a service alone, a youth worker may accompany the young person. Again, the Children's Legal Centre has some reservations about such an approach.

SEXUAL OFFENCES ACT 2003

The *Sexual Offences Act 2003*, which criminalises sexual

CASE STUDY

Katherine, who is 14 years old, has told a youth adviser at her youth club that she is pregnant. Katherine is very distraught and is certain that she wants an abortion. She gets on well with her parents, but is adamant that they must not find out that she is pregnant. Katherine has asked the Adviser for assistance.

To what extent can the Adviser assist Katherine?
The Adviser can provide Katherine with information, including telephone numbers and addresses of doctors, counselling services and abortion clinics in order to assist Katherine in deciding what to do. In doing this, the Adviser does not need to be concerned whether or not Katherine is *Gillick* competent. The Adviser could also, if Katherine requests, make the necessary appointment with a doctor. If Katherine subsequently asks the Adviser to accompany her to the abortion clinic, the Adviser should think very hard about this. In particular, the Adviser should consider that:
- if Katherine is not competent, the issue of whether or not she should have an abortion is one her parents should make after consultation with a doctor and other relevant professionals; or
- if Katherine is competent, the decision of whether to have an abortion should be made by the doctors and Katherine alone.

The Adviser should not seek to persuade Katherine one way or another.

If the doctors find Katherine to be competent, and it is decided that Katherine will have an abortion, should the Adviser accompany Katherine to the clinic where she is to have the abortion?
There is no legal restriction on the Adviser accompanying Katherine. The Adviser should, however, consider whether this is wise. If something were to happen to Katherine such as a car accident on the way to the clinic when the Adviser was driving, the Adviser's employer may be liable for any harm caused. The Adviser should also consider whether he or she is involved in deceit of the parents and taking over parental responsibility for Katherine. If the Adviser is merely acting as a 'taxi driver', it is unlikely that any problem will arise.

Can the Adviser stay with Katherine while she has the abortion and take her home?
There is nothing in law that says the Adviser should not stay with Katherine. However, in every case, the Adviser should consider the circumstances carefully. There is a difference between a 15-year-old girl estranged from her parents and leading an independent life who seeks help, and a 14-year-old living with parents with whom she has a good relationship. In the latter example, the parents have a right to exercise parental responsibility and the Adviser has no right to intervene other than to the extent necessary to safeguard and promote welfare. It is unclear whether assisting a girl to have an abortion without parental knowledge is necessarily safeguarding and promoting her welfare.

Other considerations
If a doctor or nurse at the hospital believed the youth Adviser to be responsible for Katherine and spoke to the Adviser about Katherine's after-care and the post-abortion risks, the Adviser may inadvertently take on a duty of care for Katherine. If Katherine were then dropped back at home, and the Adviser said nothing to Katherine's parents, there may be a breach of that duty. If Katherine were to suffer a haemorrhage during the night, and the Adviser had failed to indicate to Katherine's parents the likely risk of this occurring, or indeed if Katherine suffered any harm which was attributable to the abortion, the Adviser or employer may face an action for negligence. In order to prove negligence, it would be necessary to show that the harm could have been reasonably foreseen by the Adviser.

Abortion is such a sensitive issue that it would be wise to discuss appropriate action with a supervisor or manager and it is imperative that a detailed protocol is in place.

behaviour between young people under 16, does not affect the duty of care and confidentiality that health professionals and youth workers owe to young people under the age of 16[3]. Under s.73 *Sexual Offences Act 2003*, a person is not guilty of aiding, abetting or counselling a sexual offence against a child where they are acting for the purpose of:

- protecting a child from pregnancy or sexually transmitted infection;
- protecting the physical safety of a child; or
- promoting a child's emotional wellbeing by the giving of advice.

Therefore, if a youth worker were to become aware that a 14-year-old girl was having a sexual relationship with a 15-year-old boy, no offence would be committed by the worker if sexual health advice was sought and given.

EFFECT OF HAVING A CONFIDENTIAL RELATIONSHIP

As a general rule, the confidant should not disclose the confidential information to anyone else and confidential information should not be used against a young person. Where, for instance, a young person reveals to a youth worker or a counsellor in confidence that they have infringed the rules of the organisation, this information should not be passed on. This may pose particular problems where the counsellor does not have an independent identity from the institution or organisation. Records relating to a young person should be regarded as confidential. While it is acceptable to discuss a case with colleagues within the counselling or medical service for professional reasons, records should be kept separately. They should not be kept on the school record files or with any other files which may be accessed by anyone other than the service provider. It should be remembered that a child, as much as an adult, has a right to respect for private and family life under Article 8 *European Convention of Human Rights and Fundamental Freedoms*. The unnecessary breaching of a confidential relationship may violate that right.

DISCLOSURE

Many counselling and other services offer children confidentiality. Indeed, many services would be unable to attract and help children if they did not offer a confidential service. Individual youth workers, health workers or teachers may also promise a child confidentiality. However, unlike adults who are allowed to take grave risks to their health, wellbeing or even life, the need to protect children from significant harm means that no confidential service for children or young people, nor any individual, should guarantee a child absolute confidentiality. The boundaries of confidentiality should be made clear to young people before they make use of a service.

Disclosure of confidential information may arise in a number of contexts:

- a confidant who is given information which indicates

CASE STUDY

Samantha, a Year 9 pupil, had begun to behave badly at school. There were no obvious reasons for the change in her behaviour. It was suggested that she receive counselling in school from a local counselling service for young people. Samantha reluctantly agreed. The counsellor tried her best to establish a good relationship with Samantha and to ensure that she saw her as someone who could be trusted and would not pass information to the school. One day, the counsellor saw Samantha waiting for an exam with a group of friends, all of whom looked a bit nervous. Introducing herself to the group as Samantha's counsellor, she wished Samantha luck. Samantha refused to go to any further counselling sessions, and was excluded a month later.

Is this a breach of confidentiality?
Yes. Even though the counsellor did not disclose the content of her sessions with Samantha, she owed her a duty of confidence not to disclose that Samantha was accessing a counselling service.

---

that a child or young person is at risk of significant harm will have to consider whether it is in the child's best interests to disclose the information to other agencies or individuals;
- a confidant may be approached by parents, other agencies, the police or the child and asked to disclose confidential information; or
- a confidant may be ordered by the court to disclose information.

IF I AM CONCERNED ABOUT A CHILD CAN I DISCLOSE THE DETAILS AND DISCUSS THE ISSUE WITH COLLEAGUES?

If the information was given in confidence, it is acceptable to discuss the issues with your professional supervisor or manager, but you should not discuss the matter with other people in the same organisation unless you decide that the conditions for disclosure of confidential information without consent exist.

IS THERE A LEGAL DUTY TO DISCLOSE CONFIDENTIAL INFORMATION TO OTHER AGENCIES?

Local authorities are required by s.47 *Children Act 1989* to make investigations where they have reasonable cause to suspect that a child is suffering, or is likely to suffer, significant harm. There is no corresponding investigative duty on individuals, organisations or other services, nor is there any statutory duty to pass on confidential information to the local authority in circumstances where the child appears in need of immediate protection.

There is no general duty in criminal law to disclose information that criminal offences have been committed. However,

CASE STUDY

A youth advisory service was telephoned by a 14-year-old boy. The child said that neither he nor his four brothers had ever been allowed to attend school, and that they desperately wanted to be like other children and go to school. Following this conversation, the Adviser wrote a letter to the parents stating that she had been informed of the children's unhappiness, and that she wished to make an appointment with them to discuss the children's education. The Adviser agreed with the child that she would meet him at the library, give him the letter, and that he would deliver it to the parents.

Has the Adviser acted appropriately?
No. Although the Adviser placed the onus on the child to make the decision as to whether to hand the letter to his parents, the Adviser could not have known whether this would place him in immediate danger of significant harm. There may well be child protection issues in this kind of situation and the Adviser could have placed the child in danger. In addition, the young person may not have been Gillick competent, and may not have fully understood the implications of handing the letter to his parents. Before sending the letter, or making any form of contact with the parents, the Adviser should have spoken with the local authority to see whether they were aware of the family, and whether they were satisfied that the children were receiving suitable education at home.

professionals working with children and young people should be careful to avoid doing anything which could constitute aiding and abetting the commission of an offence. If a young person tells a youth worker that drugs are being sold in the youth club, and the youth worker takes no action, this could amount to aiding and abetting. Under the *Misuse of Drugs Act 1971*, it is illegal to allow premises to be used for the smoking of cannabis or opium, or the illegal consumption or supply of controlled drugs.

A MORAL DUTY TO DISCLOSE?

While there is no *legal* duty to pass on confidential information to other agencies, even where there is a likelihood that a child may be at risk of significant harm, as a matter of good practice, there is a *moral* duty to pass on such information.

CASE STUDY

A Cambridge hostel operated a policy of confidentiality under which information about homeless and vulnerable people who attended the centre would not generally be passed on to outside agencies or the police. Two workers at the hostel did not pass on information to the police that drug dealing was taking place at the centre. Both workers were prosecuted under the *Misuse of Drugs Act 1971* and given prison sentences.

There is no rule as to when there should be a disclosure of information. Each case must be judged on its individual circumstances. There are, however, a number of professional Codes of Practice, as well as Government guidance that address this issue. Government guidance, generally, encourages the passing on of confidential information, even without children's consent or against their wishes, where they may be at risk of significant harm without further help and intervention.

Some help can be gained from *Safeguarding Children in Education* (DfES 0027/2004), which applies to schools in meeting their duty to safeguard and promote children's welfare.

> *'Experience, and consultation with children, shows that they will talk about their concerns and problems to people they feel they can trust and they feel comfortable with. This will not necessarily be a teacher. It is, therefore, essential that all staff and volunteers in a school or establishment know how to respond sensitively to a child's concerns, who to approach for advice about them, and the importance of not guaranteeing complete confidentiality. Staff must be aware that they cannot promise a child complete confidentiality – instead they must explain that they may need to pass information to other professionals to help keep the child or other children safe.'*

Most non-statutory organisations and bodies interpret the moral duty to pass on confidential information narrowly. There are two situations when most feel a breach of confidence is justified:

- where there is a child protection issue (the client or other children are at risk of suffering significant harm); or
- where the life of the client or a third party is at risk.

Working together to safeguard children: a guide to inter-agency working to safeguard and promote the welfare of children (1999 DoH), states that:

> *'If somebody believes that a child may be suffering, or may be at risk of suffering, significant harm, then he or she should always refer his or her concerns to the local authority social services department.'*

Other professionals may feel safer disclosing a wider range of confidential information in situations where a young person may indicate that they have committed a crime or intend to commit a crime, or when the service the professional is providing is at risk. In deciding whether to disclose confidential information, a youth worker must consider whether the benefit of breaching confidentiality outweighs the risk that such disclosure poses.

In relation to young people under 16 engaging in sexual relationships, youth workers need to consider whether disclosure is necessary. This will depend on the nature of the relationship. Guidance issued by the Crown Prosecution Service is clear that the *Sexual Offences Act 2003* is:

> *'… designed to protect children, not punish them unnecessarily or make them subject to the criminal justice system where it is wholly inappropriate. Young people should not be prosecuted or issued with a reprimand or final warning where sexual activity was entirely mutually agreed and non-exploitative.'*[4]

> **What is personal data?**
> It is information about any identified or identifiable individual and includes their name, address and telephone number as well as any reports or records.

The *Data Protection Act 1998* only stipulates that records should be kept no longer than is necessary. There are no actual timescales imposed. It is a matter of individual judgement, taking into account the nature of the records. Organisations often impose their own timescales for the retention of data in case legal proceedings are brought, and such records are required. It is advisable for all organisations who retain data on children and young people to devise timescales to ensure consistency. Six years is a commonly used benchmark, and is compatible with limitation periods for the commencement of most legal proceedings.

Any specific queries relating to data protection issues should be directed to the Information Commissioner's Data Protection Helpline on 01625 545 745.

> **Can the Freedom of Information Act 2000 be used instead of the Data Protection Act 1998 to obtain information about an individual?**
> If individuals wish to obtain their own personal information such as educational records, local authority or youth club records, the *Data Protection Act 1998* will apply and they should make a Subject Access Request. The organisation has 40 days to provide such information. If the information being sought is not about an individual, but is related to a public authority then the *Freedom of Information Act 2000* will apply. The Act gives a general right of access to 'recorded' information held by public authorities.
>
> *For further information on the* Freedom of Information Act 2000, *see www.informationcommissioner.gov.uk*

REMEDIES WHERE CONFIDENTIALITY IS BREACHED

Where there is a confidential relationship, the person receiving the confidential information is under a duty not to pass on the information to a third party. Disclosure of confidential information can give rise to an action for breach of confidence, in which an injunction or compensation may be claimed. It is also possible that a child may make a free standing claim for breach of his or her right to respect for privacy and family life under Article 8 *European Convention of Human Rights and Fundamental Freedoms*. As in all proceedings involving children, such action must be taken by a Litigation Friend unless the child is mature enough to instruct his or her own solicitor. Where a client knows in advance that confidentiality is going to be breached, an interlocutory (interim) injunction will be the most relevant remedy. This serves to halt the disclosure while the court considers whether disclosure is preventable.

In order to get an injunction, it is necessary to show an apprehension or fear of damage, which will be difficult for most children, but not impossible. Where there is a breach of confidence in relation to a child or young person, it is unlikely that there will have been much notice of the breach and extremely unlikely that the young person will know that they could obtain an injunction or fulfil the criteria for obtaining one. Usually, a client will not have advance knowledge of an impending breach and so an injunction will be inappropriate. In this case, the obvious remedy is to claim damages (compensation), since disclosure has already taken place.

The main defence to an action for breach of confidence is to show that the disclosure was justified in the public interest. The circumstances in which this can be claimed are limited, but it was established in *Fraser v Evans [1969] 1 QB 349* that crimes, frauds and misconduct are relevant issues for disclosure:

> '... *both those committed as well as those in contemplation, provided always, and this is essential, that the disclosure is justified in the public interest. The disclosure ... must be to one who has a proper interest to receive the information. Thus it would be appropriate to disclose a crime to the police ...*'

In each instance, the court will balance whether the public interest in the protection of confidentiality is outweighed by the public interest in its disclosure.

FOOTNOTES:
1. s.8 *Family Law Reform Act 1969.*
2. *Guidance for Youth Workers on Providing Information and Referring Young People to Contraceptive and Sexual Health Services.* 2001. Teenage Pregnancy Unit.
3. *Best Practice Guidance for Doctors and Other Health Professionals on the Provision of Advice and Treatment to Young People Under 16 on Contraception, Sexual and Reproductive Health.* 2004. Department of Health.
4. *Legal Guidance: Sexual Offences Act 2003.* 2004. Crown Prosecution Service.
5. s.47(9)-(11) *Children Act 1989.*
6. *Data Protection Act 1998* and the *Data Protection (Subject Access Modification) (Health) Order 2000.*
7. *Education (Pupil Information) (England) Regulations 2000* and *Education (Pupil Information) (Wales) Regulations 2004.*
8. *Data Protection (Subject Access Modification) (Social Work) Order 2000.*
9. s.5 *Oaths Act 1978.*

Taking trips:

Responsibilities of youth organisations

The responsibility of youth groups and organisations can be a cause of anxiety when a trip away from the local base is planned. Under the *Health and Safety at Work etc Act 1974*, employers are responsible for the health, safety and welfare of employees and others connected with the organisation's activities, whether on-site or off-site. Voluntary and statutory organisations owe a duty of care to children and young people when taking them on trips and during activities off site. Recent case law has led to even greater anxiety as the Geography teacher Paul Ellis was convicted of manslaughter in 2003, when a 10-year-old in his care died as a result of his 'negligent and foolhardy' behaviour.

LEGISLATION AND LICENSING

Following the deaths of four young people at the Lyme Bay Activity Centre, the Government began to regulate the management and safety of practices of commercial activity centres through the *Activity Centres (Young Persons' Safety) Act 1995* and the *Adventure Activities Licensing Regulations 2004*[1]. These require that certain centres are licensed, especially those providing caving, climbing, trekking and water sports. Also, commercial centres selling adventure holidays must be licensed, as must educational establishments, such as youth and community centres, and schools if they provide activities for anyone other than their pupils or members. Non-commercial voluntary sector activities are exempt from licensing, as are schools providing activities for their own pupils, and organisers of activities which involve parents or guardians. Before arranging and booking a trip with an activity centre, youth organisations should check whether the activity centre is licensed[2].

The Department for Education and Skills (DfES) has produced a Good Practice Guide, *Health and Safety of Pupils on Educational Visits* (1998), which provides guidance on safety when taking children on trips. The Guidance, which applies to all activities, seeks to promote the safety of participants by providing detailed requirements on staffing, facilities, insurance and other issues. Although the Guidance is primarily aimed at staff in schools and local authorities, much of it is equally valid for staff in youth and other organisations. A copy of *Health and Safety of Pupils on Educational Visits* may be obtained free on request from DfES Publications[3]. It is supplemented by five further guidance documents from the DfES:

- *Health and Safety: Responsibilities and Powers*[4], which is aimed primarily at schools and seeks to clarify responsibilities under existing health and safety legislation;

- *Standards for LEAs in Overseeing Educational Visits*, which sets out good practice for local authorities in overseeing educational visits by schools. It recommends that local authorities have an outdoor education adviser and schools have an educational visits coordinator (youth organisations may also find this Guidance useful);
- *Standards for Adventure Activities*, aimed at teachers or youth workers who lead young people on adventure activities;
- *A Handbook for Group Leaders*, aimed at anyone who leads groups of young people on any kind of educational visit. It sets out good practice in supervision, ongoing risk assessment and emergency procedures; and
- *Group Safety at Water Margins*, aimed at anyone who organises learning activities that take place in or near water.

The DfES has recognised that amendments to the Guidance will be required from time to time. The supplementary Guidance will exist as '*living documents*', with amendments being made to the website versions[5].

GROUP LEADER

Health and Safety of Pupils on Educational Visits recommends that prior to organising a trip a group leader should be appointed. This person should have overall responsibility for the supervision and conduct of the visit and the health and safety of the group. It should be up to the group leader to define each of the supervisors' roles and ensure that all tasks are assigned. The group leader should be able to control and lead young people of the relevant age range, be suitably competent to instruct young people in activities and also be familiar with the location or centre where the activities are to take place. The group leader should also be responsible for:
- briefing parents about the trip;
- ensuring that appropriate first aid provision is available;

- undertaking the risk assessment;
- ensuring the ratio of supervisors to young people is appropriate; and
- ensuring supervisors are aware of any special educational or medical needs amongst the group.

A Handbook for Group Leaders supplements *Health and Safety of Pupils on Educational Visits* with additional information about the role and responsibilities of group leaders. The supplementary Guidance features practical information on supervision, including head counts; the buddy system; remote supervision; 'down' time and night time; ongoing risk assessment; emergency procedures; and specific activities (such as coastal visits, farm visits and swimming).

HEAD COUNTS

Whatever the length and nature of the visit, regular head counts should take place, particularly before leaving any venue. It is good practice for all supervisors to carry a register of all the young people and adults involved in the visit at all times, and ensure that participants are readily identifiable, especially if the visit is to a densely populated area. Brightly coloured caps, t-shirts or school uniforms can help identify group members more easily. Identification mechanisms that could put young people at risk, such as name badges, should not be used. Participants should be aware of rendezvous points and should know what to do if they become separated from the group.

'BUDDY' SYSTEMS

The Guidance recommends that each child should be paired with a buddy, and each should regularly check that the other is present. A variant of this is the 'circle buddy' system: the young people form a circle at the start of the visit so that each young person has a left and a right buddy, he or she will then check on these buddies when asked. This ensures that unlike when buddies are paired two young people cannot vanish together and not be missed.

EMERGENCY PROCEDURES

Given that thorough emergency planning can mitigate the trauma of being caught up in an emergency, the Guidance suggests that it is good practice for the group leader to devise an emergency plan and ensure that all members of the group know what action to take if there is a problem. If an emergency does occur during an activity, the group leader should maintain or resume control of the group overall. The leader must establish the nature and extent of the emergency as quickly as possible, and ensure that all members of the group are safe and looked after. The names of any casualties should be established and immediate medical attention sought. A supervisor should accompany any casualties to hospital and the rest of the group should be kept together and adequately supervised. The Guidance lists a number of other factors to be considered in the event of an emergency, including noti-

CASE STUDY

In September 1999, a science teacher from the independent Boundary Oak School in Fareham, Hampshire, took a party of children on a school sailing trip to Portsmouth. As the conditions were unsuitable for sailing, the teacher agreed to take nine children out in the school's dory, the engine of which had a history of stalling. When the engine stalled for the second time, the teacher told four of the pupils to start paddling. The boat capsized, leaving everyone in the water. The teacher failed to conduct a head count, and one was not taken until one of the girls realised that her twin sister was missing. She was found under the dory and died in hospital after resuscitation attempts failed. A report by the Marine Accident Investigation Branch criticised the school and the teacher's supervision of the children, although the Crown Prosecution Service decided not to prosecute either.

fying the police and parents, keeping a written account of the incident and ensuring no one in the group discusses the incident with the media.

PREPARATION AND RISK ASSESSMENT

There should be formal plans and preparations made prior to taking a trip or arranging an activity.

The purpose of such planning is to consider the risks and difficulties that may arise and make plans to reduce them. If frequent visits are made to the site, such as a swimming pool, it is not necessary to carry out a risk assessment each time, but a reassessment of risk should be made from time to time. The group leader is responsible for conducting a risk assessment or ensuring that one is carried out. Such an assessment should be made well in advance of the visit.

The risk assessment should be based on the following considerations:
- What are the possible hazards?
- Who might be affected by them?
- What safety measures need to be in place to reduce risks to an acceptable level?
- Can the group leader put the safety measures in place?
- What steps will be taken in an emergency?

The following factors should be taken into consideration when assessing risks:
- the type of activity and the level at which it is being undertaken;
- the location, routes and mode of transport;
- the competence, experience and qualifications of supervisory staff;
- the group members' ages, competence, fitness and temperament, and the suitability of the activity;
- the ratio of competent, experienced and qualified staff to children;

- the quality and suitability of the available equipment, and whether it meets specifications identified by the national governing body for that activity;
- seasonal conditions, weather and timing;
- the special educational or medical needs of the children;
- emergency procedures;
- how to cope when a young person becomes unable or unwilling to continue; and
- the need to monitor risks throughout.

Health and Safety of Pupils on Educational Visits is clear that if the risks cannot be contained, the visit must not take place.

The supplementary Guidance, *Standards for LEAs in Overseeing Educational Visits*, states that there are three levels of risk assessment for educational visits:
- generic activity risk assessments, which are likely to apply to the activity wherever and whenever it takes place;
- visit or site specific risk assessments, which will differ from place to place and group to group; and
- ongoing risk assessments, which will consist of judgements and decisions made as the need arises, taking account of, for example, illness of staff or pupils or changes in the weather.

The person carrying out the risk assessment should record it and give copies to all supervisors on the visit, with details of the measures they should take to avoid or reduce the risks.

In order to make an informed assessment of risk, *Health and Safety of Pupils on Educational Visits* recommends that an exploratory visit should be made prior to a trip or activity, especially where the plan is to take a group abroad or on a residential visit. This is particularly necessary where youth workers are to instruct or lead the group in an outdoor activity in a location that is not familiar to them. If an exploratory visit is not feasible, a risk assessment should be conducted by obtaining specific information by letter from the venue and from local organisations such as tourist boards.

If a tour operator is being used, the group leader or organisation should obtain a written or documentary assurance that the operator has assessed the risks and has appropriate safety measures in place.

WATER SAFETY

The DfES Guidance *Group Safety at Water Margins* is intended for teachers, youth workers, voluntary leaders and anyone else who might organise or lead an educational visit taking place in or near water. It covers activities such as walking along a river bank or seashore, collecting samples from ponds and streams, or paddling or walking in gentle, shallow water. It is not designed to cover swimming and other activities that require water safety or rescue qualifications and equipment, or water-going craft. The Guidance lists issues to be considered to help organisers plan and lead a safe visit, including preparing the visit, risk assessment and group control.

ADVENTURE ACTIVITIES

The supplementary Guidance, *Standards for Adventure Activities*, develops the advice on school-led adventure activities given in *Health and Safety of Pupils on Educational Visits* and concentrates on the role of the technical adviser. A technical adviser would be a person with a high level of competence in a particular activity and, therefore, able to make judgements about the technical and supervisory competence of others. They should be qualified to the level recognised as satisfactory by the Adventure Activities Licensing Authority and may be found within a local authority, through a commercial provider or professional association.

FIRST AID

For adventure activities, residential activities and visits abroad, at least one member of the supervisory staff should be competent in first aid, holding a valid first aid certificate[6]. The group leader should have a good working knowledge of first aid and ensure that an adequate first aid box is taken on the trip. All supervisory staff should know how to contact the emergency services. When assessing first aid requirements, consideration should be given to the:
- numbers in the group and the nature of the activity;
- likely injuries and how effective first aid would be; and
- distance of the nearest hospital.

SUPERVISION LEVELS

Desirable supervision levels will vary according to the activity, age group, location and experience of the supervisors. However, for groups of people under the age of 18, recommended supervisor to young people ratios are:
- one adult to 10 to 15 children aged eight to 11 and one adult for 15 to 20 children aged 11 or 12 and over for visits where the element of risk to be encountered is similar to that normally encountered in daily life (visits to sites of historic interests, field work or local walks);
- one adult to 10 group members for residential trips, trips abroad or where swimming or water sports are involved; and
- where there are children under the age of eight in the group, a minimum ratio of one adult to six group members. The same minimum ratio could apply to groups which wholly or mainly comprise children with special educational needs or disabilities, although lower ratios can be used depending on the nature of the children's disabilities.

ACCOMMODATION

Where activities include spending the night in outdoor areas, mountain huts, bunk houses, or tents standards of accommodation will vary widely. However, where residential accommodation is being used, *Health and Safety of Pupils on Educational Visits* provides useful guidance on the necessary standard of accommodation. While aimed at school trips, youth groups should apply the same standards when booking accommodation for activity courses. The youth group should consider the following:

- the group should have adjoining rooms, but male and female sleeping areas and bathroom facilities should be separate;
- there should be at least one adult from each sex for mixed groups and there should be an adequate number of supervisors on standby during the night;
- the immediate accommodation area should be exclusively for the group's use and security arrangements should be in place to stop unauthorised visitors (where possible children should not sleep in ground floor rooms and there should be locks on doors);
- there should be appropriate and safe heating and ventilation and everyone should be aware of the layout of the accommodation including fire exits;
- assurances should be sought from the manager of the accommodation that staff have been checked as suitable to work with children (see Chapter 2);
- there should be drying facilities and adequate provision for the storage of clothes, rucksacks, luggage and other outdoor equipment and for the safekeeping of valuables;
- there should be provision for young people with special needs and those who fall sick;
- balconies should be stable, windows secure and electrical connections safe;
- the fire alarm must be audible throughout the accommodation; and
- there should be recreational facilities for the group and children's particular cultural and religious needs should be met.

CONSENT FORMS

Youth groups or organisations planning to take children or young people away from the premises where they usually meet need to seek the consent of a parent or a parental responsibility holder (see Chapter 4). If it is usual to visit a local park or sports facility, it should be made clear to parents when children join the organisation or club so that they may give consent. When special activities or trips are planned, it is recommended that organisations obtain specific parental consent for children's participation.

Parents should be asked to provide details on whether their children:

- suffer from allergies and what they are;
- are taking medication and what it is, the dosage and whether it can be self-administered;
- have had, or have been in contact with, any contagious or infectious diseases within the last four weeks;
- have had other recent illnesses or suffer from other medical problems;
- have any toileting difficulties;
- have any night time tendencies (such as sleepwalking);
- suffer from travel sickness;
- can swim and what their abilities are;

- may not participate in certain activities;
- have specialist dietary requirements; and
- have any special religious or cultural requirements.

Parents should also provide:

- the name and contact address for the family GP;
- the home telephone number and address;
- an alternative telephone number and address for emergencies; and
- any other information which the organiser should know.

The Guidance provides that the consent form should also contain a section for obtaining parental agreement for children and young people receiving emergency medical treatment, including anaesthetic, as considered necessary by the medical authorities. Some parents faced with such a delegation of parental responsibility may be unwilling to sign such a wide-ranging form, fearing that treatment will go ahead without them being notified. While in the view of the Children's Legal Centre, this additional clause is not technically necessary, as doctors in the UK would provide emergency medical treatment where necessary without parental consent, the situation might not be so clear in other countries. Groups wishing to add the clause should make it clear that all attempts would be made to contact parents before the organisation would give consent to emergency medical treatment on children.

As children get older and especially once they reach 16, much of the information and even consent for medical treatment can be obtained from them rather than their parents. However, parents still hold parental responsibility in relation to a child until they are 18, and it is a wise precaution to obtain parental consent to trips and activities.

PARENTAL BRIEFING

Parents should be given full and complete written details before a residential trip and when young people are to travel abroad or engage in adventure activities. Where the trip involves overnight stays, it is also useful to provide written details of the organisation and administration of the trip, including:

- content of the programme, the mode of travel and accommodation;
- dates, times and location of the visit (including address and telephone number);
- code of conduct expected of children (such as no smoking and no drinking rules);
- procedures for children who become ill;
- staffing and security details;
- special clothing or equipment and money to be taken; and
- insurance.

WHAT IF A YOUNG PERSON BREAKS THE RULES?

Young people participating in a trip should be briefed on the behaviour code. Such codes should be drafted in consultation with the young people participating in the trip and should be realistic: banning all smoking may be unrealistic, depending on the age of the young people involved. However, setting rules about smoking and banning it from rooms and when taking part in activities may be appropriate. Similarly, banning all alcohol consumption, even where there is free leisure time in the evening, may not be realistic in relation to older members of a youth organisation.

Although the organisation may have discussed all the rules to be followed during a trip, young people may break rules while away. Some organisations state that if one of the rules is broken, the young person will be sent home. Such a policy may present both legal and practical difficulties, and the circumstances in which this policy will be implemented, and the practical arrangements, need to be carefully considered.

If a young person is to be sent home, the organisation will have to consider how it is to be accomplished. First, the staff will need to contact a parent and obtain his or her permission to send a child home. The parent may refuse to cooperate or may not be available to receive the child. Second, consideration will need to be given as to who will pay the return fare, particularly if the child is abroad. Even if a parent has signed an agreement that he or she will pay for an early return ticket if the child misbehaves, a decision will still need to be made as to who purchases the ticket. Further, the organisation may find that the parent is not willing to repay the cost of the ticket if he or she is dissatisfied and disputes the organisation's reasons for returning the child. Legal proceedings may be needed to get the money back. Third, thought will need to be given as to whether the child should be accompanied, particularly if the young person is abroad or the parents cannot collect him or her. Can the organisation spare a member of staff to accompany the child, and who will pay? Fourth, there may be an issue as to breach of contract. Where there has been a payment for the trip, the young person should only be sent home if there is a clear and serious breach of the rules by the young person.

SAFETY DURING THE TRIP

There is a duty on youth leaders and staff to safeguard and promote the welfare of young people in their care. This is sometimes referred to as being *in loco parentis*. When youth workers have care and control of young people, they have the same responsibility as a reasonable parent to ensure the young people's safety. Youth workers may, however, delegate their responsibility, for instance, to a member of staff at an activity centre.

TIME AWAY FROM THE GROUP

The Children's Legal Centre is often asked whether youth workers can allow young people some time away from the group: for example, if the group is visiting a historic site or even where the group has travelled abroad. While an organisation will be responsible for the safety of young people during a trip, this does not necessarily mean that youth workers must accompany them at all times. Staff are under a duty to act as a reasonable parent. Depending on the age of the young people on the trip and the location, it may be acceptable to allow young people some time to explore on their own. However, basic safety rules should be laid down and agreed. These should include:

- the times during which it is possible to leave the group;
- the length of time members may be out unaccompanied;
- the rule that they may not go out on their own; and
- the rule that they must tell the organisation where they are going.

These issues should be discussed before the trip, so that young people and their parents are quite clear about the rules to be applied during the trip. While organisers of trips are concerned about the safety of the young people, they should also have regard for their increasing maturity. It may be unrealistic to impose a rule that no young person is to leave the group at any time during the trip once the age of 16 or 17 is reached.

REMOTE SUPERVISION

The use of remote supervision may be effective. Remote supervision involves group work conducted away from the supervisor, but subject to stated controls. The group leader remains responsible for the young people even when not in direct contact with them. However, parents should know before hand if any form of remote supervision were going to take place. Factors to consider when remote supervision is used include:

- groups should be sufficiently trained and assessed as competent for the level of activity to be taken, including first aid and emergency procedures;
- groups should be familiar with the environment or similar environments and have details of rendezvous points and times;
- there should be clear and understandable boundaries set for the group;
- there should be monitoring of progress at appropriate levels;
- supervisors should be able to reach groups promptly should they need assistance;
- there should be a recognisable point at which the activity is completed; and
- there should be clear arrangements for the abandonment of activities where they cannot be completed safely.

TRANSPORTING CHILDREN

WHO CAN DRIVE A MINIBUS?

Individuals with a driving licence issued before 1 January 1997 can drive a minibus providing that they are over 21, the minibus has a maximum of 17 seats and is not being used for hire or reward. However, those with licences issued after January 1997 do not have automatic entitlement to drive a minibus and must meet the following requirements:

- unless they are operating under a permit they must not drive for hire or reward and must drive for a non-commercial body for social purposes;
- they must be aged 21 or over;
- they must have held a category B licence for at least two years;
- their services must be provided voluntarily; and
- the bus should be no heavier than 3.5 tonnes excluding specialist equipment (4.25 tonnes will be permitted in some circumstances such as equipment for the carriage of disabled passengers).

A driver will need to have a Passenger Carrying Vehicle entitlement, which involves taking a further driving test and meeting higher medical standards, if the driver is going to be paid to drive, a charge is made for the transport, or the minibus has more than nine seats. Further information may be found in the booklet *Passenger transport provided by voluntary groups under the Section 19 or 22 permit system*[7].

SEAT BELTS

The *Road Vehicles (Construction and Use) Regulations 1986* require that when a group of three or more children are transported in a minibus or coach on an organised trip, they must each be provided with a forward facing seat with a seat belt. For the purposes of the legislation, a child is defined as a person who is three to 15, a seat belt is a minimum of a lap belt and a seat has a minimum width of 400mm. The legislation does not define an organised trip. However, the key element is whether the journey is undertaken to transport children. School outings and trips by youth and voluntary organisations, where transporting children is the key element, are all subject to this legislation. A journey to or from a youth group, even when accompanied or driven by parents, and by road, from one part of a youth organisation's premises to another, is an organised trip. However, an organised trip using a scheduled service intended for the general population, which would operate regardless of whether children were travelling, would not be included.

While the legislation does not apply to public buses used for the general population, it does apply to all minibuses and coaches used to transport children, whether or not privately owned or used for hire or reward.

A minibus is defined as a motor vehicle constructed or adapted to carry more than eight, but not more than 16, passengers in addition to the driver. A coach is defined as a vehicle constructed or adapted to carry more than 16 passengers which has a gross weight of more than 7.5 tonnes and a maximum speed exceeding 60mph. The legislation does not apply to buses that do not meet the speed or weight criteria.

WHO IS RESPONSIBLE FOR ENSURING THAT THE CORRECT TYPE OF VEHICLE IS USED?

When a youth organisation seeks to hire a minibus or coach for a trip, the driver and his or her employer should supply a vehicle which meets the statutory standards. A failure on their part to do so would open them to legal liability for operating a vehicle which does not comply with the requirements of the legislation. However, the youth worker arranging the trip should inform the vehicle operator that the vehicle is required to transport children.

WHO IS RESPONSIBLE FOR ENSURING THAT A YOUNG PERSON WEARS A SEAT BELT?

Front and rear seats of minibuses

It is the driver's responsibility to ensure that all children under 14 wear seat belts (or seat-restraints if the child is under three) where they are available. Children of 14 and over must wear a seat belt if one is fitted, but they are responsible for doing so.

Larger minibuses and coaches

Although there is no statutory requirement that young people in the rear of larger minibuses or in coaches wear a seat belt, youth workers supervising a trip should try to ensure that the restraints are worn. A single seat belt should not be used by more than one child, nor should a belt be placed around a child who is on an adult's lap.

CAN WE STILL USE A VEHICLE WITH REAR FACING OR SIDE FACING SEATS?

The legislation requires that forward facing seats with a belt be available for each child. However, vehicles fitted with side or rear facing seats may be used as long as only the forward facing seats are used by the passengers.

Note: The legislation does not apply to children in wheelchairs. A Code of Practice entitled **The Safety of Passengers in Wheelchairs on Buses** *(VSE 87/1) is available from the Department for Transport Mobility and Inclusion Unit, Great Minster House, 76 Marsham Street, London SW1P 4DR.*

FOOTNOTES:

1. SI 2004/1309.
2. Contact the Adventure Activities Licensing Authority, 17 Lambourne Crescent, Cardiff Business Park, Llanishen, Cardiff CF14 5GF, telephone 029 2075 5715.
3. PO Box 5050, Annesley, Nottingham NG15 0DL, telephone 0845 60 222 60. (The Guide also contains a useful list of other organisations offering advice on safety for different activities.)
4. DfES 0803/2001.
5. www.teachernet.gov.uk/visits.
6. Either St John's Ambulance qualification or Red Cross.
7. www.vosa.gov.uk

USEFUL ADDRESSES:

A long list of addresses of useful bodies is contained in *Health and Safety of Pupils on Educational Visits*, but the following may be useful.

Adventure Activities Licensing Authority
17 Lambourne Crescent
Cardiff Business Park
Llanishen
Cardiff CF14 5GF
Tel: 029 2075 5715
Email: info@aala.org.uk
www.aala.org

For details of the types of licence required for drivers of minibuses, contact:
Community Transport Association
Highbank
Halton Street
Hyde
Cheshire SK14 2NY
Tel: 0870 774 3586
www.communitytransport.com
See also www.dvla.gov.uk

A Code of Practice on The Safety of Passengers in Wheelchairs on Buses (VSE87/1) *is available from:*
Department for Transport Mobility and Inclusion Unit
Great Minster House
76 Marsham Street
London SW1P 4DR
Tel: 020 7944 8300

For copies of Department for Education and Skills documents, contact:
DfES Publications
P.O. Box 5050
Annesley
Nottingham NG15 0DL
Tel: 0845 60 222 60
Fax: 0845 60 333 60
Email: dfes@prolog.uk.com

Running away

Although many young people run away from home, most of them do not appear in official statistics because they return home before the police are contacted. In addition many of those who are reported missing return home of their own free will or are easily traced. However, some young people who run away are never found and some are never even sought.

When young people run away from home or local authority care there are many factors to be considered. These include first, the urgent need to find out why they went; second, where the runaway is living to make sure that he or she is safe; third, how to help the young person without breaching either the law or professional codes of conduct; and fourth, achieving a practical solution, which will be accepted by the young person and those responsible for him or her.

This chapter provides advice on the legal position of young people who have run away; those with parental responsibility for them; and those who seek to assist them.

AT WHAT AGE MAY A YOUNG PERSON LEAVE HOME?

YOUNG PEOPLE LIVING AT HOME

There is no definite age at which young people are allowed to leave home. The *Children Act 1989* provides that parents have '*parental responsibility*' for their children until they are 18 years old. However, parental responsibility is not well defined in the *Children Act 1989* and is not necessarily the same as '*parental rights*'. Parents have limited powers to force their children to return home once they are 16 years old and below this age, although their powers are much stronger, they are not absolute.

YOUNG PEOPLE LOOKED AFTER BY THE LOCAL AUTHORITY

Some young people are looked after by the local authority on a voluntary basis, which means that there is no court order giving the local authority responsibility for them. This is called being '*accommodated*'[1]. A child who is accommodated over the age of 16 cannot be made to return to his or her parents, even though the parents may still hold parental responsibility.

Young people accommodated by a Care Order or subject to the provisions of the *Children (Leaving Care) Act 2000* will find it particularly difficult if they run away as they will not be entitled to claim social benefits: it is the responsibility of the local authority to look after them and provide financial assistance.

In situations where young people are subject to either a Care Order under s.31 *Children Act 1989*, an Emergency Protection Order under s.44 *Children Act 1989* or in police protection under s.46 *Children Act 1989*, it is a criminal offence to encourage them to run away or to abduct them[2]. Young people do not commit a criminal offence if they run away from home, the local authority, or a foster home. However, they may find themselves sought by the police and returned home, or the subject of court proceedings to secure their return. Young people looked after by the local authority may even find themselves placed in secure accommodation[3].

CHILDREN MISSING FROM CARE AND FROM HOME

The Department of Health published guidance on dealing with young runaways in November 2002. *Children Missing from Care and from Home: A guide to good practice* (2002 DoH)[4] defines childen as missing if they:

> '... *spend time away from where they ought to live without the knowledge and consent of their carers.*'

The Guidance is designed to set out good practice for agencies to follow when faced with young runaways and is divided into two sections. The first deals with children missing from care and the second with children missing from home.

CHILDREN MISSING FROM CARE

Both the law and the Department of Health Guidance provide that children's homes and foster carers should have written procedures that must be followed where a child goes missing, and that service managers in local authorities should monitor patterns of absence from individual children's homes and foster carers. In the event that a young person's absence is unauthorised, the local authority that made the placement must be informed, but there is no requirement to inform the police. The local authority has discretion as to whether it informs the parents of this.

When dealing with a persistent runaway, the manager responsible for the children's home or fostering service, in consultation with the local authority, should convene a multi-agency risk management meeting to develop a strategy about how the identified risks can be managed.

PHYSICALLY PREVENTING A CHILD FROM RUNNING AWAY

The Guidance considers it permissible to physically intervene to prevent a young person from running away, but it is clear that such action must be justified by an assessment of the risks faced if the young person does run away. Physical intervention should not be considered to be a long-term risk management strategy.

STRATEGIES AND PROCEDURES

Local authorities, the police and voluntary sector agencies, where appropriate, should draw up protocols for action to be taken where young people run away from care. According to the Guidance such protocols should:

- include details about the circumstances when it will be appropriate to contact the police;
- be compatible with other local arrangements concerned with minimising the exposure of young people to harm – in particular, local child protection procedures and protocols for safeguarding young people at risk of sexual exploitation;
- be approved and signed off by the Local Safeguarding Children Board (formerly Local Area Child Protection Committee); and
- specify senior management posts in each agency with responsibility for ensuring that the protocol is followed.

Records and logs should be kept when a looked after child runs away.

If a young person runs away and fails to return to his or her placement within a reasonable period, senior managers must be informed.

WHAT HELP CAN BE GIVEN TO YOUNG RUNAWAYS?

Organisations wishing to act as an intermediary for a young runaway should approach the appropriate local authority. However, if the response of social workers is unsatisfactory then an immediate approach should be made to the Director of Children's Services (formerly Director of Social Services). Organisations should also consider involving the Department of Health's Commission for Social Care Inspection (formerly the Social Services Inspectorate).

> 'Young people who have run from care should expect their placing local authority to respond like a concerned parent, attempting to understand the reasons that a young person has run and ensuring that they are able to access appropriate services, which might include independent advocacy.'[5]

Many young people who run away from home stay in the area, often with friends. A young person may turn to someone he or she already knows for advice and help, perhaps a teacher or a youth worker. That person may be put in the position of negotiating with parents or the local authority on behalf of the young person.

When negotiating on behalf of a young person it is important to establish the wishes of the young person: the young person may wish to live with another family, live in a supportive establishment or live independently. The young person may require help in order to work out the practical possibilities of achieving his or her plan. It should be noted that young people below the age of 16 are not regarded as being able to live independently.

It may be helpful to involve other people in the negotiations, not just the person with whom the young person is in conflict, such as the parents or local authority. It is also necessary to understand the legal boundaries, and the extent to which it is legally acceptable to conceal a child's whereabouts from a parent or carer.

Although there is no absolute duty on a youth worker, other professional or organisation to disclose the whereabouts of a young runaway, there are situations where failure to disclose information would make an individual or organisation liable to prosecution. Individuals should also consider that there may be additional disciplinary proceedings from their employer (such as the local authority), if they fail to disclose the whereabouts of a child when asked to do so. Decisions about what help to offer a runaway is particularly difficult if the runaway is young or thought to be at risk.

If a young person is under 16 (or disabled and under 18) the local authority must be informed if he or she stays more than 28 days with an individual who does not possess parental responsibility. If the young person stays more than 28 days he or she will be regarded as being 'privately fostered'[6]. Failure to inform the local authority may be considered an offence.

It is possible to commit an offence under s.2 *Child Abduction Act 1984* by concealing a child or helping a child to run away from his or her parents. A person commits an offence if, without lawful authority or reasonable excuse, he or she detains a young person below the age of 16:

> *'a) so as to remove him from the lawful control of any person having lawful control of the child; or*
> *b) so as to keep him out of the lawful control of any person entitled to lawful control of the child.'*

Taking and detaining includes inducing the young person to run away or inducing him or her to remain out of the parents' control. Convictions under this Act are rare and the law hinges on the intention of the individual. If the individual is responding to a young person's actions, rather than encouraging the young person to run away, it is doubtful whether a prosecution would be brought.

Where a Care Order has been made, the child is the subject of an Emergency Protection Order or is in police protection, a person will be guilty of an offence under s.49 *Children Act 1989* if, '*knowingly and without lawful authority or reasonable excuse*', he or she takes or keeps a child away from a responsible person, or induces, assists or incites a child to run away or stay away from the responsible person.

However, s.51 *Children Act 1989* exempts organisations providing refuges for children from charges under s.2 *Child Abduction Act 1984*, if they have a certificate from the Secretary of State, which allows them to provide refuge to children who are '*at risk*'.

All agencies should consider general policies on the kind of help they can offer young people who have runaway from home or local authority care. These policies should outline the circumstances in which they will disclose information even against the wishes of the young person[7].

WHAT ACTION CAN BE TAKEN TO RETURN RUNAWAYS HOME OR INTO LOCAL AUTHORITY CARE?

When a young person runs away the main concern of parents and the local authority is to ensure that the young person is safe. Parents may try to find their children themselves and may turn to youth organisations for help: agencies should anticipate these situations and have policies in place. Once young people are found those with parental responsibility may seek to return them to their care. In trying to enforce return, the powers of the local authority and parents differ.

THE ROLE OF THE POLICE

In many circumstances where young people run away from home or local authority care, the first response to their disappearance will be to call the police.

Children who have run away from home

Parents will be asked to file a Missing Person's Report, or if they know the whereabouts of the young person they may request the police to return the young person to their care. If the police approach an organisation seeking information on the whereabouts of a young person, there is no general duty for the organisation to reveal to the police where the young person is living. However, giving false or misleading information may result in prosecution for obstruction[8]. If an agency or worker refuses to disclose information given in confidence by a young person, or refuses to surrender a young person known to be on the premises, it is important to try to explain to the police why this is necessary, and to establish a friendly professional relationship with the police.

The extent of police action to return young runaways to their parents is largely discretionary, varying from one area to another, and according to the age and maturity of the young person in question and the circumstances of the case. Where the police do decide to locate and return a young runaway,

youth workers, or those working closely with the young person, should suggest to the police that they first interview the young person before returning him or her home. The police should only allow a return home if they are satisfied it is in the young person's best interests.

Children who have run away from a local authority

Local authorities should have joint protocols with the police and records of young people's absences should be recorded. Where a young person has run away from local authority care, the police will generally be informed and will return the young person to the children's home or foster parent. However, before being returned to local authority care, children should have access to an independent interview and their views and wishes listened to. Youth workers may act as an independent advocate in such situations or ensure that the child has access to an independent advocacy service[9].

Police protection

In emergency situations, where the police believe that a child may be at risk of '*significant harm*', they have the power to:

> '*a) remove the child to suitable accommodation and keep him there; or*
>
> *b) take such steps as are reasonable to ensure that the child's removal from any hospital, or other place, in which he is then being accommodated is prevented.*'[10]

The police may keep the child for up to 72 hours, but must move the child as soon as possible to local authority accommodation. The police must inform all carers of the child, those with parental responsibility and the police that the child has been taken into police protection and the reasons for this action. While the child is in police protection they must allow parents and others with contact or residence rights to have contact with the child as long as this contact is in the child's best interests. The police must also attempt to

---

CASE STUDY

A youth worker rang the Children's Legal Centre concerned at what she had been told by Jane. Jane, an immature 15-year-old, had been truanting from school. She had been spending the day with other teenagers and a number of older men, reading magazines and watching pornographic videos at the house of Mr and Mrs Jones. The Joneses had now asked her to come and live with them and help to look after the children. The Joneses were known to the police. There was concern that the children were being supplied with drugs, and that a paedophile ring was being run from the house. Although the youth worker was able to talk Jane out of moving in with the Joneses, and to achieve a reconciliation between her and her parents, the youth worker was so concerned about the presence of other, unidentified teenagers in the Joneses' house that she contacted the police. The police raided the premises and removed Anne and Ben, two 14-year-old runaways living there, into police protection.

'*discover the wishes and feelings of the child*' and having investigated the circumstances of the situation, the police must release the child unless there is reason to believe that the child will suffer significant harm as a result. If the police believe that a child is a further risk they may apply for an Emergency Protection Order.

EMERGENCY PROTECTION ORDERS

Anyone concerned about the welfare of a child including the police, youth workers, the local authority or a friend of the child, may apply for an Emergency Protection Order under s.44 *Children Act 1989*. A court can only make such an order if it is satisfied that there is '*reasonable cause to believe*' that the child is a risk of significant harm. Such orders are not granted lightly and will only be appropriate in cases where the likely significant harm is serious[11].

As far as runaways are concerned, it is important to note that an Emergency Protection Order might be useful as a short-term remedy, to provide a cooling-off period. The applicant for an Emergency Protection Order must inform the local authority, which must then investigate. The local authority then has the power, having consulted the applicant and child, to take over the Order and responsibility for the child[12]. An Emergency Protection Order is, therefore, more useful for a child who has run away from home than one who has run away from care, although the latter group are not excluded from the protection of Emergency Protection Orders.

An Emergency Protection Order only lasts for a maximum of eight days (local authorities can apply to renew for another seven days). The child, parents and persons with whom the child was living, can apply for a discharge after 72 hours[13]. While the Order is in force, it operates as a direction to any person who is in a position to do so, to comply with any request to produce the child to the applicant. It may also authorise the applicant to enter premises and search for the child named in the Order, or any other child in danger.

WARDSHIP AND THE INHERENT JURISDICTION OF THE COURT

Parents may apply to have their child made a ward of court or ask the court to exercise its inherent jurisdiction as a means of trying to force their child to return home. However, a local authority cannot make an application for wardship[14], instead, the local authority will seek to invoke the inherent jurisdiction of the court. The powers of the court under the inherent jurisdiction are virtually identical to those of its wardship jurisdiction. When a child is made a ward of court, the court itself takes parental responsibility for the child, and appears to have far greater parental rights than parents possess. Once warded, the court can make orders, by an injunction if necessary,

> Local authorities are frequently unwilling to take action with respect to a child over the age of 14 and may need considerable persuasion before accepting that the young person is at risk of suffering significant harm.

controlling the child's or parents' actions. Any breach of an Order is treated extremely seriously, and can even be punished by committal to prison for contempt of court.

Where a child has run away, the parents could ask the High Court to make a 'Seek and Find' Order under its inherent jurisdiction. This can be made on the application of the parents alone. When a 'Seek and Find' Order is made, the Tipstaff (the court police) will be directed to seek and find the child concerned. When the Tipstaff finds the child, they will take the child into custody and deliver the child to the person named in the Order and, when backed with a warrant, arrest any person in breach of the Order.

The wardship court cannot order that a child be placed in the care of the local authority, though it could order that the local authority investigates the child's circumstances[15].

If people are summonsed to attend court in wardship proceedings, they can be compelled to disclose information about the ward to the court. Thus, a youth worker could be forced to disclose a young person's whereabouts, although the court may listen to the worker's objections to disclosing information given in confidence. Anyone who assists a young person who has been made a ward of court, in a way which could interfere with the court's protection of the young person, could be found guilty of contempt of court.

Of course, agencies who are contacted by runaways for help may not know that a young person is a ward (and, indeed, the young person may also be unaware that he or she is a ward of the court). Unless the young person discloses this information, there is no easy way of finding out. A worker who knowingly assists a ward, contrary to a court order, would be unlikely to be found guilty of contempt, but might be summonsed to court to explain his or her actions.

RETURN OF YOUNG RUNAWAYS TO LOCAL AUTHORITY CARE

RECOVERY ORDERS

Where it appears to the court that there is reason to believe that a child who is in care, subject to an Emergency Protection Order, or police protection, has been unlawfully taken away, is being kept away unlawfully, has run away or is missing, the court may make a Recovery Order[16]. A Recovery Order:
- operates as a direction to any person who is in a position to do so to produce the child at the request of an authorised person;
- authorises the removal of a child;
- requires any person who has information as to the child's whereabouts to disclose that information if asked to do so; and
- allows the police to enter premises specified in the Order and search for the child. A person will be guilty of an offence if he or she intentionally obstructs an authorised person from removing the child.

WHAT FORMS OF ACTION CAN A YOUNG RUNAWAY TAKE?

APPROACHING THE LOCAL AUTHORITY

Local authorities quite often act as go-betweens to try to resolve differences and negotiate agreements between parents and children. Local authorities have a duty under s.47 *Children Act 1989* to make '*such enquiries as they consider necessary to enable them to decide whether they should take any action to safeguard or promote the child's welfare*', where they have reasonable cause to believe, or where they have been informed, that a child who lives or is found in their area is suffering or is likely to suffer significant harm. Some local authorities consider that, if alerted to the fact that a young person is a runaway, they must become involved in an investigation of the child's circumstances. Other local authorities are reluctant to get involved. If the youth worker or other professional thinks the intervention of the local authority would be helpful, this should be discussed with the young person and his or her consent obtained to a referral.

There is also a duty placed on other authorities (including the local education authority (LEA), the local housing authority and the health authority) to assist the local authority with their enquiries[17]. This obviously has implications for youth workers employed by, for example, the LEA who may be advising a young runaway. However, the same section specifically permits people not to assist local authorities '*where doing so would be unreasonable in all the circumstances of the case*'. It is probably sensible to involve senior management in any inter-professional conflicts of this sort.

Some young runaways have been threatened with '*being put in care*'. The local authority can only take a child into care by means of a Care Order, which must be obtained from the court under s.31 *Children Act 1989*. A court may only make a Care Order if it is satisfied that the child concerned is suffering, or is likely to suffer, significant harm and that the harm is attributable either to an unacceptable level of care by the parent(s), or the child being beyond parental control[18].

Parents cannot insist that a local authority seek a Care Order. Neither can they take legal action, other than a High Court judicial review or asking the Secretary of State to use his or her default powers, to compel the local authority to take a child or young person into care. The position is the same for young people. Some runaways do ask local authorities to take them into care, but they will only intervene if they consider the welfare of the child is at risk. However, where family proceedings are already taking place, and a question arises with respect to the welfare of the child, the court may, if it thinks it appropriate, direct the local authority to conduct an investigation of the child's circumstances[19].

Although a young person cannot force the local authority to take him or her into care, it is possible for a young person to be accommodated by the local authority. The local authority must provide a child (under 18) with accommodation if:

- there is no one with parental responsibility for him or her;
- the young person is lost or abandoned; or
- the person caring for him or her is prevented from providing the young person with suitable accommodation or care.

The young runaway could, therefore, ask the local authority for accommodation. However, where the young person is under the age of 16, a local authority may not provide accommodation if any person who has parental responsibility is willing and able to provide accommodation and objects to the local authority accommodating the young person.

Even if the parents did not object initially to the provision of accommodation, they may do so at a later stage, and may remove the child from accommodation. Where there is a real conflict between the young person and the parents, it may be possible to negotiate with the local authority, parents and the young person, for him or her to be accommodated for a limited period of time to allow a breathing space.

This is a difficult area of the law, as where one parent has a Residence Order the position changes.

The need for parents to consent to the child being accommodated disappears once the child reaches the age of 16. From that point, the young person may ask to be accommodated, agree the care plan and discharge him or herself from accommodation, without reference to parents[20]. However, the local authority is only obliged to offer accommodation to a 16-year-old where it considers that the young person is likely to be seriously prejudiced if it does not provide him or her with accommodation. In other cases, the local authority

CASE STUDY

The Children's Legal Centre was contacted by a father. His three children lived with their mother, who had been granted a Residence Order in relation to the children. The 13-year-old boy had become very difficult, taking drugs, mixing with a 'bad group' and staying out all night. The mother had asked the local authority to accommodate him. The local authority agreed and placed the boy with foster parents. The father, when he heard that the boy was accommodated, contacted him. He then rang the local authority and offered to have the boy. The mother refused to allow the boy to live with his father, and wanted him to remain with the foster parents who, she thought, would provide better care.

Because the mother had a Residence Order, the father had no power to remove the child from the accommodation. Either the boy or the father would have to return to court and obtain a new Residence Order. Once the father was granted a Residence Order, he could then object to the provision of accommodation and remove the boy.

has discretion as to whether to provide accommodation: it needs only do so if it considers it would safeguard or promote the young person's welfare. While being accommodated would undoubtedly be better for a young person than being homeless, local authorities have limited amounts of accommodation, most of which is bed and breakfast or hostel accommodation, and will need to be persuaded that it is necessary to provide such accommodation.

It is unfortunately quite common for local authorities to refuse to get involved in the cases of young runaways, but if the young person is homeless and unable to return home, the local authority should be pressed to take up its responsibilities. Where an authority refuses to offer accommodation, it is possible to make a formal complaint under s.26 *Children Act 1989*, but generally, given the emergency nature of the young person's situation it will be better to seek a judicial review of the refusal. In both instances, the young person should be encouraged to consult a solicitor on the Children Panel (details available from the Law Society).

INITIATING LEGAL PROCEEDINGS

Since the introduction of the *Children Act 1989*, young people have been able to bring their own 'private law' actions under s.8 *Children Act 1989*. The most useful of the s.8 orders for a young runaway would be a Residence Order, allowing him or her to live with a named person.

A child does not have an automatic right to apply for a Residence Order under s.8 *Children Act 1989*, but only a right to '*apply for leave*' to make such an application. The court will only grant such leave if satisfied that the child has '*sufficient understanding to make the proposed application*'. As a general rule, an application must be made initially through a

CASE STUDY

Claudia, aged 15, lived with her aunt during the week from the age of 11 to 14 while her mother was working as a nurse. She returned to live with her mother a year ago, when the mother married George. Claudia hardly knew George before the marriage and does not get on with him. There are constant arguments and fights. Claudia is also unhappy with her new school and sees little of her mother who is still working. Claudia asked her mother whether she could return to live with the aunt, who is happy to revert to the old arrangement. The mother has refused on the basis that the family should stay together. Claudia became increasingly unhappy and eventually ran away. Claudia rang the Children's Legal Centre for advice, telling us that at the moment she was living with a friend, but that she could not stay there more than a few days, and that she wanted to live with her aunt.

The Children's Legal Centre advised her that she could seek a Residence Order herself (the aunt was unwilling to take legal action against her sister) allowing her to live with her aunt.

Litigation Friend – someone over the age of 18 (legal aid will be based on the young person's means, not the Litigation Friend's). There are, however, exceptions to this rule. A child may instruct a solicitor to make the application for him or her, or apply to the court for leave to make the application him or herself. The court must consider whether any proposed application will '*risk… disrupting the child's life to such an extent that he would be harmed by it*'. It should be noted that the courts do not encourage the taking of such actions by children, on the basis that it is likely to cause even more upset and contribute to a greater breakdown of family relationships. In such cases, mediation can be very helpful in order to resolve residence issues and provide further help to the family.

It is important to note that:
- Only in '*exceptional circumstances*' can a s.8 order be made in respect of 16- or 17-year-olds.
- Where a child is subject to a Care Order, he or she can still make an application for a Residence Order to live with a named person under s.8 *Children Act 1989*.

SECURE ACCOMMODATION

Where young people are '*looked after*' by the local authority (either under a Care Order or are accommodated), the consequences of running away may be far more serious. Serial runaways may face the danger of being placed in secure accommodation: in effect being locked up in accommodation from which they are not free to leave. Under s.25 *Children Act 1989* a local authority may place a child in secure accommodation if it appears that:

> '… he has a history of absconding and is likely to abscond from any other description of accommodation; and if he absconds, he is likely to suffer significant harm.'

This section of the Act applies to all children looked after by the local authority, other than children between 16 and 21 who are accommodated by the local authority to safeguard or promote their welfare. The local authority cannot keep a young person in secure accommodation for more than 72 hours without the court's authorisation.

Secure accommodation is often an inappropriate response to absconding, which is generally the result of poor care in open facilities, a breakdown in relationships and a fear of necessary risk-taking. If a local authority is threatening to restrict a young person's liberty, it may be particularly difficult to persuade the runaway to return to care. The most useful service that can be provided in these circumstances is to investigate viable alternative placements and to identify energetic advocates for the young person. Local authorities should be reminded that they are under a duty to '*avoid the need for children … to be placed in secure accommodation*', and that alternatives should be sought and seriously considered[21].

FOOTNOTES:

1. s.20 *Children Act 1989*.

2. s.49 *Children Act 1989*.

3. see p.45.

4. Guidance. 2002. Department of Health.

5. *Children Missing from Care and from Home: A guide to good practice*. 2002. Department of Health.

6. s.66 *Children Act 1989*.

7. see chapter 5.

8. see chapter 15.

9. For details of independent advocacy services contact CROA at www.cora.org.uk

10. s.46 *Children Act 1989*.

11. chapter 10.

12. *Emergency Protection Orders (Transfer of Responsibilities) Regulations 1991*.

13. s.45 *Children Act 1989*.

14. s.100 *Children Act 1989*.

15. s.37 *Children Act 1989*.

16. s.50 *Children Act 1989*.

17. s.47 *Children Act 1989*.

18. see chapter 10.

19. s.37 *Children Act 1989*.

20. s.20 *Children Act 1989*.

21. Sched. 2, para.7 *Children Act 1989*.

Sex:

Sexual relationships, sex education and sexually transmitted infections

There is no doubt that issues associated with relationships, sex, sexual identity and sexual health are matters of major concern to most adolescents. Such relationships can also be a concern to those working with young people: especially knowing what information to provide and when to intervene in what may be an exploitative relationship or illegal sexual activity.

One of the main concerns for youth organisations, especially those which take children on overnight trips and holidays, is the extent to which they should police the sexual relationships between young people in their care and even young people and staff in the organisation. Although some organisations have instituted no-touching policies with consequences for breaking the rules, such a policy may be unrealistic and backfire by encouraging young people to continue their relationships in secret. Other organisations have no specific policy and deal with the issue as it arises. However, it is helpful for organisations to have a policy on sexual relations between its members and to discuss the reasons for such a policy with the young people and staff in order to reach a consensus.

In order to draft the policy, organisations need knowledge of the relevant law together with a degree of realism and sensitivity. The primary aim of the policy should be to ensure that young people are not exposed to unwanted or exploitative sexual activity. However, it should be sensitive to young people and resist penalising them for developing relationships, which are neither exploitative nor corrupting.

THE AGE OF CONSENT

The age of consent is set at 16 for heterosexual, homosexual and lesbian relationships in England and Wales. However, young people can commit sexual crimes from the age of 10 as this is the age of criminal responsibility[1]. A boy over the age of 10 years old is regarded by the law as capable of committing any sexual offence, including rape[2] and both males and females over 10 may be charged with any of the other sexual offences contained in the *Sexual Offences Act 2003*, except where the offence stipulates that the perpetrator has to be aged 18 or over.

CONSENSUAL SEXUAL RELATIONS BETWEEN YOUNG PEOPLE

The *Sexual Offences Act 2003* introduced new sexual offences and a range of measures to deal with them. At this stage, it is too early to make judgements about the impact of the Act. However, one of the more radical provisions relates to offences which can be committed by children and young people engaging in *consensual* sexual activity with each other.

A young person under 18 commits an offence if he or she intentionally[3]:

- engages in sexual touching of a child under the age of 16;
- causes or incites a child aged under 16 to engage in sexual activity;
- engages in sexual activity in the presence of a child under the age of 16 or in a place from which a child can observe him or her; or
- causes a child under the age of 16 to watch a third person engaging in sexual activity or to look at an image of a person engaging in sexual activity (e.g. a pornographic film).

The consent of the children is irrelevant.

WHAT DO 'SEXUAL' AND 'TOUCHING' MEAN?

The *Sexual Offences Act 2003* provides that:
> '*penetration, touching or any other activity is sexual if a reasonable person would consider that:*
> *(a) whatever its circumstances or any person's purpose in relation to it, it is because of its nature sexual; or*
> *(b) because of its nature it may be sexual and because of its*

circumstances or the purpose of any person in relation to it (or both) it is sexual.'[4]

It also provides a definition of touching:

> *'Touching includes touching:*
> *(a) with any part of the body;*
> *(b) with anything else; or*
> *(c) through anything [e.g. clothing];*
> *and in particular includes touching amounting to penetration.'*[5]

The result is that behaviour often considered as 'normal' consensual activity between two young people under 18, such as fondling and petting, is criminalised.

PROSECUTION

A young person convicted of an offence could face imprisonment for up to five years[6]. The Explanatory Notes to the Act advise that decisions about whether or not to prosecute will be made by the Crown Prosecution Service on the basis of whether or not it is in the public interest to prosecute. There is no provision about this in the Act. However, the Notes suggest that the following considerations should be taken into account:

- the ages of the parties;
- the emotional maturity of the parties;
- whether they entered into a sexual relationship willingly;
- any coercion or corruption by a person; and
- the relationship between the parties[7].

The Guidance issued by the Crown Prosecution Service[8] makes it clear that the Act is designed to protect children, not to punish them unnecessarily or make them subject to the criminal justice system where it is wholly inappropriate. Young people should not be prosecuted where sexual activity was entirely mutually agreed and non-exploitative.

UNLAWFUL SEXUAL RELATIONSHIPS

Children and young people are protected by the same laws as adults in relation to unwanted or non-consensual sexual behaviour. The range of sexual offences which can be committed against children and young people are set out in the *Sexual Offences Act 2003*. Rape is the only offence that can only be committed by a man because it relates to penile penetration. All other sexual offences can be committed by both males and females[9].

OFFENCE:	CRITERIA FOR COMMITTING THE OFFENCE:	MAXIMUM SENTENCE:
Sexual activity with a child (s.9 *Sexual Offences Act 2003*)	It is a criminal offence for a person aged 18 or over to intentionally touch a young person in a sexual manner if they are under the age of 16. Where the young person is aged 13 or over, but under 16, the prosecution must prove that the defendant did not reasonably believe that the young person was 16 or over. The consent of the young person is irrelevant. The penalties for sex offences against children under 13 are higher than penalties for offences against older children.	14 years imprisonment
Causing or inciting a child to engage in sexual activity (s.10 *Sexual Offences Act 2003*)	It is a criminal offence for a person aged 18 or over to intentionally cause or incite a young person under the age of 16 to engage in sexual activity. Where the young person is aged 13 or over, but under 16, the prosecution must prove that the defendant did not reasonably believe that the young person was 16 or over. The consent of the young person is irrelevant.	14 years imprisonment
Engaging in sexual activity in the presence of a child (s.11 *Sexual Offences Act 2003*)	It is a criminal offence for a person aged 18 or over, for the purpose of obtaining sexual gratification, to intentionally engage in sexual activity when a child under the age of 16 is present or, with the person's knowledge, able to observe the activity. Where the young person is aged 13 or over, but under 16, the prosecution must prove that the defendant did not reasonably believe that the young person was 16 or over. The consent of the young person is irrelevant.	10 years imprisonment
Causing a child to watch a sexual act (s.12 *Sexual Offences Act 2003*)	It is a criminal offence for a person aged 18 or over, for the purpose of obtaining sexual gratification, to intentionally cause a young person under the age of 16 to watch a third party engaging in sexual activity or to watch an image of	10 years imprisonment

OFFENCE:	CRITERIA FOR COMMITTING THE OFFENCE cont'd:	MAXIMUM SENTENCE:
	any person engaging in such activity. Where the young person is aged 13 or over, but under 16, the prosecution must prove that the defendant did not reasonably believe that the young person was 16 or over. The consent of the young person is irrelevant.	
Sexual assault of a child under 13 (s.7 *Sexual Offences Act 2003*)	It is a criminal offence for a person to intentionally touch in a sexual manner a child under the age of 13. The consent of the young person is irrelevant.	14 years imprisonment
Assault of a child under 13 by penetration (s.6 *Sexual Offences Act 2003*)	It is an offence for a person to intentionally penetrate sexually the vagina, anus or mouth of a child under the age of 13. This includes penetration by a part of the defendant's body, such as a finger, or anything else, such as a bottle or other object. The consent of the young person is irrelevant and it is not necessary for the young person to know what he or she was penetrated with.	Life imprisonment
Rape of a child under 13 (s.5 *Sexual Offences Act 2003*)	It is an offence for a male to intentionally penetrate with his penis the vagina, anus or mouth of a child under the age of 13. The consent of the young person is irrelevant.	Life imprisonment
Causing or inciting a child under 13 to engage in sexual activity (s.8 *Sexual Offences Act 2003*)	It is an offence for a person to intentionally cause or incite a child under the age of 13 to engage in sexual activity. This may include making the child strip or masturbate, or making him or her have intercourse with a third party by promising a reward or that such behaviour is normal. The consent of the young person is irrelevant.	14 years imprisonment

Note: The offences of unlawful sexual intercourse and indecent assault no longer exist.

ARRANGING OR FACILITATING THE COMMISSION OF A CHILD SEX OFFENCE

It is an offence for a person to intentionally arrange or facilitate any action which he or she intends to, intends another person to, or believes another person will, in any part of the world, commit an offence under the *Sexual Offences Act 2003*[10]. The maximum penalty for this offence is 14 years in prison. This provision is designed to prohibit actions such as:

- approaching an agency requesting the procurement of a child for the purpose of sexual activity with the defendant or his or her friend;
- driving a friend to meet a child with whom he or she knows the friend is going to engage in sexual activity; and
- offering a bedroom in his house to friends for the purposes of having sex with a particular child or children.

A person can be prosecuted under the Act for activities anywhere in the world, as long as the activity is an offence in the country where it takes place. However, the Act also provides that no offence is committed where a person is acting

for the purpose of:

- protecting a child from sexually transmitted infection;
- protecting the physical safety of a child;
- preventing the child from becoming pregnant; or
- promoting the child's emotional wellbeing by the giving of advice.

This exception applies provided the person concerned does not act for the purpose of sexual gratification. This exception is designed to protect youth workers, health workers, teachers and Connexions advisers. It would be relevant, for example, where a discovery was made that a 16-year-old boy was having sex with a 14-year-old girl and where a youth worker provided the girl with condoms in the belief that if contraception was not provided the couple would have unprotected sex.

MEETING A CHILD FOLLOWING SEXUAL GROOMING

It is unlawful for a person aged 18 or over to intentionally meet, or travel with the intention of meeting, a young person under the age of 16 (and whom he or she does not reasonably believe to be over the age of 16) with the intention of committing a sexual offence against the young person[11]. In order to commit this offence, the person must have met or communicated with the young person on at least two prior occasions. This provision is designed to protect children from sexual grooming: where they 'meet' an adult posing to be a young person in an internet chat room and the adult gains their trust and suggests meeting in person. The maximum sentence for this offence is 10 years imprisonment.

ABUSE OF POSITION OF TRUST

The *Sexual Offences (Amendment) Act 2000* introduced a new offence of '*abuse of position of trust*'. The aim of the offence is to protect 16- and 17-year-olds, but the offence also applies to young people under 16. The law relating to this offence has since been updated by the *Sexual Offences Act 2003*.

Abuse of position of trust arises where a person aged 18 or over who is in a '*position of trust*' intentionally:
- sexually touches a person under the age of 18;
- causes or incites a person under the age of 18 to engage in a sexual activity;
- engages in a sexual activity when a person under the age of 18 is present or does so in a place from which he or she can be observed by an under 18; or
- causes a person under the age of 18 to watch a third person engaging in an sexual activity or to look at an image of any person engaging in a sexual activity.

WHAT IS A POSITION OF TRUST?
A person is in a position of trust if he or she:
- looks after young people under the age of 18 who are detained in an institution by virtue of a court order or under an enactment (e.g. detention in a Young Offenders Institution);
- looks after young people under the age of 18 accommodated in foster care, voluntary or local authority residential care and semi-independent accommodation;
- looks after young people under the age of 18 accommodated and cared for in:
  - a hospital;
  - an independent clinic;
  - a care home, residential care home or private hospital;
  - a community home, voluntary home or children's home;
  - a private children's home receiving provision, equipment and maintenance from the State; or
  - a residential family centre.
- looks after young people under the age of 18 at an educational institution. Where a child under 18 is registered as receiving full-time education at one establishment, but attends another as part of his or her course, the older person is treated as in a position of trust if looking after the child at either establishment;
- looks after young people under the age of 18 on an individual basis in his or her capacity as, for example, a Connexions personal adviser;
- has regular unsupervised contact with young people

under the age of 18 in the context of his or her duties under s.20 and s.21 *Children Act 1989*. This covers social workers and family centre staff who visit children accommodated by social services to monitor their welfare;
- has regular unsupervised contact with young people under the age of 18 by virtue of his or her appointment as a CAFCASS Children and Family Reporter;
- looks after young people under the age of 18 on an individual basis in their capacity as a personal adviser (see chapter 1);
- supervises on an individual basis young people under the age of 18 pursuant to a Care Order, Supervision Order or Education Supervision Order;
- has regular unsupervised contact with young people under the age of 18 in the course of his or her duties as a CAFCASS Children's Guardian, a children's guardian in relation to adoption proceedings or a *guardian ad litem*; and
- supervises young people under the age of 18 who are subject to bail, a community sentence or conditions following release from detention (e.g. Youth Offending Team members)[12].

WHAT DOES 'LOOKED AFTER' MEAN?
A person 'looks after' a person under 18 years old in the circumstances above, if he or she is regularly involved in caring for, training, supervising or being in sole charge of the individual[13].

CASE STUDY

Mark is 17-years-old. He has recently been convicted of theft of a mobile phone. Mark is a heroin addict and he stole the mobile phone to help fund his habit. Part of his sentence was a six month Drug Treatment and Testing Order, which obliges Mark to undergo drug treatment and be tested regularly for drugs. Sally, aged 19, is responsible for the provision of Mark's drug treatment programme and she has been assisting him for the past six weeks. Mark and Sally have grown quite close and a couple of weeks ago, they had sexual intercourse. Sally confided in a colleague about what had happened, and the colleague is concerned that Sally may have committed an offence. Has she?

Yes. Sally has committed the offence of abuse of position of trust. She is a person in a position of trust under s.21 Sexual Offences Act 2003 because she is supervising as part of a community sentence. Although Mark is over the age of consent, the offence of abuse of position of trust was introduced to protect young people in Mark's position and of Mark's age.

DEFENCES
The offence of abuse of position of trust will not be made out where the defendant can show that he or she reasonably believed that the young person was 18 or over, unless the

child concerned is under 13 in which case any belief the defendant had in relation to the child's age is irrelevant.

CASE STUDY

A youth club takes a group of teenagers on a camping trip. The leaders of the trip include a 20-year-old male who, during the course of the holiday, forms a sexual relationship with a 17-year-old girl.

The adult male is not in a position of trust to the 17-year-old. He is not looking after her within the meaning of the Sexual Offences Act 2003. Neither does the youth club trip fall within the situations set out above when a person may be in a position of trust. However, the youth club may wish to consider whether there should be a written policy on the desirability of sexual relationships between staff and those in their care.

Those working with young people should be aware of their responsibilities. They should be alert to the fact that paedophiles are attracted to places where young people meet, such as swimming pools, camp sites, playing grounds and outside schools and youth clubs. If a person who has no known connection with any of the young people present is frequently seen around such venues, and is taking a specific interest in the young people, the police must be contacted and any suspicions or unease communicated to them.

HOMOSEXUALITY AND LESBIANISM

The age of consent for homosexual, heterosexual and lesbian activity is 16. Sexual acts between consenting adults over that age are not illegal. Thus, any act that is legal for heterosexual couples is also legal for homosexual and lesbian couples. The offences set out in the *Sexual Offences Act 2003* apply equally to heterosexual, homosexual and lesbian activity.

INFORMATION AND ADVICE ABOUT SEX AND SEXUALITY

There has always been a tendency to direct information about sexual matters to girls rather than boys. However, boys are equally confused and in need of accurate information: it is important for workers to recognise their responsibility to this group.

SHOULD YOUTH WORKERS BE PROVIDING INFORMATION AND ADVICE ABOUT SEXUAL MATTERS?

Sex education is usually provided by schools. Guidance on what should be covered is contained in *Sex and Relationship Education Guidance*[14]. Trained staff in secondary schools are able to give young people full information about different types of contraception, as well as confidential advice, counselling and treatment.

Youth workers may also give contraceptive advice or information to young people regardless of their age. The Government encourages this:

> '*Youth workers … can and should encourage young people [including under-16s] to seek advice and contraception and direct them to local services if it appears that they are, or are thinking about becoming, sexually active.*'[15]

The issue of youth workers providing confidential advice and assistance to young people is discussed in greater detail in chapter 5.

SEXUALLY TRANSMITTED INFECTIONS AND DISEASES

Youth workers should be aware of the importance of encouraging young people who think that they may have contracted a sexually transmitted disease, including the Human Immunodeficiency Virus (HIV – the virus that causes the Acquired Immunodeficiency Syndrome (AIDS)), to seek prompt professional medical advice. The National AIDS Manual makes it plain that:

> '*… [p]eople with HIV who [receive appropriate treatment] are living with HIV without symptoms, and without an AIDS diagnosis, for longer. [Furthermore], very many people who meet rigid AIDS definitions can continue to lead healthy lives for long periods.*'[16]

Most clinicians now take the firm view that it is counter-productive to view AIDS as an invariably fatal modern day equivalent to the medieval plague. Furthermore, it is clear that HIV/AIDS cannot be considered in isolation from other sexually transmitted infections (STIs). Most, if not all, STIs cause lesions in the genital areas which may facilitate the transmission of other diseases, including hepatitis and AIDS.

TESTING

Following a Practice Direction in 1994[17] all applications to test a child for the presence of the AIDS virus (HIV) had to be made to the High Court. However, in 2003, the President of the Family Division issued a new Practice Direction. This recognised that medical science had developed and that the court took the view that applications should only be made to the court in rare cases. In cases where a young person under the age of 16 is regarded as competent (See *Gillick* competence, chapter 5) and opposes proposed testing, but doctors or parents think a test is in his or her best interests, an application should be made to the High Court to determine whether testing should take place. Where all those with parental responsibility agree to the test, and the young person does not oppose such testing, no application need be made to the court.

EDUCATION AND INFORMATION

It is important that young people understand about the existence of sexually transmitted infections and the risks that they pose to health. Young people may seek advice and information about such matters on their own behalf. Workers dealing with the individual fears of young people will be well-advised to refer them to specialist health professionals who will be best equipped to inform and reassure young people about specific problems of this type.

If projects wish to include an element to cover sexual health matters in their programmes, they should seek the agreement of their management group, and the support of health professionals in ensuring that the content is accurate. The key messages for all sex educators are:

* information and knowledge about HIV/AIDS is vital;
* young people need to understand what is risky behaviour and what is not;
* sex and relationship education should inform young people about condom use and safer sex in general;
* young people need skills to enable them to avoid being pressurised into unwanted or unprotected sex (this should link with issues of peer pressure and other risk-taking behaviour, such as drugs and alcohol); and
* young people need factual information about safer sex and skills to enable them to negotiate safer sex[18].

Any information should recognise that there are more sexually transmitted infections than HIV/AIDS alone, and that the long term effects of these, if untreated, are also devastating. There should be clarity about the difference between HIV infection and the development of AIDS.

Attention should be given to the relationship between the use of injected drugs and such conditions as infection by the HIV virus and hepatitis. Discussion will inevitably involve explicit information on various sexual practices, and on the risks for drug users who share needles. It is, therefore, essential that the policy of the project includes acknowledgement of this.

FOOTNOTES:

1. s.34 *Crime and Disorder Act 1998*.
2. s.1 *Sexual Offences Act 1993*.
3. s.13 *Sexual Offences Act 2003*.
4. s.78 *Sexual Offences Act 2003*.
5. s.79 (8) *Sexual Offences Act 2003*.
6. s.13(2) *Sexual Offences Act 2003*.
7. Para 22. *Explanatory Notes to Sexual Offences Act 2003*.
8. See www.cps.gov.uk
9. Para 6, Home Office Circular 021/2004, *Guidance on Part 1 of the Sexual Offences Act 2003*.
10. s.14 *Sexual Offences Act 2003*.
11. s.15 *Sexual Offences Act 2003*.
12. s.21 *Sexual Offences Act 2003*.
13. s.22 *Sexual Offences Act 2003*.
14. DfES Circular 0116/2000.
15. *Guidance for Youth Workers on Providing Information and Referring Young People to Contraceptive and Sexual Health Services 2001. Teenage Pregnancy Unit. Department of Health*.
16. HIV Basics, Improving treatments, www.nam.org.uk
17. *Re HIV Tests* [1994] 2 FLR 116.
18. *Sex and Relationship Education Guidance*. DfES Circular 0116/2000.

The use of drugs, alcohol and cigarettes

It is important to know the law relating to the use of drugs, alcohol and cigarettes when working with young people, especially if working in an informal setting such as a youth centre or project. It is also important that the legal position is clearly explained to young people in addition to any rules that the centre or project makes in relation to their use (see chapter 1).

DRUG USE

The use of drugs by young people is not desirable and it must be recognised that drug use is an important problem in the UK (with the highest levels of drug use in Europe). European surveys show that the highest prevalence rates of Cannabis use amongst 15-year-olds is in England as 42.5% of boys and 38% of girls have tried it[1].

Youth clubs need to strike a difficult balance between one, ensuring that drug use and supply does not take place on the premises and that young people are protected from drugs; and two that they do not overreact to the occasional drug use of their members if it incurs little apparent risk of harm and takes place away from the premises. All youth organisations should have a policy on drugs, which should be made known to the young people who participate in its services, projects or activities.

CONTROLLED DRUGS

Some dangerous drugs or otherwise harmful drugs are classified as 'controlled drugs' under the *Misuse of Drugs Act 1971* and are divided into three categories according to the dangers they pose:
- *Class A* includes heroin, cocaine, LSD, ecstasy, morphine, opium, methadone and injectable amphetamines.
- *Class B* includes amphetamines and barbiturates.
- *Class C* includes cannabis (marijuana or grass), cannabis resin (hashish), cannabinol and derivatives, anabolic steroids and tranquilisers, such as (valium).

It is an offence under s.8 *Misuse of Drugs Act 1971* for an occupier, or any one involved in the management of any premises to knowingly allow the premises to be used for:

- the smoking of cannabis or opium;
- the preparation of opium; or
- the production or supply of controlled drugs.

However, in order to establish that an offence has taken place, the prosecution must prove that the defendant actually knew that these things were taking place, or had closed his or her eyes to the obvious and so had been unwilling to prevent it. This imposes a considerable duty on youth clubs to ensure that drugs are not used on their premises.

Under s.19 *Misuse of Drugs Act 1971* a youth worker can be prosecuted if he or she incites another person to commit an offence under the Act. In other words if a youth worker persuades the manager of a youth club to ignore the fact that cannabis is being smoked on the premises, both would be guilty of an offence. It is also an offence under s.18 *Misuse of Drugs Act 1971* to knowingly give false information, if questioned, in relation to an offence under the Act. In both cases, the prosecution must prove that the defendant knew what was taking place. Police may search premises for drugs with a warrant obtained from a Magistrates' Court.

While youth centres and clubs should have a policy prohibiting drug use on the premises, or on any trips organised by them, it may simply be unrealistic to control young people's habits once they are away from the centre or club.

DRUGS TESTING

Some youth clubs or projects may consider requiring young people who would like to become members to undergo a drugs test. Youth organisations should be cautious of requiring drugs tests for two reasons:
- Research conducted into cannabis use indicates that

many young people would test positive to the test. This would then lead to considering the actions which would then be taken by the youth organisation when tests are returned positive.

- Will they inform the young person of the result?
- Will the young person be given the opportunity to challenge the result?
- Will the young person's parents be informed?
- What if informing parents has negative consequences for the young person, such as being thrown out of home?
- Can the youth organisation be sure that the results are correct?

Testing may alter a young person's drug taking for the worse. Cannabis used casually can be detected in a young person's body for between two and seven days; heavy cannabis use for up to 14 days. However, heroin is only detectable in the body for between one and two days. It would be unfortunate if young people chose heroin as a drug of choice, rather than cannabis so that they were not detected.

CANNABIS

Cannabis was downgraded from a *Class B* drug to a *Class C* drug in January 2004 in order to reflect its relative danger in comparison to other drugs. This does not mean that cannabis has been legalised. However, the maximum penalties for possession have been reduced: from five to two years imprisonment. The maximum penalty for dealing or supplying remains at 14 years.

The police still have the power to arrest people for possessing cannabis. However, there is a presumption against using this power unless there are aggravating circumstances: this presumption only applies to adults, not young people under 18 years old. The Government has stressed that this does not mean that young people are being treated more strictly than adults, but it would seem that the consequences for a young person possessing cannabis are more serious. A first offence of possession is likely to lead to a young person receiving a reprimand; a second offence is likely to lead to a final warning; and subsequent offences are likely to result in charge (see also chapter 15).

TAKING POSSESSION OF DRUGS FROM YOUNG PEOPLE

There has been considerable discussion as to whether a youth worker should search a young person suspected of carrying drugs. Asking a young person to turn out his or her pockets is acceptable. However, a youth organisation needs to give thought as to what will happen if the young person refuses the request or complies and reveals that he or she has drugs.

It would be unwise for a member of staff to carry out a personal search on a young person[2]. In addition, a youth worker should not search a young person's property without his or her consent. If the youth worker feels that it is essential that a young person is searched then a request needs to be made to the police.

Under s.5 *Misuse of Drugs Act 1971*, it is an offence for a person to have a controlled drug in his or her possession. However, it is a defence if the person can prove that he or she took possession of the drug with the intention of preventing an offence from being committed. In order for this defence to succeed, the individual must have taken all reasonable steps to destroy the drug or deliver it to a person lawfully entitled to take custody of it.

There is no guidance for youth workers on procedures that should be followed after confiscating drugs. However, in *Drugs: Guidance for schools*[3] the Government sets out advice for schools in such situations. Youth organisations may wish to have regard to this Guidance, which provides that any person taking temporary possession and disposing of suspected illegal drugs should:

- ensure that a second adult witness is present throughout;
- seal the sample in a plastic bag and include details of the date and time of the seizure/find and witness present;
- store it in a secure location, such as a safe or other lockable container with access limited to particular staff members; and
- notify the police without delay, who will then collect it and store or dispose of it in line with locally agreed protocols[4].

Youth organisations should have a clear policy on the protocol to be followed in confiscating and disposing of drugs.

AN OBLIGATION TO REPORT?

There is no legal obligation on youth workers to report an incident involving drugs to the police or to disclose the names of any individual involved. However, youth organisations may wish to draw up a protocol setting out the circumstances in which disclosure will be made.

ALCOHOL USE

Young people under the age of 18 may not consume alcohol in a public place unless they are on licensed premises. However, children may drink alcohol on private premises between the ages of five and 16 (s.5 *Children and Young Persons Act 1933*). Children may also enter a pub at any age in the company of a person over the age of 18, if the licensee holds a 'children's certificate' (s.168A *Licensing Act 1964*), but may not drink alcohol. Young people over the age of 14 may enter any bar in the company of a person aged over 18. However, it is a criminal offence for a person under the age of 18 to buy, attempt to buy, or drink alcohol on a licensed premises (s.169C and s.169E *Licensing Act 1964*). It is also an offence for someone to buy alcohol on behalf of a child on licensed premises (s.169C *Licensing Act 1964*).

At 16, a young person can have beer, cider or porter with a meal in a restaurant or other room used for meals in a pub or a hotel (s.169D *Licensing Act 1964*). Only when a young person reaches the age of 18 may he or she legally buy alcohol in a pub, shop, off-license or wholesalers.

If a young person under the age of 18 is with an adult youth worker or a parent, and a police officer believes that the adult intends to give alcohol to the young person, the police officer can confiscate the alcohol (s.1 *Confiscation of Alcohol (Young Persons) Act 1997*). Although the *Confiscation of Alcohol (Young Persons) Act 1997* was intended to prevent young people drinking in town centres and causing a nuisance, the effect is that young people under the age of 18 cannot consume alcohol on a picnic, at the seaside or in any other public place.

The *Licensing Act 2003* amends the law relating to young people and the consumption and purchase of alcohol, but at the time of writing the 2003 Act was not yet in force. When the Act does come into operation, which is expected to be in November 2005, the law will change to the following:

- Children may enter a pub at any age in the company of a person over the age of 18, but may not drink alcohol (s.145 *Licensing Act 2003*).
- Once aged 16, a young person can enter a bar alone, but he or she can only purchase soft drinks (s.145 *Licensing Act 2003*).
- It is an offence for a young person under the age of 18 to buy or attempt to buy alcohol (s.149(1) *Licensing Act 2003*).
- It is an offence for someone to buy or attempt to buy alcohol for a young person under the age of 18 (s.149(3) *Licensing Act 2003*).
- A person can purchase beer, wine or cider on behalf of a young person aged 16 or 17 if the young person is going to consume the alcohol with a meal on licensed premises (s.149(5) *Licensing Act 2003*).
- A young person can only purchase alcohol on licensed premises when he or she reaches the age of 18 (s.150 *Licensing Act 2003*).

CIGARETTES

Contrary to popular belief, it is not illegal to smoke at any age. However, under s.7 *Children and Young Persons Act 1933* it is an offence to sell tobacco, cigarettes, cigarette papers or any product containing tobacco, such as flavoured pellets containing moist tobacco, to anybody under the age of 16.

Under s.7 *Children and Young Persons Act 1933* if a child or young person under the age of 16 is caught smoking in a public place, such as a park or railway station, by a uniformed police officer or park-keeper, they can seize the young person's tobacco or cigarettes.

SOLVENT ABUSE

It is not illegal to possess, use or buy solvents (aerosols, gases, glues) at any age. However, it is an offence for retailers or any other suppliers to sell any substance to a young person

---

CASE STUDY

A youth club, providing evening activities for 11- to 16-year-olds has a policy that no one should smoke on the club's premises. This is taken to include the car park and outside area of the club. A number of the children attending the club smoke, and wish to go outside during the evening so that they can have a cigarette. Due to the no-smoking policy, the children are standing in the road. The club is concerned that it should not be seen to be condoning the smoking, which it feels parents would not approve of. They are also concerned at the danger posed to the children from standing in the road.

Youth clubs should not be seen to be encouraging children to smoke. However, the primary concern of the youth club should be to safeguard the children's welfare. It is perfectly justifiable to have a policy of no-smoking in any building. It is probably justifiable to have a policy of no-smoking anywhere on the premises during club sessions. However, youth clubs need to be realistic. If a number of their members smoke, they will need to decide which is more important, their continued attendance or their refraining from smoking. If young people are to be permitted to smoke outside, however, they should be allowed to smoke somewhere safe.

---

under the age of 18 if they have reasonable cause to believe that the substance or its fumes are likely to be inhaled by the young person for the purpose of intoxication (s.1 *Intoxicating Substances (Supply) Act 1985*). It is also an offence for a shopkeeper to sell lighter fluid (butane) to under-18s, regardless of whether they believe it will be used for intoxicating purposes (Reg. 2 *Cigarette Lighter Refill (Safety) Regulations 1999*).

FOOTNOTES:

1. *Annual report 2004: the state of the drugs problem in the European Union and Norway*, European Monitoring Centre for Drugs and Drug Addiction.

2. Para 4. 10DfES Guidance 0092/2004.

3. DfES 0092/2004.

4. Para 4.7, *Drugs: Guidance for schools* (DfES 0092/2004).

Child protection

A number of children suffer abuse during their childhood. Therefore, it is likely that most professionals working with children will be approached, at some time, by a child who is being abused physically, sexually or emotionally. It is important that when a request for help is made by a child or young person, either directly or indirectly, that professionals and youth workers are able to respond in a sensitive and informed manner. This chapter seeks to outline the child protection system and provide information to help youth workers deal appropriately with situations that arise.

ORGANISATIONAL POLICY

All youth services, organisations and projects should have clear policies about the way in which youth workers should respond when approached for help by young people.

It is crucial that all youth organisations recognise that young people may be sexually or physically abused by youth workers within the organisation. Therefore, there should be clear guidelines for responding to allegations about members of staff. It is necessary to have clear and accessible procedures for young people to use in order to complain about abuse or other inappropriate behaviour by youth workers. A youth organisation's policy should also address the question of how to respond to abusive behaviour between young people who may or may not be members of the organisation.

In order to support young people suffering from abuse or who make allegations of abuse, youth workers should be well informed about the policies and practices of their own and other local agencies. It is also essential to be aware of the procedures of local authorities, the police and education services for investigating child abuse.

> It would be extremely unwise for any individual to deal with suspected child abuse on their own; for instance, by visiting the family to check out what they have been told by a young person. Such action could place the young person at risk of further harm. All organisations working with young people should make sure that their staff know how to seek advice if they suspect that a young person may be suffering abuse.

PUBLIC LAW: THE LOCAL AUTHORITY CHILD PROTECTION STRUCTURE

The local authority is under a duty to safeguard and promote children's welfare. This includes protecting children from suffering significant harm as a result of child abuse.

> *WORKING TOGETHER TO SAFEGUARD CHILDREN:*
> *A guide to inter-agency working to safeguard and promote the welfare of children* (1999 DoH)
> This document is the most important piece of Government guidance on child abuse. It describes how agencies such as the police, local authorities, education departments and health services are to work together to protect children; how investigations and assessments are to be carried out; how case conferences are to be managed; and the necessary training for staff. A new edition of this Guidance is due by the beginning of 2006.

WHAT IS CHILD ABUSE?
Working Together to Safeguard Children outlines four separate categories of abuse. However, it is unlikely that abuse will fall neatly into one category and it is common for a child to suffer more than one type of abuse.

Physical abuse involves hitting, shaking, burning, poisoning, throwing, suffocating or otherwise causing physical harm to a child.

Emotional abuse involves the persistent emotional ill-treatment of a child so as to cause severe long-lasting ill-effects on the child's emotional development. It can involve conveying to a child that they are worthless or unloved, causing a child to feel frightened or in danger (for instance, through witnessing violence), or the exploitation or corruption of a child.

Sexual abuse involves enticing or forcing a child to take part in sexual activities (whether or not the child is aware of what is happening) or encouraging a child to behave in sexually inappropriate ways. It may involve physical contact, including penetrative, non-penetrative acts or non-contact activities. It may involve a child looking at or taking part in the production of pornographic material, or watching sexual activities.

Neglect involves the persistent failure to meet a child's basic physical or psychological needs, which may result in damage to the child's health and development. It can involve failing to provide food, clothing or accommodation or failing to get medical help when needed[1].

REPORTING CHILD ABUSE

PRIVATE INDIVIDUALS
Private individuals do not have a legal duty to report child abuse, but may inform local authorities, the police or the NSPCC of their concerns about a child. The name of a person making such a report is confidential and will not be released to the family of the child about whom the report is made, or indeed anyone else apart from those responsible for the investigation that follows[2].

DUTIES OF THE LEA AND EDUCATIONAL ESTABLISHMENTS
Under s.175 *Education Act 2002* local education authorities, the governing bodies of maintained schools and further education colleges have a duty to make arrangements to ensure that their functions are exercised with a view to safeguarding and promoting the welfare of children. The practical result of this is that governing bodies of schools must now ensure that the school has an effective child protection policy. There is no specific statutory duty on teachers to report allegations of abuse, but it is likely that such a duty would be placed upon them within their own child protection policy.

OTHER PROFESSIONALS
While there is no statutory duty to report child abuse in England and Wales, an individual who fails to report suspected child abuse could be severely criticised. All youth services, cultural and leisure services and health services should have their own policies and procedures for safeguarding children. While *Working Together to Safeguard Children* requires schools, colleges, health authorities and health trusts to designate a person in their organisation with the knowledge and skills to recognise and act upon child protection concerns, there is no such requirement for voluntary organisations. However, the appointment of such a person would be beneficial for all but the smallest organisations. In any event, staff and volunteers in youth organisations need to be sure that they have a clear understanding of their organisation's child protection policy and the circumstances in which they may find it necessary to report child abuse.

Some voluntary organisations, such as the Samaritans, have a policy of never disclosing what they are told. However, most organisations working with children in the voluntary and independent sectors do currently have published policies and procedures to deal with the disclosure of information in situations where a child is at risk of significant harm.

TO WHOM SHOULD CHILD ABUSE BE REPORTED?
Allegations of child abuse may be investigated by three different agencies:
- the local authority;
- the NSPCC; or
- the police (who are required to investigate possible criminal offences).

WHAT HAPPENS WHEN CHILD ABUSE IS REPORTED?

In 2003, the Government produced guidance entitled *What to Do If You're Worried a Child Is Being Abused* (2003 DoH), which contains detailed guidance for practitioners working with children, young people and their families, particularly those working in social care, health, education and criminal justice services. The Guidance is considered to be relevant to all those working in the statutory and independent sectors and wider members of the community. It is advisable for youth organisations to refer to this Guidance when addressing child protection concerns. The document contains detailed advice on all processes involved – from reporting child abuse and information on what will happen after a referral, to what happens when a statutory service is made.

> Remember that an allegation of child abuse or neglect may lead to a criminal investigation, so nothing must be done to jeopardise a police investigation, such as asking a child leading questions or attempting to investigate the allegations of abuse yourself[3].

Stage 1: making a referral
In situations where a youth worker suspects child abuse, the concerns should be discussed with a manager. A decision should be made as to whether the concern is justified and if this decision is positive then a referral should be made to the local authority either by telephone, or by telephone and in writing. The local authority and the youth organisation should be clear about who will be taking any further action and the decision should be recorded by both parties.

Once a referral is made the local authority should make a decision about the action required within one working day. The local authority may decide to:

- conduct an initial assessment of the child's needs;
- make a referral to another agency for the provision of services;
- provide advice or information to the family; or
- take no further action.

Occasionally, the child is at such risk of significant harm, that emergency action must be taken to safeguard the child.

CASE STUDY

Alice, aged 15, a learning disabled child with an IQ of 69, told a youth worker that when she had got home the night before, her mother had not let her into the house. Her mother had left some bedding outside the house and Alice had slept in the garden shed. She did not know what she had done wrong or why her mother had done this. She also said that she was very hungry as she had not had any dinner and had not been able to wash. When questioned, Alice said that the same thing had happened to her the previous week. The youth worker rang the local authority and after some persuasion the local authority placed Alice, who they agreed was at risk of significant harm, with a foster parent while they assessed her family situation.

Stage 2: initial assessment

An initial assessment should be conducted within seven days of a referral being made to the local authority. However, the local authority frequently take much longer than seven days to undertake an assessment and may need some reminding before they carry it out. An initial assessment is generally brief, and its purpose is to determine:

> '... whether the child is in need, the nature of any services required, and whether a further, more detailed core assessment should be undertaken.'[4]

If it is felt that a fuller investigation should be made under s.47 *Children Act 1989*, this stage is likely to be very brief.

The local authority must convene a strategy discussion, if following the assessment (or at any time) there is *'reasonable cause to suspect'* that a child is suffering, or likely to suffer significant harm: *'reasonable cause to suspect'* sets a low threshold. Where some substance is found to the allegation of abuse, or where a parent refuses to address the concerns of the local authority a strategy discussion will be prompted. The strategy discussion will involve the local authority, the police and other appropriate agencies. The purpose of the discussion is to decide whether further enquiries should be carried out under s.47 *Children Act 1989*. It should also consider whether any immediate action is needed to safeguard the child[5].

The child should be seen and spoken to, as should family members. All information on the family should be considered, including any information from the nursery or school the child attends and medical information.

Stage 3: s.47 Children Act 1989 investigation

If the local authority suspects that a child is suffering or likely to suffer significant harm an investigation should commence under s.47 *Children Act 1989*. This will usually comprise of a core assessment, which is an in-depth assessment of the nature of the child's needs and the capacity of his or her parents to meet those needs within the wider family and community context. The purpose of this kind of investigation is for the local authority to determine whether they should take any action to safeguard or promote the child's welfare.

As a general rule, the local authority will need to build up a picture of the child on the basis of information from a number of sources. The child's parent or carer will be interviewed, as will the child (except in the case of babies): children should always be seen on their own. Information should also be sought from anyone who is personally or professionally connected with the child. This could include the child's youth worker, doctor or teacher[6]. There is a statutory duty placed on health, education, housing and other services to help the local authority with their enquiries if they are asked to do so.

A new provision introduced by s.53 *Children Act 2004* requires local authorities to ascertain and give due consideration to a child's wishes and feelings when deciding what action to take under s.47 *Children Act 1989*.

The outcome of the investigation should be recorded in writing and a copy given to the parents and any professionals and agencies involved in advance of any child protection conference that is convened[7].

The definition of what constitutes 'harm' includes impairment suffered from seeing or hearing the ill-treatment of another (witnessing domestic violence)[8].

The police have a general duty to investigate crimes, as well as a duty to prevent offences from being committed and to protect the general public. In exceptional cases, the police can interview a child without informing his or her parents. This is likely where a child does not yet wish his or her parents to know about the allegations, or there is a risk that the parents will threaten the child or otherwise coerce the child into silence.

When the decision is made to undertake a police interview with a child as part of a criminal investigation, the police should follow the guidance set out in *Achieving Best Evidence in Criminal Proceedings: Guidance for vulnerable or intimidated witness, including children* (2002 Home Office) (see Chapter 16).

When the concerns about the child are not substantiated there will usually be no further action taken. In a minority of cases, the family may be offered a service because the child is felt to be 'in need' under s.17 *Children Act 1989*. It is not compulsory to accept this service. However, if the child is judged to be at risk of continuing significant harm, the local authority should convene a child protection conference.

Stage 4: Child Protection Conference

A child protection conference is designed to enable the professionals involved in a case to assess all the relevant information and plan how to safeguard the child and promote his or her welfare.

There are various people, who will attend the conference, including:
- local authority staff who have undertaken an assessment of the child and family;
- foster carers (current or former);
- professionals involved with the child (health visitor, midwife, school nurse, Children's Guardian (if appointed), doctor, teacher, nursery staff);
- professionals involved with the family (adult mental health services, the GP, probation services, family support services);
- those involved in the enquiries (the police);
- local authority legal services (as legal adviser to the conference, rather than as a full participant);
- NSPCC or other involved voluntary organisations; and
- family members (including the wider family)[9].

While youth workers are not specifically included in the list of people to be invited set out in *Working Together to Safeguard Children*, they will generally fall within the category of '*other voluntary organisations*'. In addition, there is no reason why a youth worker should not contact the local authority and ask to attend.

Children should be given the opportunity to attend their child protection conferences and to bring an advocate or friend if they wish (see chapter 3). It is extremely useful for children to have advocates to support them and there may be occasions when a youth worker could fulfil this role. Alternatively, a youth worker might suggest to a child that he or she, if mature enough, contacts a solicitor and obtains legal representation. If a child does not want to attend, or it is not appropriate for a child to attend, a social worker who is closely involved with the child should ascertain what the child's wishes are and explain these to the conference[10]. A youth worker could help the child in presenting his or her views to a social worker.

The task of a child protection conference is to:
- pool and analyse information about the child's background and consider the parent's capacity to provide suitable care and a safe living environment for the child;
- evaluate whether the child is likely to suffer significant harm in the future; and

- decide on action to safeguard the child and promote his or her welfare, how this is to be achieved and any specific outcomes required[11].

The principal question for the child protection conference to consider is whether or not the child is at continuing risk of significant harm. The actions available to the conference are to:
- determine that no further action is necessary;
- place the child's name on the child protection register under the specific category of abuse;
- prepare a child protection plan, identifying the needs of the child and the appropriate services to meet them, the objectives needed to safeguard and promote the child's welfare, roles and responsibilities for the professionals and timescale for the work;
- make recommendations for joint working between the family and agencies to safeguard the child from harm. Specific actions will include appointing a key worker and designating a core group of professionals and family to implement the child protection plan; and
- identify any further assessments needed.

The key worker with the family should make sure that the family understands the child protection plan and that they accept it and are willing to work to it. If the child is unhappy with the plan, it is possible to complain.

Any child protection plan should:
- assess the likelihood of the child suffering significant harm and ways in which the child can be protected;
- establish short-term and longer-term aims and objectives that are clearly linked to reducing the likelihood of harm to the child and promoting the child's welfare;
- clarify who will have responsibility for what actions and within what timescale;
- outline ways of monitoring and evaluating progress; and
- establish which professional will be responsible for checking that the required changes have taken place[12].

If a child's name is placed on the child protection register, a child protection review conference should be held within three months of the initial conference. There should then be follow-up conferences every six months for as long as the child's name remains on the child protection register. The purpose of the review conference is to ensure that plans for the child are up to date and that action is being carried out as agreed, and to consider whether the child protection plan should be changed.

It is not possible to appeal the decision of the child protection conference to a higher body or court. Any complaint should be made, in the first instance, to the conference chair[13]. The only remedy for a young person or parent dissatisfied with the decision reached is to make a complaint or to start an action for judicial review (for which the young person or parent would need to contact a solicitor).

Stage 5: Child Protection Register

There is a child protection register for each local authority area. It lists all the children living in the area who have been identified by a child protection conference as being at risk of significant harm.

Children are registered under one or more of the categories of physical, emotional, sexual abuse, or neglect.

A child protection review conference may decide that a child should be deregistered. It will only make this decision if it decides that the child is no longer at risk of significant harm. When the decision is made, the child's name may be removed from the register. A young person will also be removed from the register once he or she turns 18.

CAN A CHILD OR A PARENT SEE THE RECORDS?

Young people can apply for access to data or personal information held about themselves by the local authority on computer and in some paper records (s.7 and s.68 *Data Protection Act 1998*). There is no set age at which young people can make applications for disclosure of data held. However, in each case the data controller (the person in charge of dealing with disclosure of records) must be satisfied that the young person is of sufficient understanding to exercise the right to disclosure.

If the local authority decides that a young person does not understand, then a parental responsibility holder may apply on the young person's behalf. If a parent applies, the local authority should satisfy itself that the young person lacks the understanding to apply him or herself. If the parent does apply, the local authority must be satisfied that the request is in the young person's interests. If a young person is refused access to his or her records, he or she may appeal to the data controller, the Information Commissioner or the courts.

URGENT ACTION TO PROTECT A YOUNG PERSON

It is rare for a decision to be made that a young person is in such danger that it warrants immediate removal from home. It should also be remembered that sudden removal from home and separation from parents may be extremely traumatic for a young person, and suitable alternative care may be difficult to arrange.

Courts are only likely to grant an emergency order removing a child when there is clear evidence of abuse, whether physical, sexual, or severe neglect, and it is evident that one or both of the immediate carers are actively involved in the abuse.

There are also situations, in which young people are at risk of significant harm, but where a hasty reaction may cause further damage. It may be that young people involved in prostitution will not necessarily cooperate with their removal to a place of safety and the use of secure accommodation may be inappropriate for them.

Local authorities do not have the power to force an entry into a family home. If they wish to obtain access or to remove a young person, they must first obtain a court order.

Emergency Protection Orders

Unlike most child protection orders, anyone can apply to the court for an Emergency Protection Order under s.44 *Children Act 1989*. Most orders are made by the local authority, but may be made by an individual if the local authority does not appear to be taking their concerns seriously.

It is open to a youth worker to apply for an Emergency Protection Order where he or she considers that a young person may be at risk and the local authority is not taking appropriate steps to protect the young person. However, under the *Emergency Protection Order (Transfer of Responsibilities) Regulations 1991*, local authorities must take over responsibility for the Emergency Protection Order if they consider that this is in the best interests of the child. In making this decision, the local authority must consult with the applicant and take into account a number of factors, including the young person's wishes and feelings, the circumstances that gave rise to the Emergency Protection Order being made and any plans made by the applicant.

An Emergency Protection Order is a very serious measure as it grants the local authority parental responsibility in relation to the child and allows them to remove the child from the parents' care. The court may make such an order if it is satisfied that there is reasonable cause to believe that the child is likely to suffer significant harm:
- if he or she is not removed into local authority accommodation; or
- if he or she does not stay in the place (such as a hospital or foster home), where he or she is currently being cared for[14].

The court can also grant such an order to a local authority applicant if enquiries being made by the local authority under s.47 *Children Act 1989* are being frustrated by access to the young person being unreasonably refused.

An Emergency Protection Order lasts for up to eight days, but it can be extended once for a period of not more than seven days[15]. Such orders are often made without notice being given to the young person or the parents or carers. In some cases, children can simply be told at school that an order has been made and they are to move to a foster parent or a children's home for the duration of the Order.

The *Children Act 1989* also requires that, while the Order is in force, the young person should be given reasonable contact with his or her family, unless the court orders otherwise.

The court can restrict contact and will do so in certain circumstances. If there is a possibility that criminal charges will be brought against the parents, or there is a fear that the parents may try to persuade or threaten the young person not to say anything about the family, contact is likely to be restricted until the young person has been interviewed by the local authority or the police.

When the court makes an Emergency Protection Order, it can order a medical or psychiatric assessment. However, the young person may refuse treatment if he of she is deemed competent; young people frequently do refuse treatment[16].

Police protection

The police have the general authority to remove young people from danger and place them in suitable accommodation or prevent their removal to somewhere unsafe if they have '*reasonable cause to believe that a child would otherwise be likely to suffer significant harm*'[17]. This is referred to as taking a young person into 'police protection'.

This may happen, for instance, if the police find a young person left at home alone, in the charge of a parent who is drunk and incapable, or at immediate risk of abuse or in the company of known child sex offenders. Where a young person understands what the police are seeking to do, and refuses to go with the police constable, it is unclear whether the police have the power to insist on the young person leaving the home. Removal against the wishes of the young person could amount to a breach of family life under Article 8 and the right to a fair trial under Article 6 (l) *European Convention on Human Rights and Fundamental Freedoms*. In such circumstances, the police would probably advise the local authority to obtain an Emergency Protection Order from the court.

Generally, the police will take the young person to the police station. Once there, the police must:
* inform the local authority in whose area the young person was found of the steps that have been taken or are proposed to be taken and the reason for these actions;
* inform the local authority in whose area the young person is usually resident of where the young person is being accommodated;
* inform the young person of the steps that have been taken and what further steps may be taken, if the young person appears to be capable of understanding;
* take reasonable practicable steps to discover the young person's wishes and feelings about what is going to happen;
* arrange for the young person to be moved to local authority accommodation, unless this has already been done;
* inform the young person's parents or any others with parental responsibility; and
* organise for the case to be taken by an officer designated by the Chief Constable (usually a police officer from the child protection unit)[18].

The police do not acquire parental responsibility for the duration of the police protection order. They must allow contact between the young person and his or her parents and others to the extent that is reasonable and in the young person's best interests[19].

After conducting an investigation, the appointed police officer may decide to allow a young person to go home. In any event, the police cannot keep a young person in police protection for more than 72 hours[20]. However, if the police consider that there is still reasonable cause for believing that a young person would be likely to suffer significant harm if released, they may apply for an Emergency Protection Order in respect of the young person[21].

Accommodating a child

Parents may agree to a child being removed from the family home and 'accommodated' by the local authority, under s.20 *Children Act 1989*, while an investigation and assessment are carried out. Such an agreement is not uncommon. It shows willingness on the part of the parents to work cooperatively and in partnership with the local authority and may prevent an application for an Emergency Protection Order or an Interim Care Order being pursued. It is also useful where a young person has fallen out with parents, as it allows both the child and the parents breathing space.

> Police protection powers should only be used in exceptional circumstances where there is insufficient time to seek an Emergency Protection Order or for reasons relating to the immediate safety of a child[22].

While a child is accommodated, parents retain full parental responsibility: parents should always be told where the child is living, and the local authority should ensure regular contact. See Chapter 4 for more information on accommodation under s.20 *Children Act 1989*.

Exclusion Orders

If the local authority believes that the significant harm being suffered by a child is due to the presence of one particular person in a house, it may be possible to negotiate with the family so that the alleged abuser leaves the home. In some instances, the local authority may be willing to help with the deposit for alternative accommodation or rent. If the alleged abuser is unwilling to move, the local authority may consider obtaining an order to remove the abuser from the home. The purpose of such an order is to allow the young person to remain at home, rather than being removed into the care of the local authority.

An Exclusion Order can only be attached to an Interim Care Order or an Emergency Protection Order,[23] and will only be made if the court is satisfied that:
* There is reasonable cause to believe that if the person is excluded from the home the young person would cease

to suffer, or cease to be likely to suffer, significant harm.
- Another person living in the home is able and willing to give the young person the care and consents to the exclusion requirement.

The local authority will only apply for an Exclusion Order if the remaining parent is cooperative and can be depended upon to keep the abuser out of the home. Such orders are not frequent.

Collaboration in criminal investigations: the police and local authority

In some cases, the need to discover whether a crime has been committed and the need to ensure the welfare of a child overlap. In such cases, the police and the local authority may decide to carry out a joint investigation. The way in which such investigations are to be carried out will be in the local procedures prepared by the Local Area Child Protection Committee (these will be known as Local Safeguarding Children Boards once the provisions of the *Children Act 2004* come into force).

Where a child makes an allegation amounting to a criminal offence against another person, the child will be interviewed in accordance with the guidance set out in *Achieving Best Evidence in Criminal Proceedings: Guidance for Vulnerable or Intimidated Witnesses, including Children* (see Chapter 16). Interviews are usually carried out by specialist police officers and social workers and will take place as soon as possible after the child makes an allegation.

LONGER TERM MEASURES FOR PROTECTING CHILDREN

CARE PROCEEDINGS

If the local authority has reasonable cause to believe, after the investigation, that a young person remains at risk, it may apply for a Care Order. A court may only issue a Care Order if it is satisfied that threshold criteria have been met:

'(a)   *that the child concerned is suffering, or is likely to suffer, significant harm; and*

(b)   *that the harm, or likelihood of harm, is attributable to:*
(i) the care given to the child, or likely to be given to him if the order were not made, not being what it would be reasonable to expect a parent to give to him; or
(ii) the child's being beyond parental control.'[24]

Young people cannot ask the court to make a Care Order no matter how unhappy they are at home. Such an Order can only be applied for by the local authority or the NSPCC[25].

In addition to satisfying the threshold criteria, the court must apply the welfare principle together with the statutory welfare checklist in s.1(3) *Children Act 1989*, when deciding whether to make a Care Order. The court must also be satisfied that making an order would be in the best interests of the child[26].

A Care Order may not be made once the young person has reached the age of 17 (or 16 in the case of a young person who is married)[27]. An Order lasts until the young person is 18 years old unless it is discharged before this date on the application of a parent or the young person[28].

While a young person is in care, the local authority has parental responsibility for the child, which it shares with the parents. Parental responsibility is not shared equally, as the local authority have the power to restrict the exercise of parental responsibility by the parent[29]. However, the local authority may not change the child's religion or surname, remove the child from the UK or consent to the child's adoption. All these elements of parental responsibility remain with the parent. As a child gets older, especially over the age of 14, the less likely a local authority is to seek a Care Order, though it will do so in exceptional cases.

SUPERVISION ORDER

There are occasions when the threshold criteria are met for a Care Order to be made, but the young person does not need the same level of protection. In such instances, the court may make a Supervision Order. This generally runs for one year, although it may be extended to three years[30]. The Order does not extend beyond the child's eighteenth birthday. Parental responsibility remains with the parents, but the local authority will advise, assist and befriend the child. In practice, this means that a social worker will visit the child, usually at intervals of between four weeks and three months, for the duration of the Supervision Order. The young person may also be required to participate in certain activities during the course of the Order.

REPRESENTATION OF YOUNG PEOPLE

CHILDREN'S GUARDIANS

Young people are party to care proceedings and are entitled to legal representation. Usually a Children's Guardian will also be appointed by the court. Children's Guardians are part of the Children and Family Court Advisory and Support Service (CAFCASS). CAFCASS is responsible for safeguarding and promoting the welfare of children involved in family court proceedings.

A Children's Guardian is independent of all other parties involved in the case. The Guardian will:
- appoint a solicitor for the child who specialises in working with children and families;
- advise the court about what work needs to be done before the court makes its decision; and
- write a report for the court saying what he or she thinks would be best for the child: this report must tell the court the child's wishes and feelings.

The Guardian and the young person's solicitor work in partnership. However, there is sometimes a conflict between the views of the young person and the recommendations of the

Guardian. In such a case, the young person should tell the Guardian and the solicitor that he or she does not accept the recommendations of the Guardian. Once aware of the conflict, the solicitor should make it clear to the Guardian that he or she cannot continue to represent both. The Guardian should, at this point, seek to appoint his or her own solicitor, leaving the young person's solicitor to represent the young person's views and wishes. The young person will, of course, only be able to instruct the solicitor if the solicitor is satisfied that he or she has the understanding to give instructions. Where the young person does not have that maturity, the Guardian and the young person will continue to share a solicitor, but the Guardian should ensure that the young person's views and wishes are made clear to the court.

At the interim stage or at the final hearing, the court may decide not to make a Care or Supervision Order, but a Residence Order in favour of a member of the extended family or any other person with a concern for the young person's welfare[31]. The Children's Guardian should advise the court about any such person. Again, a youth worker could be of assistance in exploring with the young person the possibility of a particular person putting him or herself forward, as well as the possibility of the young person applying for a Residence Order on his or her own behalf (see chapter 4).

AFTER THE FINAL HEARING

THE CARE PLAN
If a Care Order is made, the local authority will implement the care plan for the child. This will set out what the local authority considers to be in the best interests of the child. It will contain details of the place of residence and who will look after the child. In some cases, the plan may be to return the child to the parents. Alternatively, the local authority may place the child with relatives, long-term foster parents, seek adoptive parents, or place the child in a children's home.

CAN THE FAMILY SEE THE CHILD?
The local authority is required to allow parents reasonable contact with their children[32], unless to do so will not safeguard or promote the young person's welfare. Disputes about contact may be resolved by recourse to the courts. There is no right of contact for siblings, grandparents or other relatives.

DOES THE CHILD HAVE ANY SAY?
A young person in care who is unhappy with his or her care plan may make an application to court for:
- the discharge of the Care Order[33]; or
- leave (permission) to apply for a Residence, Contact or other Order[34].

The court will grant the young person leave if it is satisfied that:
- the child has sufficient understanding to make the application[35]; and
- there is an arguable case.

For example, the child may wish to live with relatives or perhaps former foster parents who are not eligible to make the application themselves[36]: such applications are rare.

HOW LONG DOES A CARE ORDER LAST?
A Care Order lasts until the child is 18 or until the Care Order is discharged. The local authority occasionally applies to discharge Care Orders, especially if the young person has continued to live with the parent and the local authority feels that it no longer needs to share parental responsibility with the parent.

RIGHTS OF CHILDREN 'LOOKED AFTER' BY LOCAL AUTHORITIES

WHO ARE 'LOOKED AFTER' CHILDREN?
The group of young people 'looked after' by the local authority include:
- those who are the subject of a Care Order made under s.31 *Children Act 1989*;
- those accommodated at their own or their parents' request under s.20 *Children Act 1989*; and
- those in police protection or detention, or remanded to the local authority by the courts under s.21 *Children Act 1989*.

DECISION-MAKING
The local authority owes all three groups of children the same duties under s.22 *Children Act 1989*. The local authority must safeguard and promote the welfare of any young person it is looking after and must consult young people when making decisions. The local authority should take into consideration the wishes and feelings of children in light of their age and understanding as well as the wishes and feelings of parents and others whose views the authority considers to be relevant, as well as the young person's racial origin, religious and cultural background[37]. There is no indication of the weight that should be attached to the views of young people.

SHOULD PARENTS KNOW WHERE THEIR CHILDREN ARE LIVING?
Local authorities must inform parents about their children's whereabouts where they are accommodated, detained or remanded. Where the child is under a Care Order, the situation is different[38]. Although the local authority shares parental responsibility with the parents, there may be times when they decide not to allow a parent to know where the child is living. This may happen when they think that the parent will destabilise a placement or where the child has been placed with prospective adopters.

REVIEWS
The *Review of Children's Cases Regulations 1991* requires local authorities to conduct regular case reviews in relation to children looked after by them[39]. Such reviews must be chaired by an independent reviewing officer[40] and should occur:

CASE STUDY

John was placed in a children's home following the making of a Care Order. The home was some distance away, in another county, but John was extremely happy there, and was doing well at the local school. The local authority decided that John should move to an in-county children's home. He was given a week's notice of the impending move. John was extremely unhappy about the move and rang the Children's Legal Centre.

He was advised that the local authority were under a duty to consult him, and that their failure to do so was grounds for taking an action for judicial review to force the local authority to consult him fully on the move, and take his views and wishes into account.

* within four weeks of the date from which the young person began to be looked after;
* not more than three months from the first review; and
* not more than six months from the previous review[41].

Young people have no absolute right to attend the review meeting (this is limited by the discretion of the local authority), but the *Children Act 1989 Guidance and Regulations (Volume 3)* (1997 DoH), provides that attendance of the child should be the norm rather than the exception. Independent Reviewing Officers should ensure that children are given the oppor-tunity to make meaningful contributions to their reviews. If children are able and willing to speak for themselves at the meeting, the Independent Reviewing Officer should facilitate this. Children should also be given the opportunity to provide a written contribution to the meeting if they cannot or do not wish to attend[42].

Young people may be accompanied to a planning or review meeting by someone who is able to provide friendly support. This may be a function that youth workers feels able to undertake. If the young person does not want to attend, the youth worker could assist the young person by conveying his or her views to the social worker.

CONTACT

Where children are looked after by the local authority, the *Children Act 1989* imposes a duty on the local authority to promote contact between young people and their parents, extended family and friends wherever possible, unless it is inconsistent with their welfare[43]. There is also a presumption that there should be contact between young people in care and their parents and other relevant persons, such as their grandparents[44]. The local authority may make payments to a young person to cover travel costs or other expenses, to enable contact to take place[45].

If a child is subject to a Care Order, local authorities cannot stop or refuse contact without going back to court and obtaining an order to this effect. If there is an emergency contact may be stopped for seven days[46].

Young people should not be forced to have contact with anyone that they do not wish to see, including parents, although social workers should fully explore why this view is held.

Young people in care have the right to apply for a Contact Order in favour of any named person, such as a member of the extended family, or perhaps more importantly, a sibling or friend. Where siblings are in care, contact can be lost very quickly. Young people may also apply for an order that there be no contact between them and a named person.

EDUCATION OF 'LOOKED AFTER' CHILDREN

Young people who are looked after often have particular difficulty obtaining a school place and achieving to the same level as their peers. The Government has published *Guidance on the Education of Young People in Public Care*[47], which addresses these issues. All 'looked after' children should have a personal education plan and where a child has to be moved as an emergency or where education provision breaks down, the local authority must secure an education placement for the child within 20 school days. Non-emergency placements should include arrangements for a suitable education.

INDEPENDENT VISITORS

Research shows that young people in care can lose contact with their natural family very quickly. This leaves such young people very isolated with nobody to represent their interests. Where it appears to the local authority that a young person has little communication with parents and he or she has not been visited by them for the last 12 months, and where it would appear to be in the young person's best interests, the local authority must appoint an independent visitor for the young person[48]. There is no reason why such visitors should not be provided before 12 months have passed, and a youth worker could seek to fulfil this role. The restrictions on the recruitment of independent visitors are set out in the *Definition of Independent Visitors (Children) Regulations 1991*.

CONTROL AND DISCIPLINE

Measures of control and discipline in relation to looked after young people is one of the most difficult areas of care to manage. The *Fostering Services Regulations 2002* require fostering service providers (both private and local authority) to have a written policy on acceptable measures of control, restraint and discipline of children placed with foster carers. The Regulations specifically require fostering service providers to ensure that a child placed with foster parents:
* is not subjected to any form of corporal punishment;
* is not subjected to excessive or unreasonable measures of control, restraint or discipline; and
* is only physically restrained where it is necessary to prevent likely injury to the child or another person, or serious damage to property[49].

Children's homes are also required to have a behaviour management policy setting out the measures of control, restraint and discipline which may be used in the home[50]. These Regulations, which are more detailed than those relating to foster placements, prohibit the use of certain forms of control and discipline in children's homes, including:

- any excessive or unreasonable measure of control, restraint or discipline;
- any form of corporal punishment;
- any punishment relating to the consumption or deprivation of food;
- the restriction of contact with, or visits from, parents, relatives or friends (or the prevention of visits with a social worker, solicitor or Children's Guardian or access to a telephone helpline for counselling);
- any requirement to wear distinctive or inappropriate clothing;
- the withholding of medication or treatment;
- the intentional deprivation of sleep; and
- the withholding of aids or equipment needed by a disabled child[51].

However, staff are allowed to use physical restraint where young people are putting themselves or others at risk or are likely to seriously damage property[52]. Any use of physical restraint should only be carried out by trained staff and should always be recorded.

Physical restraint may also be used where a young person is lawfully detained (those who have been remanded) in order to prevent him or her running away from an open unit.

FOOTNOTES:

1. Paras 2.3-2.7 *Working Together to Safeguard Children*. 1999 DoH.
2. *D v NSPCC [1978] AC 171.*
3. Para 10.2, *What To Do If You're Worried A Child Is Being Abused*. 2003 DoH.
4. Para 3.9, *Framework for the Assessment of Children in Need and their Families*. 2000 DoH.
5. Para 5.28-5.32 *Working Together to Safeguard Children*. 1999 DoH.
6. Para 5.34 *Working Together to Safeguard Children*. 1999 DoH.
7. Para 5.45 *Working Together to Safeguard Children*. 1999 DoH.
8. s.120 *Adoption and Children Act 2002.*
9. Para 5.55 *Working Together to Safeguard Children*. 1999 DoH.
10. Para 5.57 *Working Together to Safeguard Children*. 1999 DoH.
11. Para 5.53 *Working Together to Safeguard Children*. 1999 DoH.
12. Para 49 *What To Do If You're Worried A Child Is Being Abused*. 2003 DoH.
13. Para 5.72 *Working Together to Safeguard Children*. 1999 DoH.
14. s.44(1) *Children Act 1989.*
15. s.45 *Children Act 1989.*
16. s.44 *Children Act 1989.*
17. s.46(1) *Children Act 1989.*
18. s.46(3) *Children Act 1989.*
19. s.46(10) *Children Act 1989.*
20. s.46(6) *Children Act 1989.*
21. s.44 *Children Act 1989.*
22. Para 3.8 *Guidance on Investigating Child Abuse and Safeguarding Children* 2005, ACPO.
23. s.44A *Children Act 1989.*
24. s.31(2) *Children Act 1989.*
25. s.31(1) *Children Act 1989.*
26. s.1(5) *Children Act 1989.*
27. s.31(3) *Children Act 1989.*
28. s.39(1) *Children Act 1989.*
29. s.33(3) *Children Act 1989.*
30. Schedule 3, para 6 *Children Act 1989.*
31. s.10(1)(b) *Children Act 1989.*
32. s.34(1) *Children Act 1989.*
33. s.39 *Children Act 1989.*
34. s.8 *Children Act 1989.*
35. s.10 *Children Act 1989.*
36. s.10 *Children Act 1989.*
37. s.22(4)-(5) *Children Act 1989.*
38. Schedule 2, para 15 *Children Act 1989.*
39. Reg 2 *Review of Children's Cases Regulations 1991.*
40. Reg 2A *Review of Children's Cases Regulations 1991.*
41. Reg 3 *Review of Children's Cases Regulations 1991.*
42. *Independent Reviewing Officers Guidance: Adoption and Children Act 2002.* DfES 2004.
43. Schedule 2, para 15 *Children Act 1989.*
44. s.34(1) *Children Act 1989.*
45. Schedule 2, para 16 *Children Act 1989.*
46. s.34(6) *Children Act 1989.*
47. LAC (2000) 13. www.doh.gov.uk or from Office of Public Sector Information.
48. Schedule 2, para 17 *Children Act 1989.*
49. Reg 13 *Fostering Services Regulations 2002.*
50. Reg 17(2) *Children's Homes Regulations 2001.*
51. Reg 17 *Children's Homes Regulations 2001.*
52. Reg 17(6)(b) *Children's Homes Regulations 2001.*

Young people estranged from their families

There are growing numbers of young people who, for various reasons, are estranged from their families, either temporarily or permanently. Some of these young people are able to live independently provided that they can find somewhere to live and can obtain employment or access financial support to remain in education. Others are far more vulnerable, are not able to look after themselves, and will need a greater level of support. This chapter focuses on the duties of the local authority towards this specific group of young people.

The local authority has a general duty under s.17 *Children Act 1989* to:
> '...safeguard and promote the welfare of children within their area who are in need and so far as is consistent with that duty, to promote the upbringing of such children by their families, by providing a range and level of services appropriate to those children's needs.'

A young person under the age of 18 who is estranged from his or her parents is likely to fall under this definition.

WHO IS A CHILD IN NEED?

A child will be 'in need'[1] if:
- the child will not achieve or maintain a reasonable standard of health or development unless he or she receives services from the local authority;
- the child's health or development is likely to be significantly impaired, or further impaired, without the provision of such services; or
- the child is disabled.

What do 'disabled', 'health' and 'development' mean?

Disabled: under the *Children Act 1989*, a child is disabled if he or she is blind, deaf or dumb, suffers from a mental disorder of any kind (all of which require medical evidence), or is substantially and permanently handicapped by illness, injury or congenital deformity or other such disability as may be prescribed.

Health: this means physical or mental health.

Development: this means physical, intellectual, emotional, social or behavioural development.

'*Safeguarding*' has two parts:
- a duty to protect children from being ill-treated; and
- a duty to prevent children's development from being impaired because they have not had access to services that might help prevent this[2].

'*Promoting welfare*' has a wider, more positive approach which is intended to ensure that children have access to opportunities that will support them into adult life, and that they grow up in circumstances in which they will get safe and effective care[3].

Local authorities also have a more specific duty: s.20(1) *Children Act 1989* imposes a duty on local authorities to provide accommodation for any child in need in their area who seems to them to require it, because:
- there is no one with parental responsibility for him or her;
- he or she is lost or has been abandoned; or
- the person who has been caring for the child has been prevented (whether or not permanently, and for whatever reason) from providing him or her with suitable accommodation or care.

The duties owed to children and young people estranged from their families differ according to whether or not they are under or over 16 – and when over 16, whether they are able to live independently or not.

CHILDREN UNDER THE AGE OF 16

Children under the age of 16 who are estranged from their

parents often stay with friends. This is usually an acceptable arrangement for short term estrangement, but may not be acceptable in the long term. Where it is unlikely that a child will return to his or her family in the short-term, the host family may be able to reach an agreement with the child's parents on caring for the child and financial support. If no agreement can be reached for support of the child, and the host family feel that they cannot continue to care for the child without some financial support, there are a limited range of options:

- they can ask that the child benefit payment be transferred to them[4]; or
- a referral could be made to the local authority.

In situations where there is a referral, local authorities must carry out an assessment to determine whether the child is in need and whether services should be provided to meet those needs. If the child cannot return home, or will not return home, the local authority should consider whether the child should be accommodated by the local authority under s.20 *Children Act 1989*. Local authorities can consider placing children with friends or family, who will act as foster parents and may be supported by means of a fostering allowance.

WHAT DOES 'ACCOMMODATED' MEAN?

'Accommodated' children are looked after by local authorities[5]. However, local authorities do not have parental responsibility for accommodated children. Parental responsibility remains with the parents. Local authorities may not accommodate a child under 16 when a person with parental responsibility objects to the accommodation and is willing to provide or arrange accommodation for the child[6]. Thus, until the young person reaches the age of 16 a parent or other parental responsibility holder is entitled to remove him or her from local authority accommodation at any time, regardless of the views of the young person[7]. A young person under the age of 16 cannot ask the local authority to continue to accommodate him or her without the parents' permission.

The host family could make an application to the court for a Residence Order and ask for financial support from the parent. If the host family are not entitled to pubic funding this could be an expensive option. If the child is deemed to be of sufficient maturity he or she may instruct a solicitor to make an application on his or her behalf. The courts do not encourage such applications by a child, but they are not unknown.

> It is not possible for children under the age of 16 to obtain housing from the housing authority.

YOUNG PEOPLE AGED 16 TO 18

The duty to accommodate homeless 16- and 17-year-olds can fall either on the local authority or the local housing authority. In the majority of cases, responsibility falls on the housing authority.

CASE STUDY

Miranda, aged 14, has been accommodated by the local authority for the last three months as her mother has been an in-patient at a local psychiatric unit. Her mother is much better, but is unable to have Miranda living with her. Miranda sees her mother regularly and hopes to return to live with her once her mother has recovered. Miranda lost touch with her father following her parents' divorce and has not seen him since she was nine years old. The local authority recently contacted her father to inform him of Miranda's circumstances. He has told them that he does not wish Miranda to be accommodated, and has expressed his willingness to have Miranda living with him. Miranda remembers her father as a violent man who used to hit her mother, and is unwilling to live with him. The local authority has told Miranda that because her father objects to her being accommodated, she cannot stay with the foster parents that she is currently living with, and will have to live with her father.

In such a case, the local authority is unable to continue to provide Miranda with accommodation in the face of her father's objection. Miranda should ask for an advocate and should be referred to a Children Panel solicitor. Her options are limited as her father has parental responsibility for her. She could seek a Residence Order to allow her to live with her current foster parents. However, she would need permission from the High Court to start such an action. Further, it would mean that the foster parents would lose their fostering allowance for her, and the local authority would be unlikely to pay them a residence allowance. Alternatively, the advocate and solicitor could negotiate with the father. The solicitor could seek the father's consent to Miranda continuing to be accommodated for a further period while the feasibility of her moving to live with him is explored and father and daughter get to know one another better.

THE LOCAL AUTHORITY

If a young person aged between 16 and 19 feels that he or she is unable to live independently and needs support, a referral for services should be made to the local authority. The local authority should undertake an initial assessment to decide whether the young person is a child in need, and how those needs can be met. The local authority may decide that the young person is not a child in need, in which case, no services will be offered. Alternatively, if the initial assessment concludes that the child is a child in need, it must determine what services should be provided to the young person. Local authorities are often reluctant to undertake an assessment, but they are obliged to do so. Youth workers could assist a young person in need by making a referral. A note should be kept of the referral and a response should be received from the local authority within one working day.

At 16, a young person may ask to be accommodated by the local authority under s.20 *Children Act 1989*, even against the express wishes of his or her parents. Further, the local

Framework for Assessment of Children in Need and their families (2002 DoH)

Paragraph 3.8:

'There is an expectation that within one working day of a referral being received … there will be a decision about what response is required. A referral is defined as a request for services to be provided by the social services department.'

Paragraph 3.9:

'A decision to gather more information constitutes an initial assessment. An initial assessment is defined as a brief assessment of each child referred to social services with a request for services to be provided. This should be under-taken within a maximum of seven working days but could be very brief depending on the child's circum-stances. It should address the dimensions of the Assessment Framework, determining whether the child is in need, the nature of any services required, from where and within what timescales, and whether a further, more detailed core assessment should be undertaken. An initial assessment is deemed to have commenced at the point of referral to the social services department or when new information on an open case indicates an initial assess-ment should be repeated …' [emphasis supplied]

authority may continue to accommodate the young person, even where the parents object, if the young person wishes to remain accommodated by the local authority.

Local authorities are often very reluctant to accommodate young people of 16 years and over, especially if they have not previously been looked after. This reluctance is particularly evident when a local authority decides that the young person's estrangement from the family is temporary. However, the local authority has a duty under s.20(3) *Children Act 1989* to provide accommodation to any child within its area who has reached the age of 16 and whose welfare the authority considers is likely to be seriously prejudiced if it does not provide him or her with accommodation. Under s.20(5) *Children Act 1989*, it may also, at its discretion, accommodate young people aged 16 to 21, if it considers that to do so may safeguard and promote a young person's welfare.

Note: It is often difficult to persuade the local authority to provide accommodation for 16- and 17-year-olds who have decided that they can no longer live at home. There are very few foster placements available for such children, and those who are provided with accommodation may find themselves in bed and breakfast or hostel accommodation.

Young people who have reached the age of 16 and have nowhere to live, often because they have fallen out with their parents, and do not have an extended family network who are able to offer them support, will frequently need the help of the local authority. If they are still receiving full-time education, or some form of vocational training, they will generally be regarded as seriously prejudiced if they are not offered accommodation. As local authorities are often reluctant to provide accommodation a young person may well

need the help of a youth worker to advocate on his or her behalf. Where a young person is going to be accommodated by the local authority, or is already accommodated, the local authority shall, under s.20 (6) *Children Act 1989*, as far as is reasonably practicable and consistent with the young person's welfare, ascertain his or her wishes regarding the provision of accommodation and give due consideration to such wishes.

CASE STUDY

Sam, aged 16, who has had a poor relationship with her family for some time, was told to leave home by her father and step-mother. She stayed with a friend for a couple of nights but cannot stay there any longer. She has been treated for depression and, having slept rough for a night, is now hungry and distressed. She has told her youth worker that she just does not know what to do. The youth worker calls the local authority who say that they are unable to help. The social worker recommends that Sam returns home and suggests that the youth work-er accompanies her and sorts matters out with her parents. Sam absolutely refuses to go home.

The youth worker should impress on the social worker the responsibility of the local authority to provide immediate accommodation for Sam. She has nowhere to go, is only 16-years-old and, without the provision of accommoda-tion, financial assistance and help in deciding her future, her welfare is likely to be seriously prejudiced. The youth worker should also make it clear to the local authority that he or she is making a formal referral for services.

If the local authority refuses to help, Sam should be referred to an advocacy service and/or a solicitor. Sam should be assessed and, if it is impossible for her to return to her family, accommodated under s.20 Children Act 1989. If the local authority continues to refuse assis-tance, the solicitor may need to consider taking judicial review proceedings.

RESPONSIBILITY OF THE HOUSING AUTHORITY

Rather than accommodate young people under s.20 *Children Act 1989*, local authorities often refer them to the local housing authority. The duties of local housing authorities focus on the issue of '*priority need*' and whether a young person is '*intentionally homeless*'.

Article 3 *Homelessness (Priority Need for Accommodation) (England) Order 2002* provides that 16- and 17-year-olds are automatically classed as being in '*priority need*' unless they are a '*relevant child*' (see p.74) or the local authority has a duty to accommodate them under s.20 *Children Act 1989*. If the housing authority determines that, having carried out an assessment, a young person is vulnerable and falls within the s.20 *Children Act 1989* criteria, it will refuse to provide housing on the basis that the local authority is responsible. The local authority will then need to make a decision as to whether they will accommodate the young person as a looked after child under s.20 *Children Act 1989*, or whether they will provide accommodation and support under s.17 *Children Act 1989*. If they decide to support the young person under s.17 *Children Act 1989*, the child will not be a looked after child, and will not benefit from the leaving care provisions once he or she reaches 18 years old.

Under s.188(1) *Housing Act 1996*, housing authorities have an interim duty to accommodate 16- and 17-year-olds in priority need whilst they make a decision as to what duties they owe under the *Housing Act 1996*. Thus, a housing authority can and should provide some housing on a temporary basis while it decides whether the child should be housed by it or accommodated under s.20 *Children Act 1989*.

In deciding what duties it owes, the housing authority will consider whether the young person is intentionally homeless. Under s.191(1) *Housing Act 1996*, a person becomes homeless intentionally:

> '... *if he deliberately does or fails to do anything in consequence of which he ceases to occupy accommodation which is available for his occupation and which it would have been reasonable for him to continue to occupy.*'

This covers situations where a young person has, for example, broken '*house rules*' in the family home resulting in a breakdown of family relationships. Such a young person genuinely may have nowhere to live, but under the *Housing Act 1996*, he or she is intentionally homeless. Where a young person is considered intentionally homeless, the housing authority's only duty under s.190 (2) *Housing Act 1996* is to provide the young person with:

- accommodation for such period as they consider will give him or her a reasonable opportunity of securing accommodation for his or her occupation; and
- advice and assistance in securing accommodation.

Thus, the housing authority cannot simply turn a homeless 16- or 17-year-old away because he or she is intentionally homeless.

Where a 16- or 17-year-old with nowhere to live is not considered to be intentionally homeless, the housing authority has a duty under s.193(1) *Housing Act 1996* to provide the young person with accommodation until he or she turns 18, unless the young person makes him or herself intentionally homeless prior to that.

Homelessness Code of Guidance for Local Authorities (2002)
'*Responsibility for providing suitable accommodation for a relevant child or a child in need to whom a local authority owes a duty under section 20 of the Children Act 1989 rests with the social services authority. In all cases of uncertainty as to whether a 16 or 17 year old applicant may be a relevant child or a child in need, the housing authority should contact the relevant social services authority. It is recommended that a framework for joint assessment of 16 and 17 year olds is established by housing and social services authorities to facilitate the seamless discharge of duties and appropriate services to this client group*' (para 8.37).

FOOTNOTES:
1. s.17 (10) *Children Act 1989*.
2. Para 1.15 *Framework for the Assessment of Children in Need and their Families*. 2000. DoH.
3. Para 1.17 *Framework for the Assessment of Children in Need and their Families*. 2000. DoH.
4. Contact Child Benefit Office (GB), PO Box 1, Newcastle upon Tyne, NE88 1AA. Tel 0845 302 1444.
5. s.22(1) *Children Act 1989*.
6. s.20(7) *Children Act 1989*.
7. s.20(8) *Children Act 1989*.

Support for care leavers

The *Children Act 1989*[1] and the *Children (Leaving Care) (England) Regulations 2001* set out the duties of local authorities towards *'looked after'* children as they exit the care system. These duties are further explained in the *Children (Leaving Care) Act 2000 Regulations and Guidance*, which must be observed by local authorities. In essence, the leaving care provisions in the *Children Act 1989* require a local authority to assess and meet the care and support needs of this group of young people with a view to ensuring that they make a smooth transition to adulthood and independent living.

The leaving care provisions are complex and depending on which of three categories a child belongs to, they impose different duties on local authorities. The three categories are: eligible children; relevant children; and former relevant children.

WHICH YOUNG PEOPLE ARE AFFECTED?

Essentially, the young people affected are those aged 16 and over[2] who have been looked after by a local authority for at least 13 weeks after they became 14-years-old. Those weeks can be continuous or made up of separate episodes of care, apart from any short term placements which have been organised as respite care. The Act covers both young people who have been subject to a Care Order under s.31 *Children Act 1989*, or were accommodated under s.20 *Children Act 1989*, as well as looked after children who were detained in a young offender institution, a remand or secure training centre, or who were in hospital on their sixteenth birthday[3].

Under Regulation 4 *Children (Leaving Care) (England) Regulations 2001*, children who have been accommodated and have made a successful return to their families – that is, a household containing either a parent or someone with parental responsibility for them – will not be regarded as *'relevant'* children once their return has lasted for more than six months. It will, however, be the duty of the local authority to keep in touch with such children and, if their arrangements break down, they may become relevant children once more.

WHO IS THE RESPONSIBLE AUTHORITY?

Under s.23A (4) *Children Act 1989* this is the local authority that last looked after the child, regardless of where that child is currently living. The responsible authority will be the young person's primary income provider, and will fund the young person to the levels agreed and set out in the pathway plan[4].

WHEN SHOULD AN ASSESSMENT TAKE PLACE?

If the child is an eligible child, an assessment should take place not more than three months after the child becomes 16 years old. If the child is a relevant child who does not already have a pathway plan, the assessment must be completed not more than three months after the date on which he or she became a relevant child.

WHAT SHOULD AN ASSESSMENT INCLUDE?

It should contain a great deal of detail drawing on earlier assessments and records of the child, and the child's current situation and needs. Regulation 7 *Children (Leaving Care) (England) Regulations 2001* and the *Children (Leaving Care) (Wales) Regulations 2001* require that the local authority include in the assessment:

* health and development;
* education, training or employment;
* the support available to the child from family and other persons;
* financial needs;
* the extent to which the child possesses the skills necessary for independent living; and
* the need for care, support and accommodation.

WHAT IS A PERSONAL ADVISER?

Under s.23D *Children Act 1989* local authorities must appoint a personal adviser for eligible, relevant and former relevant children. The personal adviser must:

- provide personal and practical advice and support to the young person;
- be involved in the assessment of the young person's needs and the production and reviews of the pathway plan;
- liaise with the responsible authority over the implementation of the pathway plan;
- coordinate the provision of services and make sure that the young person can make use of such services;
- keep informed about the young person's progress and wellbeing; and
- keep written records of contact with the young person[5].

WHAT IS A PATHWAY PLAN?

All eligible, relevant and former relevant children must have a pathway plan. This should be drafted as soon as possible after the assessment is completed and must clearly identify the child's needs, what is to be done about them, by whom and when. It should, therefore, detail the advice, assistance and support the child should have, both while being looked after and once he or she ceases to be looked after by the local authority.

It is not part of the personal adviser's function to undertake the statutory assessment of a young person about to leave care, nor is it permissible for the personal adviser to prepare the pathway plan – that is the job of the local authority. However, it is not unlawful to appoint as a personal adviser an officer of employee of the local authority acting as corporate parent, provided that the local authority and the personal adviser recognise the nature of the role and ensure that there is no conflict: see *R (on the application of J) v Caerphilly [2005] EWHC 586 (admin) [2005] All ER (D) 94 (April) per Munby J.*

The pathway plan represents an agreement between the child and the local authority as to what his or her needs are, what his or her future plans are and how the authority will support him or her to meet those needs and fulfil those plans[6]. It will set out a career path with milestones such as education, training, career plans, a planned date for leaving care and where and how the young person will live thereafter. The pathway plan must include:

- the nature and level of contact and personal support to be provided, and by whom, to the young person;
- details of the accommodation to be provided for the young person;
- a detailed plan for education or training and the support to be provided for those in, or seeking, employment;
- the support for the young person in developing and sustaining family relationships;
- a programme to develop the personal and practical skills necessary for independent living;
- the financial support to be provided;
- the young person's health needs, including mental health needs, and how these will be met; and
- contingency plans for action if the pathway plan does not work[7].

Under Regulation 9 *Children (Leaving Care) (England) Regulations 2001* pathway plans must be reviewed at least every six months, or earlier if the child or the personal adviser asks for this.

When drafting the pathway plan, the local authority must have regard to the young person's views and wishes and take steps to ensure that the young person is able to attend and participate in any meetings at which his or her case is considered. The local authority must also *without delay* provide the young person with the results of his or her assessment, pathway plan or review of the pathway plan, and shall, as far as is reasonably practicable, ensure that the contents of these documents are explained to the young person[8]. Young people are often helped by having an advocate to assist them at this time, as well as a personal adviser. Youth workers can be of help to children in formulating their views and wishes and making them known.

The fact that a child is uncooperative, does not turn up to meetings and will not engage with his or her social worker is not a good reason for failing to draw up a detailed pathway plan. Munby J held in *R (on the application of J) v Caerphilly [2005] EWHC 586 (admin) [2005] All ER (D) 94 (April)* that:

> 'The fact that a child is uncooperative and unwilling to engage, is no reason for the local authority not to carry out its obligations under the Act and the Regulations. After all, a disturbed child's unwillingness to engage with those who are trying to help is often merely a part of the overall problem which justified the local authority's statutory intervention in the first place. The local authority must do its best.'

CASE STUDY

J, aged 15, had been in care since the age of 11. Described, as having a wretched childhood and with special needs, J was given a Detention and Training Order. J was due to be released before his sixteenth birthday, but no assessment or pathway plan had been completed for him. When completed, the section on accommodation merely provided that the local authority would continue to explore options in preparation for his release. The pathway plan did not contain an action plan for meeting identified needs in literacy or numeracy, or for education, training or employment. While recognising that J suffered from depression and paranoia the only action to be taken was to register J with a GP and 'facilitate a health assessment'. Although acknowledging that J had complex needs it did not contain any details of specialist support to be provided to meet those needs. The pathway plan was held by the court to be merely descriptive and inadequate. There was insufficient detail as to how the child's needs were to be met, by what date and by whom.

CATEGORIES UNDER THE CHILDREN (LEAVING CARE) ACT 2000

CATEGORY OF YOUNG PERSON

ELIGIBLE CHILDREN
(Schedule 2, para 19B *Children Act 1989*,
Reg. 3 *Children (Leaving Care) (England) Regulations 2001*)

RELEVANT CHILDREN
(s.23A *Children Act 1989*, Reg. 4 *Children (Leaving Care) (England) Regulations 2001*)

FORMER RELEVANT CHILDREN
(s.23C *Children Act 1989*)

CRITERIA AND SERVICES TO BE PROVIDED

Children aged 16-17 looked after for at least 13 weeks since they were 14 years old and who continue to be looked after.
Provisions
• all existing duties for looked after children;
• assessment of needs, including information about education, health and development;
• a pathway plan; and
• a personal adviser.

Children aged 16-17 who are no longer looked after by the local authority, but who were looked after for at least 13 weeks after the age of 14 years, have been looked after at some time while they were aged 16 and 17, and who have left care. Also, children who would have been relevant, but for the fact that they were either in hospital or detained in the criminal justice system, and children who have returned to their families, but whose arrangements have broken down. Children on respite care arrangements are excluded.
Provisions
• a personal adviser;
• an assessment of needs;
• provision of accommodation and maintenance;
• assistance to achieve the goals (education, training or employment goals) set out in the pathway plan; and
• the responsible authority is to keep in touch with the young person.

Young people between the ages of 18 and 21, who have been either eligible or relevant children. A young person whose pathway plan sets out a programme of education or training which runs beyond his or her twenty-first birthday will be a former relevant child until the end of the programme, even if he or she is then over the age of 21. Reasonable breaks in a programme will not disqualify the young person from support.
Provisions
• a personal adviser;
• a pathway plan;
• the responsible authority must keep in touch with the young person;
• help with expenses associated with employment, education and training;
• assistance in general (in kind or exceptionally in cash); and
• the provision of, or funds to secure the provision of, vacation accommodation for those in full-time higher or further education, if needed.

ADVICE AND ASSISTANCE

Young people who do not fall within the three categories may be entitled to advice and assistance under s.24 and s.24A *Children Act 1989*.

A young person qualifies for advice and assistance if he or she is under 21 and has, after the age of 16 (but before the age of 18), ceased to be looked after, accommodated or fostered. Looked after, accommodated and fostered are defined as:
- looked after by a local authority;
- accommodated by or on behalf of a voluntary organisation;
- accommodated in a children's home;
- accommodated by any health or education authority for at least three months (even if this began before the child was 16); or
- privately fostered.

In the case of a young person formerly looked after by the local authority, the local authority that last looked after him or her must take steps to keep in touch. For other qualifying children, the responsible local authority will be the one for the area in which the young person resides at the time the request is made.

Where there is a qualifying child within the area of the local authority who was looked after or accommodated by the local authority or by a voluntary organisation, and appears to be in need of advice or befriending, the local authority shall advise and befriend the young person. However, in situations where a young person may be looked after by a person who appears not to have the necessary facilities to advise or befriend him or her, the local authority *may* advise or befriend the young person.

Where the local authority is under a duty or empowered to advise and befriend, it *may* also give the young person assistance in kind or, in exceptional circumstances, in cash. The local authority may also contribute to expenses incurred by him or her in living near his or her place of employment.

The local authority may also contribute to the cost of education and training. If a qualifying child is in full-time further or higher education, and needs accommodation during a vacation because term time accommodation is not available, the local authority must assist the young person by providing accommodation or providing funds for accommodation.

WELFARE BENEFITS

Under s.6 *Children (Leaving Care) Act 2000*, the *Jobseekers Act 1995* and the *Social Security Contributions and Benefits Act 1992* are amended with the effect that eligible and relevant children cannot claim Income Support, Jobseeker's Allowance or Housing Benefit. Income Support and Jobseekers Allowance are still available for sick or disabled children and single parents, and non-means tested benefits, such as Disability Living Allowance, are still payable to care leavers who qualify.

FINANCIAL SUPPORT

Section 23B (8) *Children Act 1989* provides that while a child is a relevant child, the responsible authority will normally be his or her primary source of income. The income will cover a young person's general costs including, accommodation, maintenance, travel and leisure. However, financial support for relevant children will be means tested according to Income Support criteria. Under this system, any capital up to £3,000 will be disregarded[9]. Capital between £3,000 and £8,000 will be assessed to form a weekly contribution against local authority support. Capital over £8,000 will mean that the relevant child is not eligible for financial support, although the other provisions of the Act, such as the personal adviser, the pathway plan and the duty to keep in contact, continue to apply.

The system could be seen as a counter-incentive for young people to undertake part-time work, which would build up their savings prior to their eighteenth birthday, as any sum accrued over £3,000 would, in effect, become part of their income and liable to be assessed.

Children (Leaving Care) Act 2000 Regulations and Guidance suggests that some of the items which the local authority should consider funding are:
- education and training costs including travel, materials and special equipment or any other relevant costs;
- costs associated with special needs, such as disability or pregnancy;
- childcare costs;
- clothing;
- contact with family or other important relationships;
- cultural and religious needs;
- counselling and therapeutic needs; and
- hobbies and holidays[10].

Normal rules relating to benefit entitlement and such entitlements as student loans apply when the young person reaches 18 years old.

EMERGENCY ASSISTANCE

Guidance states that where an eligible or relevant child appears in another local authority's area and needs help, then the second authority should provide assistance on a short term basis using their powers under s.17 *Children Act 1989*. The second authority should liaise with the responsible authority over the appropriate long-term needs of the child[11].

COMPLAINTS AND REPRESENTATIONS

The *Children (Leaving Care) Act 2000* inserted s.24D into the *Children Act 1989*. This requires local authorities to establish arrangements for dealing with complaints made to them about their services by relevant and former relevant children, and those who qualify for advice and assistance under s.24 and s.24A *Children Act 1989*.

The *Advocacy Services and Representations Procedure (Children) (Amendment) Regulations 2002* stipulate that where a local authority receives such a complaint, or becomes aware that such a complaint is going to be made, the local authority must:

- provide the complainant with information about advocacy services; and
- offer him or her help in obtaining an advocate[12].

For more information on the role of advocates and advocacy services, see chapter 3.

Regulation 13 *Children (Leaving Care) (England) Regulations 2001* amends the *Representations Procedure (Children) Regulations 1991* by inserting a new Regulation 3A which provides that where a local authority receives a complaint from a relevant or former relevant child, or a child who qualifies for advice and assistance, the authority shall pass the complaint to its complaints officer and endeavour to reach a settlement to the satisfaction of the complainant within 14 days. If no settlement can be reached, the procedure for investigating a formal complaint should be followed as set out in the *Representations Procedure (Children) Regulations 1991*.

VOLUNTARY ORGANISATIONS

Voluntary organisations providing care for children and young people have a duty under s.24C *Children Act 1989* to notify the responsible local authority (i.e. the department within whose area the child proposes to live) when a young person aged 16 or over leaves the voluntary organisation's care. This notification is to allow the local authority to consider whether it has a duty to that child as a qualifying child.

The *Children (Leaving Care) Act 2000 Regulations and Guidance* suggests that, although there is no statutory duty to do so, where a voluntary organisation provides accommodation for young people, it should also consider as a matter of good practice the need for after-care services for young people leaving its care after the age of 16. It should also advise them of any statutory facilities for which they may be eligible[13].

It is essential for youth workers in the voluntary and the statutory sector who are involved with young people to be aware of the leaving care provisions, which place substantial duties on local authorities. They can also pose significant problems. A young person who does not wish to work or be in contact with the local authority may be compelled to do so if he or she has no family and no other means of support, as the young person will not have access to the benefits system. Youth workers may find that they are in the position of negotiating support for such young people, who may be extremely vulnerable without this kind of assistance.

FOOTNOTES:

1. As amended by the *Children (Leaving Care) Act 2000*.
2. In certain circumstances, it can apply to a person until the age of 24.
3. Reg. 4 *Children (Leaving Care) (England) Regulations 2001*.
4. s.23 (B) *Children Act 1989*.
5. Reg. 12 *Children (Leaving Care) (England) Regulations 2001*.
6. Para 22, Explanatory Notes to *Children Leaving Care Act 2000*.
7. Schedule to the *Children (Leaving Care) (England) Regulations 2001*.
8. Reg 6 *Children (Leaving Care) (England) Regulations 2001* and *Children (Leaving Care) (Wales) Regulations 2001*.
9. There are exemptions, such as any payment by the Criminal Injuries Compensation Authority, which will not be included in calculating capital.
10. *Children (Leaving Care) Act 2000 Regulations and Guidance*, p.63.
11. *Children (Leaving Care) Act 2000 Regulations and Guidance*, p.65.
12. Reg. 4 *Advocacy Services and Representations Procedure (Children) (Amendment) Regulations 2002*.
13. *Children (Leaving Care) Act 2000 Regulations and Guidance*, p.19.

The rights of refugee and asylum seeking children

Youth workers are increasingly likely to come into contact with refugee and asylum seeking children and young people. These children and young people are often extremely vulnerable and may turn to youth workers for advice, assistance or guidance. This chapter provides an overview of the main problems that such children face and the services available to assist them.

ASYLUM AND IMMIGRATION LAW: CONTEXT

WHAT ARE ASYLUM SEEKERS?
Asylum seekers are individuals who have applied to the Government of a country other than their own, for protection or refuge, because they are unable or unwilling to seek the protection of their own Government.

ASYLUM IN THE UK
Applications for asylum in the UK can only be made once individuals are actually in the country. Asylum seekers are granted Temporary Admission, or may be detained at an Immigration Removal Centre until a decision is made on their asylum application. It is rare for children, whether with their families or unaccompanied, to be detained.

Once individuals have claimed asylum '*they cannot be removed from the country until their claim has been determined*'[1]. While applications are being processed, provision must be made to meet the basic needs of applicants.

Applications are refused when applicants do not meet the criteria to be given '*refugee status*' under the provisions of the *Convention relating to the Status of Refugees 1951* (*Refugee Convention*). However, applicants may be granted either Discretionary Leave to Remain or Humanitarian Protection[2], which allow them to remain in the UK for a limited period of time and are subject to review at the end of that period. Any form of leave entitles the holder to work or claim benefits.

WHAT ARE UNACCOMPANIED ASYLUM SEEKING CHILDREN?
Unaccompanied Asylum Seeking Children (UASC) are children:

> '… *who, at the time of making the asylum application is, or (if there is no proof) appears to be, under eighteen, is applying for asylum in their own right and has no adult relative or guardian to turn to in this country.*'[3]

The Home Office sets out specific reasons for granting Discretionary Leave to Remain. One of these is that the applicant is a UASC '*for whom adequate reception arrangements in their country are not available.*'[4]

Discretionary Leave is usually granted for three years or until UASC reach 18 years old. However, UASC from Albania, Bangladesh, Bulgaria, Jamaica, Macedonia, Moldova, Romania, Serbia and Montenegro and Sri Lanka are now only granted one year's leave in the first instance, as these countries are now deemed safe. If a young person is granted leave for a year or less, he or she cannot appeal against the refusal to grant asylum. However, if leave is granted, and this brings the total period of leave to more than one year, a right of appeal against refusal of asylum will be triggered.

CASE STUDY

L, an Albanian boy aged 16, has sought asylum on arrival at Harwich. He is refused asylum by the Home Office and is granted one year's Discretionary Leave under the concession to unaccompanied minors. At this point he has no right of appeal against refusal of asylum. Shortly before the end of the one year's leave, he applies for an extension and since no suitable reception arrangements have been identified in Albania, and he is still a child under the age of 18, he is granted a further one year period of leave. Since his aggregated period of leave totals more than one year, this triggers a right of appeal against the initial refusal of asylum.

A recent development announced by the Home Office is the Returns Programme for UASC[5]. The programme aims to return children prior to their eighteenth birthday by providing '*suitable arrangements*' for their reception in their country of origin. The programme is shortly to be piloted with Albanian children and is to be 'rolled out' when arrangements are in place to meet the programme targets.

MAKING AN ASYLUM APPLICATION FOR A CHILD

UNACCOMPANIED ASYLUM SEEKING CHILDREN

Unaccompanied children may apply for asylum on arrival in the country or thereafter. The Home Office has a target of resolving their applications within two months of the application being lodged. However, claims by unaccompanied children are disproportionately refused for two reasons: first, specific forms of persecution experienced by children do not fit neatly with *Refugee Convention* criteria; second, decision-makers at the Home Office may give less 'anxious scrutiny' to children's claims because they know that they will receive the temporary protection of Discretionary Leave in any event.

ACCOMPANIED CHILDREN

Children who are accompanied by an adult do not need to claim asylum in their own right, they will be treated as dependents of their parents or guardians and will be granted or refused leave to remain in line with the decision made about the principal applicant. It is possible for accompanied children to claim asylum in their own right. An immigration lawyer should be consulted where this is thought to be desirable.

AGE ASSESSMENTS

DEFINITION OF A CHILD

The decision about whether or not an asylum seeker is a child is not necessarily straight forward. Domestic and international legislation define a child as any person under the age of 18, but the immigration rules stipulate that:

> '[A] child means a person who is under 18 years of age or who, in the absence of documentary evidence establishing age, appears to be under that age.'[6]

Any UASC who has not already claimed asylum should seek the assistance of an immigration lawyer.

A UASC must lodge an asylum claim *in person* to an immigration officer at any port of entry to the UK. If the child is already in the UK, this must be done at one of the Asylum Screening Units in Croydon, Leeds or Liverpool.

At the point of making the claim, the child will be given a SEF (minor) form, which the child must return in person to the Asylum Screening Unit within one month of issue.

No interview is required and the child's application will be decided on the contents of the form. The child should receive help to complete the application, preferably from a specialist immigration lawyer. When the SEF (minor) form is returned, the child will be issued with an Asylum Registration Card.

Occasionally, a child will be interviewed in connection with an asylum claim, but this is rare. Interviews of UASC are being piloted and may be used for those identified as suitable for the Returns Programme for UASC.

If a child is interviewed, a responsible adult must be present. This may be a parent, guardian, representative, or other adult with responsibility for the child, but not an immigration officer.

Many asylum seeking children who come to the UK have no documentation that establishes their age, nationality or identity. In many cases this is because they are scared of being apprehended by their national authorities or because they have been smuggled or trafficked into the country. They may also destroy their travel documents *en route* to make it more difficult for the authorities to remove them[7]: this does not mean that they do not have legitimate claims or genuine fear.

In situations where the age of a young person is not believed or cannot be ascertained with certainty, the responsible authorities make a judgment on the matter.

WHY IS AGE ASSESSMENT IMPORTANT?

The assessment and determination of the age of UASC determines the services they are entitled to receive, such as accommodation provided by the local authority.

Important factors affecting age disputed UASC include:
- children assessed as being under 18 will receive a period of Discretionary Leave even if their asylum claim or claim for Humanitarian Protection fails;
- children have one month in which to return their SEF (minor) forms, whereas people over 18 only have 10 days. If forms are not returned within the time limit, the Home Office is likely to refuse them on grounds of non-compliance;

- children and demonstrably vulnerable people are inter viewed about their claims in the presence of a solicitor: people treated as competent adults are not;
- children are unlikely to be detained while their applications are being processed; and
- children assessed as being over 16, will not benefit from compulsory full-time education.

AGE DISPUTES AND LOCAL AUTHORITY POLICY

Home Office policy on age disputes involving UASC states that:

'Where an applicant claims to be a child but his/her appearance strongly suggests that he/she is over 18, IND's policy is to treat the applicant as an adult and offer NASS support (if appropriate) until there is credible documentary or medical evidence to demonstrate the age claimed. These applications are flagged as 'disputed minors' and they are treated as adult cases throughout the asylum process, or until we accept evidence to the contrary. In borderline cases IND gives the applicant the benefit of the doubt and treats the applicant as a minor.'

The Home Office usually confirms in writing that an individual is to be treated as an adult. The letter will also inform the individual that they have the right to approach a local authority for a '*social work assessment*'. It is Home Office policy to accept this assessment.

If the local authority age assessment confirms the claim that the individual is indeed a child, there are arrangements in place for altering the age recorded by the Home Office. Thereafter, the Home Office should treat the individual as a child for the purpose of the asylum claim. The child should be granted Discretionary Leave, even if the asylum claim fails.

There is no statutory guidance on the process of age assessment. However, criteria are set out in *R (on the application of B) v London Borough of Merton*[8].

If a young person is unhappy with the outcome of an age assessment, redress may be obtained either through the complaints procedure or judicial review. Advice should be sought from a family or community care solicitor. This is a separate matter from the asylum claim and does not need to be conducted by an immigration lawyer.

HOW QUICKLY MUST A LOCAL AUTHORITY CONDUCT AN ASSESSMENT OF AGE?

There are often arrangements in place for the local authority departments to be present at the airport to conduct an assessment. This is not ideal as young people may be tired, confused or frightened by new surroundings and unsure of the different roles of immigration officers and social workers. Other young people claiming asylum at a 'screening unit', once inside the country, may be referred to the local authority.

A response of 'no action' to a request for an age assessment would be unlawful and open to challenge, unless an assessment had been carried out previously by another local authority.

WELFARE PROVISION FOR ASYLUM SEEKING CHILDREN

All destitute adult asylum seekers, whether single or with families (including dependent children) now receive support through the National Asylum Support Scheme (NASS). Asylum support may be in designated accommodation with subsistence payments, or may be subsistence only for those who are accommodated by family or friends.

Asylum applicants and failed asylum seekers are prohibited from working and prohibited from claiming benefits as a condition of their Temporary Admission and are therefore reliant on asylum support unless they have independent means.

Children in asylum seeking families receiving asylum support are expected to live with their parents or care giver: this continues even when the child becomes 18 as they will continue to be considered a dependent as they were under 18 when the application was made.

Children of asylum seekers are not permitted to take any paid employment.

DISABLED CHILDREN

Disabled children living in households receiving asylum support are *also* eligible for support under s.17 *Children Act 1989* and the *Chronically Sick and Disabled Persons Act 1970*. The essential living needs will be provided by NASS, but any additional needs arising from disabilities are met by the local authority. The immigration status of children does not prevent a local authority from providing support.

UNACCOMPANIED ASYLUM SEEKING CHILDREN

The local authority is responsible for the care of UASC. The immigration status of UASC does not affect the duty on local authorities to care for children under 18 years old. However, it may play a part in the withdrawal or withholding of leaving care services in certain circumstances.

By definition UASC will meet one or more of the requirements that trigger the duty of the local authority to accommodate. Although it is usually less appropriate, it is lawful to assist some unaccompanied children (generally older children) with accommodation under s.17 *Children Act 1989*. In situations where s.17 is used young people are not considered to be looked after and so are not entitled to leaving care services once they reach 18 years old.

Leaving care provisions of the Children Act 1989

Unaccompanied children who have been accommodated under s.20 *Children Act 1989* are entitled to leaving care

A local authority can provide accommodation and support to children under either s.17 or s.20 *Children Act 1989* (see chapters 4 and 11).

Section 17:
(1) It shall be the general duty of every local authority (in addition to the other duties imposed on them by this Part) –
(a) to safeguard and promote the welfare of children within their area who are in need; and
(b) so far as is consistent with that duty, to promote the upbringing of such children by their families, by providing a range and level of services appropriate to those children's needs.

Section 20:
(1) Every local authority shall provide accommodation for any child in need within their area who appears to them to require accommodation as a result of –
(a) there being no person who has parental responsibility for him;
(b) his being lost or abandoned; or
(c) the person who has been caring for him being prevented (whether or not permanently, and for what ever reason) from providing him with suitable accommodation or care.

support as long as they have been accommodated under this section for more than 13 weeks and were accommodated on their sixteenth birthday. The services should be identical to those provided for a British child (see chapter 12).

Impact of immigration status
If a UASC is given Discretionary Leave to Remain in the UK, the restrictions on working and receiving benefits are lifted. For a UASC, who is looked after under s.20 *Children Act 1989*, this will mean that he or she will be entitled to benefits at the age of 18 years old. A child who has been assisted under s.17 *Children Act 1989* will be eligible for benefits once he or she reaches the age of 16.

Children, who are granted Discretionary Leave until they are 18 years old, may only receive benefits while their leave is current. The entitlement to benefits ends with the expiry of their Leave to Remain, unless an application for extension is made before the leave expires: in which case the leave is automatically extended by statute. However, benefits offices will sometimes need to be shown evidence that the application for an extension has been made before they will agree to provide benefits. A local authority looking after a child who has been granted Discretionary Leave until the age of 18 should make an application to extend the period for the child prior to the child's eighteenth birthday.

Responsibility for providing accommodation and support to a young person over the age of 18, whose application or appeal for asylum is still pending, generally lies with NASS (the National Asylum and Support Service). However, where the young person was looked after before the age of

CASE STUDY

K from Afghanistan arrived in the UK as an unaccompanied asylum seeking minor, aged 15, and has been supported by his local authority, first in a children's home and then in semi-supported accommodation. He was granted Refugee Status and indefinite leave to remain when he was 16. He did well at school and transferred to a local college at the age of 17, where he has been studying to gain further qualifications that would enable him to enter higher education. K has recently had his eighteenth birthday and the local authority have indicated that they no longer wish to support him. K is not entitled to income support or housing benefit as he is studying full time. K's solicitor approached the local authority for continued assistance with his accommodation and living expenses while he completed his further education programme. The solicitor also enquired about his status and whether he had been looked after by the local authority under s.20 *Children Act 1989*. After initially refusing to support K, and telling him that he would have to work to support himself and abandon his full time studies, the authority accepted that he had been accommodated under s.20 and was, therefore, a 'looked after' child entitled to benefit from the leaving care provisions (see chapter 12). The local authority were persuaded that they had ongoing duties under the leaving care provisions of the *Children Act 1989* and agreed to pay for his accommodation and support to enable him to finish his course.

18, the local authority will retain responsibilities under the leaving care provisions for assisting with accommodation and support, but NASS will reimburse its costs.

UASC looked after under s.20 *Children Act 1989* will not be dispersed to dispersal accommodation. However, unaccompanied children may be dispersed if they have been assisted under s.17 *Children Act 1989*.

ENTITLEMENT TO EDUCATION

YOUNG PEOPLE OF COMPULSORY SCHOOL AGE
Local authorities have a legal duty to provide education to all children of compulsory school age regardless of their immigration status. Such education must be appropriate to age, ability, aptitude and any Special Educational Needs. This duty does not extend to children living in accommodation centres where education is provided.

Children whose parents are supported by NASS or by their local authority under the Interim Support Scheme are entitled to receive free school meals and are entitled to the same assistance with school transport and school uniforms as other pupils.

YOUNG PEOPLE OVER COMPULSORY SCHOOL AGE
There is no duty on the local authority to provide education to UASC and children of asylum seekers over the age of 16,

though they may study at school sixth forms, sixth form colleges or colleges of further education provided that there are places available, and that they satisfy the school or college's academic requirements.

Asylum seeking children whose parents receive support from NASS or assistance under the *Children Act 1989* or the *National Assistance Act 1948*, and UASC aged 16 to 18 who receive support from or who are looked after by the local authority are regarded as home students and are only liable to pay home fees for further education courses[9]. All young people aged 16, 17 or 18 who are regarded as home students can apply for fee remission when studying on a Learning and Skills Council[10] funded course[11].

The Education Maintenance Allowance is not available to either accompanied or unaccompanied asylum seeking children, or to those with Limited Leave to Remain. It is, however, available to non-British nationals who have been granted Indefinite Leave to Remain, whether this is as a result of refugee status or other reason (irrespective of the length of time spent living in the UK). This would apply both to former UASC recognised as refugees and the dependant children of those granted Indefinite Leave to Remain (who will be given the same status as their parents). Young people are still subject to the means test applicable to all applicants.

Since September 2003 all young people, including UASC who are entitled to be regarded as home students, and who are aged 16, 17 or 18 on the 31 August in the calendar year when they begin their programme of study, can apply for Learning Support Funds[12]. Support is available under this Fund to young people studying in FE colleges, school sixth forms and sixth form colleges whose access to, or completion of, education might be inhibited by financial considerations (LSF can also be paid in certain circumstances to students studying in Higher Education institutions, see LSF Funding Guidance 2003/04 and the new LSF Funding Guidance for 2005/06). They can be paid in addition to the Education Maintenance Allowance.

There are three different types of LSF:
- general learner support/hardship funds, which can be used towards course related costs (such as the purchase of books and equipment) as well as any emergencies affecting living arrangements. Transport costs can also be paid via the hardship funds;
- residential allowances (i.e. Residential Bursaries); and
- childcare allowances (i.e. 'Care to Learn')[13] .

ENTITLEMENTS OF UNACCOMPANIED ASYLUM SEEKING CHILDREN WHEN THEY REACH 18

CHILDREN ACT 1989

A child reaches adulthood on his or her eighteenth birthday. This has an impact on both those accommodated under s.20

Children Act 1989 and those assisted under s.17 *Children Act 1989*. For those assisted under s.17 *Children Act 1989*, the local authority ceases to have a duty to provide them with support and assistance, and they will need to seek support from the benefits agency or NASS as appropriate (see below). For those who were accommodated under s.20 *Children Act 1989*, support will continue to be provided, albeit possibly in a lesser form, under the leaving care provisions (see chapter 12). In addition some young people formally supported under s.20 *Children Act 1989* will become eligible for mainstream benefits (see below).

DISCRETIONARY LEAVE

At the age of 18, not only does the protection afforded by s.17 and s.20 *Children Act 1989* stop, but children's Discretionary Leave to Remain will normally expire. All children granted Discretionary Leave until aged 18 are strongly advised to apply for an extension of that leave *before* they reach their eighteenth birthday. Where they do so, a grant of a further period of leave must be considered by the Home Office and this will result in one of the following outcomes:
- a decision may be made to grant further leave;
- a decision may be made to refuse further leave, but an appeal may be brought against this decision; and
- where an appeal is brought against the refusal to grant further leave, and this is dismissed, there is an onward challenge 'with permission' to the Tribunal. Where permission is not granted by the Tribunal, there is no further right of appeal.

OTHER ENTITLEMENTS WHERE AN 'IN TIME' APPLICATION TO EXTEND LEAVE IS MADE
Continued eligibility to work
By making an '*in time*' application to extend leave, the leave is automatically extended on the same terms as before until a new decision is reached, and where the decision is to refuse further leave, until any appeal from that decision is finally determined. During this period there is no restriction on taking or changing employment. However, young people may find it difficult to convince a new employer of their continued eligibility, as the Home Office only send out a letter acknowledging receipt of the application to extend leave and this does not include any specific acknowledgement of a continued right to work.

Housing
A young person who continues to have leave because he or she has made an '*in time*' application for an extension of that leave, will be entitled, in some circumstances, to local authority housing and will remain entitled to housing benefit while the extension application and any further appeal are outstanding.

Where accommodation cannot be secured through a private landlord, or continued through the local authority, '*in-time*' applicants may be eligible for social housing or homelessness assistance from the housing authority.

All former UASC who have an outstanding extension application or appeal – irrespective of their previous status as assisted under s.20 or s.17 *Children Act 1989* – will be eligible for social housing. In addition, those who were previously accommodated under s.20 *Children Act 1989* will fall within the definition of 'priority need' under the *Homelessness (Priority Need for Accommodation) England Order 2002*, and will often meet the other criteria allowing them to receive 'homelessness assistance' where appropriate.

WITHHOLDING AND WITHDRAWAL OF SUPPORT

Section 54 and Schedule 3 *Nationality, Immigration and Asylum Act 2002* are the central provisions concerning withholding and withdrawal of support to failed asylum seekers and those '*unlawfully in the United Kingdom*'. The provisions concern not only withdrawal of NASS support to single adult asylum seekers and asylum seeking families, but also the withholding or withdrawal of most kinds of support otherwise available to local authorities under their statutory powers and duties. This includes provision to former unaccompanied children, whether or not they were given Discretionary Leave until age 18.

WITHDRAWING OR WITHHOLDING SUPPORT FROM FORMER UASC WHO HAD DISCRETIONARY LEAVE

UASC may be provided for under either s.20 or s.17 *Children Act 1989*. However, at the age of 18, this support is terminated. After the age of 18, local authority support will only be provided to young people who were accommodated under s.20 *Children Act 1989* whilst under the age of 18. This will be done under the leaving care provisions of the *Children Act 1989*. However, support will only be available if the young person's leave is '*current*': where an '*in-time*' application for an extension of leave remains under consideration and while any appeal arising from a refusal of an extension of leave remains to be determined.

Schedule 3 *Nationality, Immigration and Asylum Act 2002* states that '*failed asylum seekers*'[14] and '*persons unlawfully in the UK*'[15] are ineligible for continued support under the leaving care provisions. If a UASC has not applied for an extension of leave by the time he or she reaches his or her eighteenth birthday, he or she will become an '*overstayer*' (even where he or she then applies '*out of time*' for an extension of leave and the application is being considered by the Home Office). He or she will, at this point, become '*unlawfully present*' and will lose any entitlement to '*leaving care*' support, along with any entitlement to benefits and housing assistance from the time that the original leave expires.

CONTINUED SUPPORT UNDER CHILDREN ACT 1989 FOR THOSE NOT GRANTED DISCRETIONARY LEAVE

Some UASC may reach the age of 18 without their asylum claim or appeal against refusal of asylum having been determined (for example if they arrive and claim asylum shortly

An application to extend Discretionary Leave to Remain can be made at any time before or after it expires. An application made *before* the expiry of Discretionary Leave ('*in time*') allows for continued eligibility for benefits and/or *Children Act 1989* support until a decision is made and any further appeal is disposed of. Where new leave is granted, eligibility continues.

Where an application is not made until after the leave expires, it is referred to as an '*out of time*' application. Further Leave to Remain can be granted in such situations, but the applicant becomes an '*overstayer*'. As an '*overstayer*' the applicant looses all right to benefits and any entitlement to '*leaving care*' support under the *Children Act 1989*. If further leave is granted as a result of an '*out of time*' application, entitlements to benefits and *Children Act 1989* (leaving care) support is restored.

before their eighteenth birthday). They will not therefore be granted any period of Discretionary Leave and will still be considered as 'asylum seekers' when they turn 18. In such a case, a post-18 UASC is entitled to continue to receive support under the leaving care provisions of the *Children Act 1989* (if they were accommodated under s.20 *Children Act 1989*) because they are still asylum seekers.

Children Act 1989 support (under the '*leaving care*' provisions) should continue until a young person becomes a '*failed asylum seeker*' (when he or she has no further appeal right against refusal of asylum) AND, in addition, he or she '*fails to cooperate with removal directions issued in respect of him*'. Both of these conditions must be met before leaving care provision under the *Children Act 1989* can be withdrawn.

Note: Former UASC assisted under s.17 Children Act 1989 until their eighteenth birthday are not entitled to Children Act 1989 support beyond that age (whether or not granted a period of Discretionary Leave).

ENTITLEMENT TO 'ASYLUM SUPPORT' (NASS SUPPORT) FOR ASYLUM SEEKING FAMILIES WITH CHILDREN

The National Asylum Support Service (NASS) provides what is known as '*asylum support*' to single adult asylum seekers and asylum-seeking families with children. Asylum seeker's entitlement to '*asylum support*' ends:
* if they withdraw their asylum claim; or
* if the claim is refused and there is no outstanding appeal.

Where asylum or some form of limited Leave results from the asylum application or appeal, the asylum seeker is entitled to benefits and may seek work and (in the case of a grant of asylum) seek an '*integration loan*'. Those with children are entitled to Child benefit and Child Tax Credit if they apply within three months of the grant of asylum. Whether the asylum claim is refused or granted, a former asylum seeker becomes ineligible for asylum support 14 days after he or she is notified of the decision by the Secretary of State.

WITHDRAWAL OF 'ASYLUM SUPPORT' (NASS SUPPORT) FOR ASYLUM SEEKING FAMILIES WITH CHILDREN

By virtue of s.9 *Asylum and Immigration (Treatment of Claimants etc) Act 2004* families with children will have their support terminated:

> '... *where the secretary of state 'certifies' that in his opinion the person has failed without reasonable excuse to take reasonable steps- (i) to leave the United Kingdom voluntarily or; (ii) to place himself in a position in which he is able to leave the United Kingdom voluntarily.*'

Schedule 3 *Nationality, Immigration and Asylum Act 2002* allows continued support to be provided under the *Children Act 1989* to the children only of the families of failed asylum seekers, raising the prospect of the separation of children from their parents. At the time of going to press, a pilot scheme to implement s.9 *Asylum and Immigration (Treatment of Claimants etc) Act 2004* is being conducted in several areas and has resulted in widespread opposition from professionals and their representative bodies. No family of failed asylum seekers has yet had their children taken into care as a result of this legislation though the power to do so remains.

FOOTNOTES:

1. *Convention relating to the Status of Refugees* 1951.

2. These replaced Exceptional Leave to Remain after 1 April 2003.

3. www.ind.homeoffice.gov.uk

4. *UASC Policy Guidance*, Home Office.

5. *Unaccompanied Asylum Seeking Children (UASC) Returns Programme – Policy Framework Document.* February 2005.

6. Para 349, *Immigration Rules*.

7. It is now a criminal offence if, at a 'leave' or asylum interview, a person does not have, without a reasonable excuse, a document which satisfactorily establishes identity, nationality and citizenship. These cases are now being prosecuted under s.2 *Asylum and Immigration (Treatment of Claimants etc.) Act 2004.*

8. [2003] EWCH 1689.

9. Paras 309 and 310, *LSC Funding Guidance for Further Education in 2004/05.*

10. The Learning and Skills Council is responsible for funding and planning education and training (other than at University) for over 16-year-olds in England.

11. Para 175, *LSC Funding Guidance for Further Education in 2004/05.*

12. Paras 3 and 15, *LSC LSF Funding Guidance for 2003/04.*

13. More details can be obtained about this funding from www.childrenslegalcentre.com (refugees and asylum seekers) and www.dfes.gov.uk.

14. Para 6 Schedule 3 *Nationality, Immigration and Asylum Act 2002.*

15. Para 7 Schedule 3 *Nationality, Immigration and Asylum Act 2002.*

Child employment

It is unknown exactly how many young people have part-time jobs. However, it is thought that at any one time around 1.5 million children and young people of compulsory school age are working. The majority of young people that youth workers come into contact with are likely to have experienced work or will do so at some point. Thus, it is important that youth workers have some knowledge of the law relating to child employment.

The laws regulating this area are complex, confusing and difficult to find. They are contained in a number of Statutes, Regulations, Codes of Practice and Government Guidance.

It is a common misconception that exploitative child employment takes place only in developing world sweatshops. However, the illegal employment of children is also a huge problem in the UK, and a number of large, well-known companies have repeatedly been found guilty of breaching child employment laws.

In July 2001, a McDonald's franchised restaurant in Camberley, Surrey, was fined more than £12,400 for employing schoolchildren illegally. Child employment officers discovered more than 50 breaches of the law. None of the young employees had work permits and they were working overtime and late on school nights. One 15-year-old had worked 16 hours on a Saturday, seven hours over the legal limit. Another 16-year-old had worked from 5.00pm until 2.00am on a school day, when legally she should not have worked after 7.00pm.

WHEN IS A CHILD EMPLOYED?

Any child who assists in a trade or occupation run for profit, even if he or she is not paid, is deemed to be employed. Babysitting or offering to wash a car for charity would not amount to employment, but helping out a local tradesman by delivering leaflets would amount to employment, as would helping out in the family shop.

AT WHAT AGE CAN A CHILD WORK?

Section 18 *Children and Young Persons Act 1933 (CYPA 1933)* sets 14 as the minimum age at which a child may take part-time employment, but there are restrictions on the type of work that may be taken and the hours that can be worked. However, although the law states that the minimum age for part-time employment is 14, 13-year-olds are also allowed to take part-time employment, on a more restricted basis, *if* local byelaws (made by their local authority), covering the area in which they work, permit it. Under s.18(2) *CYPA 1933* byelaws may authorise the employment of 13-year-olds:

- on an occasional basis by their parents in light agricultural or horticultural work; or
- in categories of light work specified in the byelaw.

No definition is provided in the Act for '*occasional basis*', but it must, inevitably, mean '*not on a regular basis*'.

Where a local authority byelaw does not specify whether 13-year-olds can work, it means they cannot be employed – 13-year-olds do not have a '*right*' to work.

CHILDREN UNDER THE AGE OF 13
As a general rule, children under the age of 13 may not be employed at all. However, there are a few exceptions to this rule. Under Part II *Children and Young Persons Act 1963 (CYPA 1963)*, under-13s can take part in performances, sports and modelling where a payment is made for their participation.

Performances
Performances are defined in s.37(2) *CYPA 1963* and cover those in connection with which a charge is made; any performance in licensed premises; any broadcast performance;

any performance included in a programme service; any performance recorded with a view to its use in a broadcast or such a service or in a film intended for public exhibition.

Section 37(1) *CYPA 1963* requires a child of compulsory school age who is engaging in such a performance to have a licence granted by the local authority unless:

- no payment other than for defraying expenses is made to the child or another person; and
- in the six months preceding the performance, the child has not taken part in other performances for more than three days; or
- the performance is given under arrangements made by a school or made by a body of persons approved by the Secretary of State or the local authority in whose area the performance takes place.

The fact that a licence is required where '*payment in connection with which a charge is made*' means that if an admission fee is charged for a performance, a licence is required regardless of whether the child him or herself is paid for his or her participation. The same rule applies under s.37(2) *CYPA 1963*, if a charge is made for the hire of a hall or theatre in which the performance takes place or if payment is made to another person such as a choreographer. It is, therefore, likely that most performances, whether for profit or not, will require a licence.

The provisions relating to performances are relevant to youth organisations that put on any kind of production involving children. They will need to be certain that they do not require a licence from the local authority (i.e. that they fall within the exceptions above).

Where a licence is required, the employer must apply for a licence to the local authority in whose area the child resides. A licence will only be granted if the local authority is satisfied that the child is fit to undertake the work, that proper provision has been made to secure his or her health and '*kind treatment*' and his or her education will not suffer. If it is so satisfied, and it has power to grant a licence, the local authority shall not refuse to grant the licence. '*Kind treatment*' is not defined in the Act. It is not clear whether this would be considered as a positive duty to act in the best interests of a child or whether it is simply a requirement not to harm the health and safety of the child. If in doubt as to whether or not a young person needs a performance licence, youth workers should ring their local authority and request information. Alternatively information can be obtained from the National Network for Child Employment and Entertainment at www.buckscc.gov.uk.

Performances of a dangerous nature
Once a child reaches the age of 12, he or she may be trained to take part in performances of a dangerous nature – i.e. acrobatics and contortionism – under, and in accordance with, a licence granted by the local authority[1]. The licence shall specify the places at which the person is to be trained

and shall contain such conditions as are, in the opinion of the local authority, necessary for the protection of the child. However, a licence shall not be refused if the person is satisfied that the child is fit and willing to be trained and that proper provision has been made to secure his or her health and kind treatment[2]. There is no indication as to how the '*willingness*' of the child is to be ascertained or by whom.

WHAT HOURS CAN A CHILD WORK?

CHILDREN UNDER 13
Where children under the age of 13 are employed in the entertainment industry, the hours that can be worked and the rest periods are set out in the *Children (Performances) Regulations 1968*.

13-YEAR-OLDS
Section 18(2)(c) *CYPA 1933* permits local authorities to prescribe in their byelaws the number of hours in each day, or in each week, a 13-year-old may work, and the time of day at which they may be employed. The hours of work should be no greater than for 14-year-olds, but may, if the local authority choose, be the same. Local authorities may also set intervals for rest and meal breaks, holidays and any other conditions to be observed in their employment.

14-YEAR-OLDS
Section 18(1) *CYPA 1933* stipulates that, on a school day, a 14-year-old may not work
- before 7.00am or after 7.00pm;
- for more than two hours on a school day. They can either work for one hour before school and one hour after school, or two hours after school; or
- for more than 12 hours in any week in which he or she attends school.

In addition, a 14-year-old may not work:
- for more than five hours on a Saturday or any other day (other than a Sunday) during school holidays; or
- for more than two hours on a Sunday.

During school holidays, a 14-year-old may not work for more than 25 hours in any week or for more than four hours in any day without a rest break of one hour.

Further, a child must have at least two consecutive non-school weeks without employment in any one year.

15- AND 16-YEAR-OLDS (UNDER SCHOOL LEAVING AGE)
The restrictions on hours of work for those aged 15 and 16 who have not reached school leaving age are essentially the same as those that apply to 14-year-olds: not before the close of school hours on any day he or she is required to attend school; not before 7.00am or after 7.00pm; not for more than two hours on any school day or 12 hours in any school week; not for more than four hours in any day without a

rest break of one hour; and a requirement to have a period of at least two consecutive weeks without employment during school holidays. However, at 15 and 16, a child may work for up to eight hours on a weekday when he or she is not at school or on a Saturday, and for up to 35 hours during the school holidays (s.18(1) *CYPA 1933*).

FULL-TIME EMPLOYMENT

A young person can only work on a full time basis when he or she becomes of school leaving age. This is the last Friday in June of the school year in which he or she reaches the age of 16.

TYPES OF WORK

WHAT IS LIGHT WORK?

Light work is defined in s.18(2A) *CYPA 1933* as:

> '… *work which, on account of the inherent nature of the tasks which it involves and the particular conditions under which they are performed:*
>
> *a) is not likely to be harmful to the safety, health or development of children; and*
>
> *b) is not such as to be harmful to their attendance at school or to their participation in work experience in accordance with section 560 of the* Education Act 1996, *or their capacity to benefit from the instruction received or, as the case may be, the experience gained.*'

Generally, byelaws specify what forms of work constitute light work. These can differ from authority to authority. Byelaws also specify forbidden types of work. These normally include a ban on employment:

- in a cinema, theatre, discotheque, dance hall or night club, except in connection with a performance given entirely by children;
- selling or delivering alcohol, except in sealed containers;
- delivering milk;
- delivering fuel oils;
- in a commercial kitchen;
- collecting or sorting refuse;
- which is more than three metres above ground level or, in the case of internal work, more than three metres above floor level;
- involving harmful exposure to physical, biological or chemical agents;
- collecting money, selling or canvassing door-to-door, except under the supervision of an adult;
- involving exposure to adult material or in situations which are for this reason otherwise unsuitable for children;
- in telephone sales;
- in any slaughter house or in that part of any butcher's shop or other premises connected with the killing of livestock, butchery, or the preparation of carcasses or meat for sale; or
- as an attendant or assistant in a fairground or amusement arcade, or in any other premises used for the purpose of public amusement by means of automatic machines, games of chance or skill or similar devices.

There are also certain types of employment that are specifically forbidden or restricted by national legislation. These include:

Street trading

Under s.20 *CYPA 1933* no child shall engage or be employed in street trading. However, a local authority may make byelaws authorising children who have attained the age of 14 years to be employed by their parents in street trading to such extent as may be specified in the byelaws.

Industrial undertakings

Under s.1 *Employment of Women, Children and Young Persons Act 1920* no child under the age of 14 may be employed in either a private or public industrial undertaking. However, an exception is made for an undertaking in which only members of the same family are employed. Industrial undertakings include mines, quarries and other mineral extraction works; industries in which articles are manufactured; construction work; and transport of passengers or goods by road, rail or inland waterway.

Performing abroad

Under s.25(1) *CYPA 1933* and s.42 *CYPA 1963* no person having responsibility for a child under the age of 18 shall allow him or her to go abroad for the purpose of singing, playing, performing or being exhibited for profit or for the purpose of taking part in a sport, or working as a model, where payment other than expenses is made, either to the child or another person, unless a licence has been granted by a justice of the peace.

Scrap metal

Under s.5(1) *Scrap Metal Dealers Act 1964* a child under the age of 16 cannot be employed to sell scrap metal.

Betting shops

Under s.21 *Betting, Gaming and Lotteries Act 1963* children under the age of 18 cannot work in a betting shop.

Charitable collections

Under *House to House Collections Regulations 1947*, under-16-year-olds may not take employment as a house to house collector of money for charitable purposes.

TERMS AND CONDITIONS OF EMPLOYMENT

Section 1 *Employment Rights Act 1996* requires all employees to be given a statement of the main terms and conditions of their employment within two months of starting work. This requirement extends to all workers, including child workers, but is often not implemented. The terms of the statement should include:

- the actual agreement between the worker and the employer (the express terms);
- terms derived from the legislation and the common law (implied terms); and
- collective agreements made between trade unions and employers.

It is rare for children to be given a written contract of employment. If a child is given a contract, it is normally impossible to challenge that contract on the grounds that it is not fair. Further, substantive rights relating to holidays and hours have been held not to apply to workers under 15, and a National Minimum Wage does not apply to workers under 18 unless they are above school leaving age.

HOLIDAY PAY

Although the legislation states that children must have two weeks each year without employment, children are not entitled to holiday pay, even if they work regularly for an employer.

SICK PAY

With regard to sick pay, there are two overlapping schemes; the contractual scheme and the Statutory Sick Pay scheme (SSP). If an employee is entitled to sick pay under his or her contract of employment, that entitlement subsists irrespective, it would seem, of the age of the person. However, under Regulation 16 *Statutory Sick Pay (General) Regulations 1982*, only those over the age of 16 are entitled to SSP. Thus, a child under school leaving age is not entitled to SSP and, in reality, is unlikely to receive contractual sick pay, even if prevented from working by illness.

INCOME TAX

The amount of income tax a person pays depends on how much they earn. Everyone can earn a certain amount each year before paying tax. This is called the personal allowance and, for the tax year April 2005 to April 2006, it is set at £4,895. Workers who are still at school are unlikely to pay income tax as they will probably not earn more than the personal allowance.

TRADE UNIONS

Many trade unions will accept children as members as soon as they start work, regardless of their age. However, this would have to be checked with the individual trade union to which a child wished to become a member.

INSURANCE
Is a child who is not registered with the local authority covered by the employer's liability insurance?

The Association of British Insurers takes the view that provided the *insurer* is aware of the child's employment, then employers' liability insurance would cover a child who suffers injury at work regardless of whether he or she is registered with the local authority. However, if the insurer is unaware of the child's employment, the insurance policy may not be triggered. This would leave a child unprotected if he or she suffered injury. The child's only course of action would be to sue the employer. However, of course, the employer may not have sufficient funds to compensate the child adequately.

DUTIES OF THE EMPLOYER

RISK ASSESSMENT

Before a child is employed, the employer must complete a risk assessment under Regulation 3 *Management of Health and Safety*

CASE STUDY

In April 2002, a 14-year-old paperboy brought a case in the Employment Tribunal against his employer, Herts and Essex Newspapers Ltd, claiming that he was entitled to paid holiday leave[3]. Edward Des Clayes based his claim on the *Working Time Regulations 1998*, which implement the *EU Working Time Directive*. However, the Employment Tribunal held that he could not claim holiday pay because the *Working Time Regulations 1998* do not apply to children under the age of 15. It would seem from the Des Clayes case, therefore, that the Tribunals are prepared to acknowledge that young people are covered by the provisions of the *Working Time Regulations 1998* from their 15th birthday. Thus, arguably, a 15-year-old paperboy could claim holiday pay under the Regulations, but anyone under that age cannot.

at Work Regulations 1999. This should be a suitable and sufficient assessment of the risks to the health and safety of the young person to which he or she is exposed whilst at work.

In making a risk assessment, particular account should be taken of:
- the inexperience, lack of awareness of risks and immaturity of young people;
- the fitting-out and layout of the workplace and the workstation;
- the nature, degree and duration of exposure to physical, biological and chemical agents;
- the form, range and use of work equipment and the way in which it is handled;
- the organisation of processes and activities;
- the extent of the health and safety training provided, or to be provided, to young people; and
- risks from agents, processes and work listed in the Annex to *Council Directive 94/33/EC* on the protection of young people at work.

The result of the risk assessment must be conveyed to the parent or carer under Regulation 10(2) *Management of Health and Safety at Work Regulations 1999*, although there is little evidence that this is a common practice. Confirmation that a risk assessment has been carried out is generally required on the application form for a work permit.

The *Management of Health and Safety at Work Regulations 1999* may not be sufficient to protect children. Children who undertake newspaper deliveries on busy roads on dark nights are not generally regarded as being at risk of harm. However, there is a risk of real harm to children in such circumstances.

APPLYING FOR A WORK PERMIT

The law relating to child employment does not stipulate that a work permit has to be applied for where an employer wishes to employ a school age child. However, the Government has published a model byelaw, which most local authorities have adopted and amended to suit local circumstances. This model byelaw provides that any person wishing to employ a child must apply to the local authority for a work permit. Although this requirement is not set out in national legislation, if it is contained in the local byelaw for the area in which the child wishes to work, a failure to apply for a permit will be a breach of the law.

Responsibility for applying for a work permit rests with the employer not the child.

DUTIES OF THE LOCAL AUTHORITY

Local authorities are responsible for registering employers and issuing permits for each young person employed. **All employment which is not registered and for which no employment permit has been issued is illegal.**

BREACHES OF THE LAW

SECTION 559 EDUCATION ACT 1996

If it appears to a local authority that a school pupil is undertaking work that may be prejudicial to his or her health, or is preventing him or her from obtaining the full benefit of education, the local authority may serve a notice in writing on the employer:
- preventing the employer from employing the child; or
- imposing such restrictions upon the employment in the interests of the child.

It is an offence for an employer to employ a child in contravention of any prohibition or restriction imposed by the local authority.

A local authority may also serve a notice in writing on the parent or employer of a child requiring the parent or employer to provide it with information to enable it to ascertain whether the child is being employed in such a manner that he or she will be unable to benefit fully from education. It is an offence for a parent or employer to fail to comply with the requirements of such a notice.

> Employers can be prosecuted and fined by the local authority if they:
> - employ school age children in a prohibited occupation; or
> - allow school age children to work outside the hours set out in local byelaws.

EMPLOYMENT TRIBUNALS

The primary forum for the resolution of employment disputes is the Employment Tribunal. Provided that the normal rules for qualification are observed, there are no provisions which prevent children from taking complaints to the Employment Tribunal. For more information, contact the Employment Tribunals public enquiry line on 0845 795 9775.

FOOTNOTES:
1. s.41 *CYPA 1963.* Where the local authority refuses, revokes or varies a licence, they must state the grounds for so doing in writing to the applicant and the applicant may appeal to a Magistrates' Court.
2. s.24 *CYPA 1933.*
3. *Des Clayes v Herts and Essex Newspapers Ltd. Case Number 3200897/2002.* Decision of the Employment Tribunal.

Young people and the police

This chapter sets out the law relevant to youth workers and other professionals who come into contact with the police through their work with young people. Decisions about allowing the police access to premises, cooperation with the police, confidentiality of information, attendance at the police station and protecting young people can all present difficulties to a youth worker contacted by the police.

As a matter of good practice, youth organisations and projects should agree a policy covering liaison with the police. This policy should be made known and be discussed with young people in the club or project. It is advantageous to ensure that the local police understand the functions of youth organisations and projects as this can help mitigate potential conflicts. It may also be useful to reach general agreements about how the police and youth organisations relate to each other. Although the police cannot be bound by such an agreement if the circumstances require otherwise, it may be possible to reach an agreement, for instance, that youth workers will be warned in advance if the police are to visit the club or project.

The police are generally receptive to new initiatives to improve inter-agency relationships and to reach common understanding. In addition, the work of the local Youth Offending Team, which is made up of representatives from a wide range of services aims to foster inter-agency cooperation.

MUST YOUTH WORKERS ASSIST POLICE WITH THEIR ENQUIRIES?

One of the most common questions asked by youth workers is whether they are under a duty to assist the police with their enquiries, particularly in relation to one of the young people in their club or project.

There is no legal duty to report an offence to the police, or to give information about an offence if questioned by the police: any individual has the right to refuse to answer questions put to him or her by the police. However, giving false or misleading information can lead to prosecution for obstructing the police. Also, youth workers may be liable to prosecution if it can be shown that any 'consideration' (i.e. money or goods) were given by a young person or someone connected to him or her, in return for not disclosing information. Although it is an offence to agree for a sum of money not to disclose information about a young person's involvement in a criminal offence, it is not an offence to accept money as repayment, or some form of reparation, for loss or injury caused by an offence, rather than reporting the matter to the police. For example, if a young person steals equipment from a project and a youth worker discovers who was responsible, the project may decide to accept payment from the young person to cover the replacement of the equipment, rather than reporting the offence to the police.

Note: If payment is received for not disclosing the information to the police, then the offence of concealing information is committed.

IS THERE A DUTY TO ASSIST PHYSICALLY?

There is a great deal of confusion about the extent to which there is a legal duty to assist the police. A youth worker cannot be prosecuted merely for failing to cooperate in an investigation. However, there is an exception to this: the law states that any person who is physically capable of helping, must assist a constable acting in the '*execution of his or her duty*' when called upon to do so in the following circumstances:

- where there is a breach of the peace, for example a fight; or
- when the constable is assaulted or obstructed when making an arrest.

If a person fails to assist when asked, he or she will commit an offence.

The key factors to remember are that:
- the police officer must have asked for help; and
- the person asked must be physically capable of helping.

This second requirement has rarely been tested, but a slightly

built woman asked to assist in the arrest of an aggressive male teenager high on drugs may be considered not physically capable. Similarly, a child or young person may be physically incapable of assisting in the arrest of a violent adult.

Parents and those who work with children and young people may find themselves faced with a conflict of interest if asked to assist a police officer in the arrest of their own child or one for whom they have responsibility. Prosecutions for failing to assist a police officer are rare and are likely to be restricted to cases where a police officer or some other person is seriously hurt by the person being arrested. Those parents and youth workers who find themselves in this difficult situation should, nevertheless, be aware of the possible consequences of failing to help when called upon to do so.

WHAT IS OBSTRUCTION OF THE POLICE?

Under s.89 (2) *Police Act 1996*, '*Any person who resists or wilfully obstructs a constable in the execution of his duty … shall be guilty of an offence*'. To constitute wilful obstruction, the behaviour must be deliberate, intentional and positive even if not necessarily aimed at or hostile to the police; for example, giving the police false or misleading information with the intention of protecting a child or young person from a police investigation. Thus, telling the police that a particular child was present at the youth club all evening, knowing this to be untrue, would be sufficient to constitute obstruction. Even a well-meant intervention on behalf of a person being arrested may amount to an obstruction.

> ### CASE STUDY
>
> During a fight at a football match, a man intervened to stop a police officer arresting someone he believed was innocent. The court decided that his good intentions were irrelevant: by laying his hand on the officer's arm he had obstructed the officer in the lawful execution of his duty (*Hill v Ellis [1983] 1 All ER 667*).

Refusing to answer police questions about a young person in connection with an offence does not, of itself, constitute an obstruction. It is obviously important that such a refusal should be given politely and, where appropriate, it should perhaps be accompanied by an explanation, for example, of the project's policy on confidentiality.

There is a separate offence of '*harbouring*' persons wanted for an arrestable offence (see '*arrestable offences*'). In order to commit this offence, it would need to be shown that the person hiding or assisting an offender had some knowledge that the alleged offender was wanted for an offence.

Parents or youth workers would commit an offence if, knowing that a young person had unlawfully stolen and crashed a number of cars, and knowing that the police were

trying to find the young person, they nevertheless took the young person to hide at a friend's house.

WHEN CAN THE POLICE SEARCH A YOUNG PERSON?

Under the *Police and Criminal Evidence Act 1984* (*PACE 1984*), a police officer in a public place can stop and search any person or motor vehicle for stolen or prohibited articles. Before doing so, the police officer must have reasonable grounds for believing that he or she will find such articles as a result of the search. Prohibited articles include knives or articles to be used for burglary and theft. The definition of prohibited articles was extended in January 2004 to include any article made, adapted or intended for use in causing criminal damage (e.g. can of spray paint). There is also a power to stop and search a young person for controlled drugs under s.23 *Misuse of Drugs Act 1971*.

Sometimes, police officers may ask young people if they would consent to being searched, even when they have no reasonable grounds for believing that the young person has stolen, prohibited articles or drugs on them. Young people are deemed to be persons who are incapable of giving informed consent and they should not be subjected to a voluntary search.

WHEN CAN A POLICE OFFICER MAKE AN ARREST?

The law in England and Wales grants the police extensive powers to make arrests with or (more commonly) without a warrant signed by a magistrate. Under the common law, the police have the power to arrest anyone for breach of the peace[1]. Most arrests, however, are made under the powers given to the police by *PACE 1984*. Under this Act the powers of arrest fall into three categories:

1. Arrestable offences
Arrestable offences are defined as:
- offences for which a person aged 21 or over may be sentenced to imprisonment for five years or more. Even though juveniles (young people who have not attained the age of 17) cannot be sent to an adult prison for committing such an offence, they still fall within the power of arrest;
- offences for which the sentence is fixed by law, such as life imprisonment for murder;
- possession of cannabis or cannabis resin has been downgraded to a class C drug, but is nevertheless an arrestable offence;
- certain other offences, such as taking a vehicle without consent;
- having an article with a blade or point in a public place;
- having an offensive weapon on school premises; and
- failing to comply with a requirement to remove a disguise.

Note: The age of criminal responsibility is 10. Under this age, a child cannot be convicted of committing a criminal offence and there is no power of arrest, even if they are suspected of committing a crime.

A police officer may arrest without a warrant:
- anyone who is, or who he or she has reasonable grounds for suspecting to be, committing an arrestable offence (such as where a police officer sees a person lighting a fire in a building using petrol soaked rags);
- anyone he or she has reasonable grounds for suspecting has committed an arrestable offence (such as where a police officer knows a fire has been started in a building and sees a person nearby with petrol soaked rags); and
- anyone who is, or who he or she has reasonable grounds for suspecting to be, about to commit an arrestable offence (such as where a police officer receives reliable information that a person is on his or her way to spray graffiti on a building and finds the person in the street carrying a spray paint can)[2].

It is important to note that in order to make an arrest for an '*arrestable offence*', such as criminal damage, the police officer needs only a suspicion that the person concerned is responsible. This is a much lower standard than '*knowing*', or even '*believing*', that the person is responsible. However, there must be some objective '*grounds*' for the arrest; for example, the person may fit the description of the suspect and may be found in the vicinity of the offence a short time after its commission.

2. Conditional Power of Arrest
PACE 1984 also gives the police the power to arrest for certain offences, but only where specific conditions apply. The most widely used of these is the offence of using threatening, abusive or insulting words or behaviour with intent, under s.4 *Public Order Act 1986*. The law allows a police constable to arrest a person if he or she is found committing the offence.

EXAMPLES

1 A police officer at a football match sees a young person in the act of using threatening behaviour towards a rival fan: he or she is actually committing the offence and can be arrested.

2 Following a violent incident at a football match, a police officer studies a video recording and sees a person using threatening behaviour towards a rival fan. The officer later sees the person in the street. That person is not at that moment committing the offence, and so the police officer cannot arrest him under the *Public Order Act 1986*.

---

3. General Power of Arrest
The police also have a general power to arrest for any criminal offence, including local byelaws, where one of the following '*general arrest conditions*' apply:
- the police officer does not know and cannot find out the suspect's name;
- the police officer believes that the name given is false or that the suspect will not stay long enough for a summons

to be served and there is not an address where someone else – for example, a social worker – will accept a summons for the suspect; and
- the police officer believes that the arrest is necessary to prevent the suspect causing harm to him or herself or others, damage to property, an offence against public decency, an unlawful obstruction of the highway, or to protect a child or other vulnerable person from the suspect[3].

An arrested person may be bailed to attend at a designated police station and released at the scene rather than being taken straight to a police station, this is called Street Bail.

WHAT HAPPENS WHEN THERE IS NO POWER OF ARREST?
Other than in the relatively rare cases where the '*general arrest conditions*' apply (see above), most offences carry no power of arrest. For example, there is no power of arrest for the offences of dropping litter, urinating in a public place or minor driving offences. In these cases, a police officer will usually inform the offender that he or she will be '*reported*' – i.e. the officer submits a report for the question of prosecution to be considered. This process normally consists of two stages:
1 A police adjudicator decides to:
- refer the report to the Crown Prosecution Service so it may consider the question of prosecution;
- offer the offender a reprimand or final warning; or
- take no further action.

2 If referred to the Crown Prosecution Service it may decide to:
- prosecute the offender and arrange for a summons to attend court to be served; or
- take no further action.

WHAT IS A BREACH OF THE PEACE?

A breach of the peace can happen in both public and private, and whenever:
- harm is actually done to a person, in his or her presence or to his or her property;
- harm is likely to be done to a person or his or her property; or
- a person is genuinely in fear of being harmed through an assault, affray, riot, unlawful assembly or disturbance.

The common thread throughout the definition is the use or threat of violence to a person or property. This means that the definition would not cover simply playing loud music, but may cover young people acting in a disorderly manner in the street.

The common law power to arrest for breach of the peace is long-established and allows any person to arrest someone if they are committing, or are about to commit, a breach of the peace or if a breach of the peace has been committed and they believe that arrest is necessary to prevent a further breach of the peace. A police officer can use this power to

stop a fight. However, the power of arrest goes much further: where perhaps there has been a fight a police officer may arrest someone and continue to hold on to the individual after the fight if he or she thinks the fight is going to start again. The person arrested can only expect to be released after the risk of the fight re-starting has passed.

WHEN CAN THE POLICE HAVE LAWFUL ENTRY TO PREMISES?

The police do not always have an automatic right of entry to premises. Obviously, they can enter if a person entitled to grant entry to the premises consents. Permission to enter granted by a child or young person would not constitute a valid consent. The police are entitled, however, to enter premises if they want to make an arrest for an arrestable offence, have a search warrant or a warrant of arrest. The police may use force to enter if necessary, but the *PACE 1984 Codes of Practice 2004* (Home Office) state that the police should seek cooperation from the occupier, unless this would frustrate the purpose of the search: for example, if evidence may be lost or destroyed if their entry is delayed or announced. The police also have the power to enter premises to prevent or stop a breach of the peace.

If the police have been issued with a warrant for arrest by a magistrate, they may enter and search any premises where there is reason to suspect that the person specified on the warrant is present. The police do not have to produce an arrest warrant before entry, though it must be shown, if requested, as soon as practicable after the arrest.

A warrant to search premises will specify the premises concerned on the warrant. A copy of the warrant, together with a list of anything seized, must be given to the occupier at the time, or left in the premises if unoccupied.

WHAT ABOUT SEARCHES OF PREMISES AFTER ARREST?

Following arrest, the police have a power to search the premises in which the suspect is arrested, or where the suspect was immediately prior to the arrest. Their search in these circumstances is limited to searching for evidence of the offence for which the suspect is arrested. The arresting officer needs no special authority to conduct this search. The police may also search for evidence of some other arrestable offence which is connected with or similar to that offence.

Powers to search are limited in private houses or children's homes to those areas of the building occupied by the suspect: for example, the suspect's bedroom and communal areas, such as the kitchen or bathroom. It would not include, for example, the parents' bedroom or staff accommodation at a residential unit. The police can only search to the extent necessary to find what they are looking for. For example, they should not look in a small chest of drawers when searching for a stolen television.

WHAT ABOUT SEARCHES OF THE PERSON AFTER ARREST?

Police officers may search a person after arrest if they have grounds to believe they will find evidence of any offence, or evidence relating to an offence, articles that will cause danger (e.g. knives), or articles that the person may use to escape from the police. Reasonable force may be used to conduct the search. The police can ask for removal of outer coat, jacket or gloves in public and search a person's mouth.

Suspects may also be subjected to a further search when they arrive at the police station to determine what property they have on them and for the custody officer to determine whether they can keep such property safely whilst in custody.

WHAT ABOUT LIABILITY IN RESPECT OF STOLEN PROPERTY?

Under s.22 *Theft Act 1968* it is an offence if a person '*handles stolen goods*'. This offence relates to anyone who dishonestly receives stolen goods or dishonestly undertakes or assists in their retention, removal, disposal, realisation (turning the goods into profit), or arranges to do any of these things.

Knowledge or belief that the goods are stolen, and a dishonest intention must be shown for a person to be convicted of the offence. Therefore, if a youth worker takes stolen goods from a young person with the honest intention of handing the goods over to the police or the owner, the youth worker would not commit an offence. However, if the stolen goods are not handed over to the police or to the rightful owner as soon as reasonably practicable, a youth worker could face an accusation of handling stolen goods. The mere presence of stolen goods on the premises alone would not normally be sufficient evidence to show that the responsible youth worker was guilty of this offence.

WHAT HAPPENS AT THE POLICE STATION WHEN A PERSON HAS BEEN ARRESTED?

Young people may only be detained at a police station if they have been arrested. On arrival at the station, the custody officer has to decide if there are '*grounds*' for detention. These grounds will be:
* to secure or preserve evidence relating to the offence, for example, to take forensic evidence from the suspect, such as glass fragments from a jacket;
* to obtain evidence by questioning, as an interview with the suspect may be necessary to determine his or her part in the alleged offence; or
* to prepare charges.

If there are no '*grounds*' for detention, the custody officer must release the suspect immediately. If detention is authorised, the suspect's legal rights should be made clear to him or her. These rights include:
* access to free and independent legal advice (in person, or on the telephone);

- the right to have someone informed of the arrest; and
- the right to consult a copy of the *PACE 1984 Codes of Practice 2004*, which is a book setting out how people should be treated while in custody.

For juveniles (a young person under the age of 17), an appropriate adult must be called as soon as possible.

WHO CAN BE AN APPROPRIATE ADULT?

In most cases, this will be the parent or step-parent with whom the young person lives. However, in the absence of a parent or legal guardian, or if the child is looked after by the local authority, the appropriate adult may be a care worker, a social worker, or other responsible adult over 18 years of age, who is not employed by the police. If parents are unable or unwilling to attend, then the police should ask a social worker or any other appropriate adult to attend.

If possible, a youth worker who is going to act as the appropriate adult should inform the custody officer of his or her expected time of arrival and should take along some form of identification. On arrival at the police station, the youth worker should try to find out as much as possible about the case from the custody officer, or the officer dealing with the young person, known as '*the officer in the case*'.

The custody officer must repeat the grounds for arrest and the detained person's rights in the presence of the appropriate adult, who will then be asked to sign the custody record to certify that this has been done. The appropriate adult may then see the young person alone.

A young person must not be interviewed, or asked to provide or sign a written statement, in the absence of an appropriate adult. In exceptional circumstances, the police can, with the approval of a senior police officer, question the young person without an appropriate adult being present: for instance, if the police think the delay in waiting for an appropriate adult would involve an immediate risk of harm to others, or serious loss of or damage to property.

THE ROLE OF AN APPROPRIATE ADULT

Appropriate adults should be told before the interview that they are not there simply to act as an observer, but to advise the young person being questioned, to observe whether the interview is being conducted properly and fairly, and to facilitate communication with the person being interviewed. This may mean interpreting unusual words or phrases used by the young person, the meaning of which may be unclear to the interviewing officer. Appropriate adults should also make sure that young people understand what is happening to them and that there is no sign of mistreatment.

WHEN WILL A YOUNG PERSON IN CUSTODY NEED A SOLICITOR?

When a child or young person first arrives under arrest at a police station, he or she will be seen by the custody officer and offered the free services of a solicitor. The custody officer must repeat this '*right*' to the child or young person in the presence of a parent or appropriate adult. A duty solicitor is available around the clock, and those in custody and those responsible for their welfare are strongly advised to seek a solicitor's help. This may be done over the telephone and/or in person at the police station.

Solicitors and their clerks (who may represent the solicitor at the police station, especially if the solicitor is engaged in court or if it is late at night) know the law and procedures governing the arrest and detention of a person suspected of a crime, and are best placed to advise on these matters and to act as a go-between with the police officers handling the case.

Once a solicitor has been requested, police officers may not commence an interview or ask the young person to provide or sign a written statement in the absence of the solicitor. In exceptional circumstances, the police can, with the approval of a senior police officer, question the young person without a solicitor being present: for instance, if they think the delay in waiting for a solicitor would involve an immediate risk of harm to others, or serious loss of or damage to property.

A person in custody is entitled to speak privately with his or her solicitor, whether on the telephone or in person. The appropriate adult may be invited to be present at the consultation with the solicitor, or the young person may see the solicitor alone. Such conversations are said to be '*privileged*'. This means that the solicitor will not reveal what was said to the police or to any other person.

FINGERPRINTS, PHOTOGRAPHS AND BODY SAMPLES

The police may take fingerprints (including palms) and photographs of children and young people where they have been charged or reported. The *PACE 1984 Codes of Practice 2004* requires that an appropriate adult should be present when fingerprints or photographs are taken. Fingerprints may, in certain circumstances, be taken before the young person is charged, if authorised by a senior officer. This may happen, for example, when the taking of the fingerprints may determine the person's involvement in an offence.

Where the young person is under the age of 14, consent to the taking of fingerprints, photographs and body samples must be given by the parent or guardian. Between the ages of 14 and 17, consent must be given by the young person and the parent or guardian, and for those over 17, the required consent must come from the young person[4]. Fingerprints may be taken by force, if necessary, but photographs may not.

The police may wish to take '*samples*' from young people in order to help prove or disprove their involvement in an offence; these may be either '*intimate*' or '*non-intimate*'. An example of an '*intimate*' sample would be blood, while head hair is an example of a '*non-intimate*' sample. *PACE 1984* and

the accompanying *Codes of Practice 2004* are very specific about when such samples may be taken. Where the police wish to take an intimate sample from a juvenile, an appropriate adult must be present during the taking of such a sample. However, if the situation involves the removal of clothing in embarrassing circumstances the juvenile may indicate, in the presence of and with the agreement of the appropriate adult, that he or she prefers that the appropriate adult were not present.

If the police wish to carry out an intimate search this must be carried out by a doctor or nurse and only in the presence of an appropriate adult of the same sex (unless the young person an appropriate adult of the other sex or no appropriate adult).

HOW LONG CAN A YOUNG PERSON BE HELD PRIOR TO BEING CHARGED?

PACE 1984 does not distinguish between adults and young people as far as detention times are concerned. However, the custody officer must be continually satisfied of the need for a young person to be kept in custody. For most offences, the maximum time that a suspect may be held before being charged is 36 hours. Throughout this period, the detention must be reviewed by an officer of at least Inspector rank, who is known as the '*review officer*'. The officer must be satisfied that the investigation is being carried out expeditiously and that the '*grounds*' for detention still apply. The review process must take place within six hours of the custody officer first authorising detention and then at least every nine hours. The review also gives an opportunity for the young person, the appropriate adult, or the solicitor to make any representations about the young person's detention and treatment.

Details of each review and other information about the young person's treatment at the police station, including reason for arrest, grounds for detention, visits and meals will be kept in a '*custody record*'. Any complaints about the treatment of the young person should be made in the first instance to the custody officer. The appropriate adult should ask for an entry to be made in the young person's custody record to this effect, giving details of the grounds for concern.

The *Codes of Practice 2004* impose restrictions on placing young people in cells. A young person should not be put in a police cell unless there is no other accommodation available. A young person must never be placed in a cell with an adult.

WHAT ABOUT THE RIGHT TO SILENCE?

Everyone has the right to silence. There is no obligation to answer questions or make a statement. However, young people should be fully aware of the implications if they exercise their right to silence. Since the *Criminal Justice and Public Order Act 1994*, saying nothing or '*no comment*' in a properly conducted interview may have consequences at court.

The new caution states:
'*You do not have to say anything, but it may harm your*

CASE STUDY

The police are told by an informant that Tom, aged 16, was responsible for stealing the car that was used in a 'ram raid' on an electrical goods warehouse. When arrested and interviewed, Tom answered '*no comment*', to every question asked. At his trial at the Crown Court, Tom tells the jury that, at the time of the offence, he was staying with his uncle and was many miles away from the scene of the crime. The Judge is unimpressed by Tom's sudden alibi and advises the jury thus:
'*… why did he not tell the police about this alibi when he was interviewed? You may take the view that he made up this story at a later time.*'

The Court may draw an adverse inference from Tom's failure to mention the alibi when originally questioned if the only sensible explanation for his failure is that he had no answer at the time, or none that would stand up to scrutiny. The Judge is entitled to cast doubt on the alibi when given at this late stage, and the jury (or magistrates in a Youth Court) may choose to discount the alibi.

---

defence if you do not mention when questioned something which you later rely on in court. Anything you do say may be given in evidence.'

Note: People have been known to say virtually anything in response to police questions in the mistaken belief that it will get them out of the police station quickly. Under pressure, a young person may make contradictory statements and even admit to something he or she has not done. This is why it is so important that a young person consults with a solicitor BEFORE being interviewed.

WHAT HAPPENS IN AN INTERVIEW?

The police must make an accurate record of each interview with the young person. All interviews with suspects are now tape recorded (unless the machinery is broken or the interview rooms are all full – and to wait would cause unnecessary delay – in which case the interview will be recorded in writing). At the start of the interview, while the tape is running, the police officer will complete a number of formalities and will ask each person present in the room, including the appropriate adult, to identify themselves. The young person will be reminded of the caution and of their right to legal advice. The officer will then proceed to ask questions relating to the alleged offence.

The officer in the case will later make a '*record of interview*' by listening to the tape and writing down what is said. This record may then be used in evidence.

It is the right of any suspect to also make a formal written statement if they so wish. Legal advice should be taken on this matter. If a written statement is made, it will be written down (usually by the police officer), whilst the tape machine is still running.

The police should give the young person the opportunity to check the written statement and then sign it if it is accurate. The appropriate adult should also sign it.

Is the young person entitled to a copy of the tape?

The interviewed person is entitled to obtain a copy of the interview tape. This is usually done through his or her solicitor, but an individual who is unrepresented may also obtain a copy. The police should hand the suspect a written notice at the end of the interview which explains how to do this.

DOES THE YOUNG PERSON HAVE TO TAKE PART IN AN IDENTITY PARADE?

Where a young person is under the age of 14, an identity parade will only be held if the parent or guardian consents. Between the ages of 14 and 17, the consent of the young person and the parent or guardian is required, and over the age of 17, only the consent of the young person is required. If an identification procedure is to be held a video identification (VIPER) will initially be offered. A witness will be shown moving images of a known suspect together with similar images of others who resemble the suspect. The parade must take place in the presence of the appropriate adult. The parade must consist of at least eight volunteers who, so far as possible, resemble the suspect in age, height, general appearance and position in life.

A refusal to take part in an identity parade may result in the police seeking identification evidence in other ways. A solicitor's advice should be taken before refusing.

WHAT HAPPENS NEXT?

When the investigation at the police station is complete, the custody officer needs to decide if there is sufficient evidence to justify a charge, which will lead to the young person appearing before a court.

1 If the custody officer thinks there is insufficient evidence, and there are no further enquiries for the officers to make, the suspect will be released without charge.

2 If the custody officer decides there are further enquiries that need completing, in order to decide whether to charge or not, the suspect may be released on police bail. This means that the suspect is under a legal obligation to return to the police station at a time and date in the future, when the enquiries are complete. This sort of bail can also be used to give the police time to seek legal advice, or to refer the case to a multi-agency Youth Offender Panel which will decide on the appropriate disposal of the case.

3 If there is sufficient evidence, the police can charge the suspect who, in most cases, will be released on bail to the local Youth Court (or Magistrates' Court if charged jointly with an adult). This means the suspect is given a time and date to attend the court for the case to be heard. Custody officers now have the power to impose bail conditions on people who are charged. An example

of a bail condition might be that the person has to reside at a particular address, or is prevented from going to certain locations during the period of bail. Occasionally, bail may be refused (see p.96).

4 Where the young person has admitted an offence, the police may decide to deal with them by a reprimand or final warning (see below).

5 A further option to charging is for the detainee to be '*reported*' and released from custody pending a decision: the police and the Crown Prosecution Service will review the case before deciding whether to proceed to court.

What is a reprimand?

The police can deal with a first-time minor offence by means of a reprimand, provided that the young person has not previously been reprimanded or given a final warning. A reprimand is an alternative to prosecution through the courts. It is not a conviction and a young person who receives a reprimand will not, as a result, have a criminal record[5]. However, the police can keep a record of reprimands for up to seven years in case the young person offends again. The criteria for the administering of a reprimand are:

- there is evidence against the young person sufficient to give a realistic prospect of conviction if he or she were to be prosecuted;
- the young person admits the offence and has consented to being given the reprimand (for children and young people under the age of 17, parental consent is required). Where a parent is not available, the decision to accept a reprimand will rest with the appropriate adult;
- the young person has not previously been convicted of an offence; and
- it is not in the public interest for the offender to be prosecuted.

A reprimand must be given orally by a police officer, and is usually (although not necessarily) given at a police station. It must be supplemented by written information that clearly explains its implications. The police officer will normally be in uniform. If the young person is under the age of 17, a parent, guardian or other appropriate adult must be present.

What is a final warning?

The officer may give a final warning to the young offender if:

- the young offender has not previously been warned; or
- the offender has previously been warned more than two years before the current offence and the police officer considers the offence not so serious as to require the offender to be charged.

This opportunity will not be permitted more than once. A final warning may be given even when a young offender has not previously been reprimanded, but only in those cases where the police officer considers the offence to be so serious as to require a final warning.

The criteria for administering a final warning are the same as those for a reprimand. As with reprimands, final warnings

may only be given by a police officer in the presence of a parent or appropriate adult and will usually (although not necessarily) be given at a police station. However, when an officer gives a final warning, the young offender is then referred to the Youth Offending Team. The Team will assess the young offender's suitability to be included in a rehabilitation programme. The programme may include short term counselling or group work, reparation to victims, supervised youth activities, or work to improve school attendance. The purpose of the programme is to prevent re-offending.

What are the implications of receiving a reprimand or a final warning?

It should be recognised that neither a reprimand nor a final warning is a soft option. Both are recorded by the police and are retained on police files for up to seven years. The police will also take fingerprints and a photograph that they are entitled to retain. The circumstances of the reprimand or final warning can be cited at court if the person is convicted of a similar offence in any subsequent court proceedings. In addition, many potential employers and insurance companies require applicants to disclose any previous convictions, reprimands or final warnings.

If a young offender accepts a final warning, he or she will have to participate in a rehabilitation programme. If a young offender refuses to participate in a programme, he or she cannot be prosecuted, but the refusal may be referred to in any future criminal proceedings.

The advice of a solicitor is especially important when the police decide whether to charge, reprimand or warn a young person. The experience of the Children's Legal Centre is that young people or their parents are inclined to accept a police reprimand or final warning when it is offered without always carefully considering whether this is the right course of action. This happens for two reasons:

- a desire to get out of the police station and get it 'all over and done with'; and
- out of relief that the police have decided not to take the matter any further.

However, calls and letters to the Children's Legal Centre indicate that reprimands or final warnings are sometimes given in situations where it is not clear that a criminal offence has been committed. It is important to be aware that the acceptance of a reprimand or final warning is an admission of guilt and an admission that the offence was committed. Where a reprimand or final warning is offered, it should be discussed with the solicitor who will make an assessment of the available evidence before recommending acceptance or otherwise. For certain sexual offences it can give rise to a requirement to sign the Sex Offenders' Register. If a reprimand or final warning is accepted, this will be recorded by the police.

Note: Think carefully before accepting a reprimand or a final warning, as these may be revealed to certain employers later in life, and have an impact on sentencing if a further offence is committed.

WHAT HAPPENS IF BAIL IS REFUSED?

A young person can only be refused bail in the most serious of cases, for example, where the public or the young person would be at serious risk if released. A young person, who once released continues to commit burglaries or continues to steal and drive away cars, may fall into this category. Other reasons would include where the identity of the young person cannot be established, or if there is good reason to believe the young person will fail to attend court.

Bail will not be refused simply because a child or young person has no place to live. In such cases, perhaps where the young person's parent(s) refuse to house him or her, the custody officer must bail the child or young person and release him or her into the custody of the local authority. The local authority representative, a social worker, will place the child or young person into temporary foster care or other accommodation until the first court appearance.

In serious cases, where the young person is 12 years old or over, the custody officer may refuse to grant bail and may then arrange for the young person to be removed into local authority secure accommodation until his or her first court appearance (usually the next day)[6]. This would only happen if the custody officer considers that release could result in harm to the public.

The social worker, acting on behalf of the local authority, must exhaust all possibilities (and certify in writing that he or she has done so) in attempting to house the child or young person in secure accommodation. If none is available, or if for some other genuine reason it is impracticable to do so, such as severe weather conditions, the child or young person will remain at the police station.

Where the child or young person has to remain at the police station, the custody officer will place him or her alone in a secure detention room set aside for people of that age group. If none are available, the child or young person will be placed in a cell in the adult area. The custody officer should try to ensure that the child or young person is segregated from adult prisoners. For example, if all the cells in the adult female area are unoccupied, a male child or young person may be placed in that area to ensure segregation from adult male prisoners. While in custody, the child or young person will be provided with adequate food and drink and may be provided with reading and writing materials and allowed visitors.

Note: For many children and young people, the time spent locked in a police cell is a lonely and traumatic experience. The importance of the role of the appropriate adult in providing support to a child or young person at this time cannot be over stated.

ACCOMPANYING A YOUNG PERSON TO COURT

Youth workers often accompany young people to court, either because the parents cannot or will not attend, or because the additional presence of a youth worker provides helpful extra support to the family. Parents should always be encouraged to attend court with a young person if this is possible. Parents should also be aware that the court can order them to attend. If a youth worker accompanies a young person to court, it is advisable for the youth worker to inform the clerk of the court and identify him or herself before the hearing begins, as there are restrictions on people admitted into Youth Courts.

COMPLAINTS AGAINST THE POLICE

Although making a complaint against the police is relatively straightforward, it is a good idea for a young person to be supported in making a complaint as this can be a daunting and unsettling experience for them. Neither the young person nor a youth worker need to have specific knowledge of the law, nor a precise understanding of what constitutes a wrong-doing by a police officer in order to complain. A youth worker may make a complaint on behalf of a young person as long as the young person agrees in writing for them to do so. Alternatively, complaints may be submitted in writing and signed by the individual to show that they agree to the youth worker taking the matter further.

A young person may complain about the way that they have been treated by any rank of police officer, or any other member of the police staff. Generally the police station at which the complaint is aimed shall deal with the complaint. However, as of April 2004, where complaints are not dealt with adequately, it is the Independent Police Complaints Commission (IPCC) that has the duty to investigate complaints about the police. The IPCC has produced a leaflet *Step by Step: how to make a complaint against the police* (2005 IPCC), which is available from the IPCC website[7] and may be obtained from police stations. The advice contained in this leaflet is summarised below and supplemented by The Children's Legal Centre.

HOW TO COMPLAIN?
There are a number of ways a young person may complain these include:
- approaching the police station;
- contacting the police station by telephone, post, email or fax;
- approaching the local Citizens' Advice Bureau, the Racial Equality Council, a Connexions Adviser, or young people's advice services and advocates;
- requesting a solicitor or MP to make the claim on behalf of a young person; or
- contacting the IPCC.

When making a complaint a young person will need to provide personal and contact details such as his or her name and address. The young person will also need to explain:
- what happened, including what was said or done and whether there are any damages;
- when it happened;
- who was involved; and

- whether there were witnesses and how to contact them.

The young person will also have to agree to the complaint being passed on to the police force and consent to it being '*recorded*'.

LOCAL RESOLUTION
Most complaints can be resolved locally. This is called '*local resolution*' and will be used for complaints that can be resolved with an apology and local actions to ensure that the problem is dealt with and will not reoccur. However, if the complaint is serious a more formal investigation will be necessary.

FORMAL INVESTIGATIONS
If a complaint is serious such as involving an injury or death while in contact with the police a formal investigation will be conducted. In such situations the IPCC will oversee the police investigation, or handle the complaint using their own independent investigators.

As an investigation is being conducted the individual who has made the complaint is entitled to be kept informed and once an investigation is complete he or she has the right to details of the outcome and the decisions that have been made. Possible decisions that may be arrived at after an investigation include:
- improvements or changes to police procedures;
- disciplinary action against a member of the police force; or
- information may be passed onto the Crown Prosecution Service, which will decide whether there is enough evidence for the criminal court.

If a young person is unhappy with the outcome of the investigation and no more action is to be taken, they may appeal to the IPCC for further investigation.

TACKLING ANTI-SOCIAL BEHAVIOUR

PARENTING ORDERS
Parenting Orders were designed to help parents or guardians address their child's anti-social behaviour or offending behaviour. They may be imposed by a criminal court, Family Court or Magistrates' Court when:
- a child safety order has been made;
- a court makes an anti-social behaviour or sex offender order in respect of a child or young person;
- a child or young person has been convicted of an offence;
- a referral order is made and a Youth Offender Panel refers a parent back to court for failing to attend panel meetings; or
- an individual has been convicted under s.443 or s.444 *Education Act 1996*: failure to comply with a school attendance order and failure to secure regular attendance at school of registered pupil respectively.

In addition, Parenting Orders are available on application to the adult Magistrates' Court by a Youth Offending Team

(YOT), where a child or young person has engaged in criminal conduct or anti-social behaviour and has been referred to the YOT, or by a local education authority (LEA), where a child has been excluded from school on disciplinary grounds, or has truanted.

A Parenting Order primarily requires the parent or guardian to attend counselling or guidance sessions for up to three months. Such sessions are designed to help parents address their child's or children's misbehaviour. The Order can also impose specific requirements, according to individual circumstances, encouraging the parent or guardian to exercise a degree of control over the child, for example, by ensuring school attendance. Residential parenting courses have also been in operation since February 2004 and courts can require a parent to attend such a course providing that it is likely to be more effective than a non-residential course and that any interference with family life is proportionate[8].

Failure to comply with any requirement included in the Order, or specified in directions given by the responsible officer, carries the penalty, on summary conviction, of a fine.

Parenting Orders have been supported by a number of children's organisations as an effective way of combating anti-social behaviour. Poor parenting has been labelled as a root cause of anti-social behaviour among young people. Barnardos, for instance, has claimed that work with parents:

'... is an important preventative measure, and is particularly effective when used in relation to children at risk of anti-social behaviour or offending behaviour rather than post-conviction.'[9]

However, the necessity for the coercive nature of Parenting Orders has been questioned. Although giving parents parenting advice is a positive and effective preventative measure, the coercive nature of the Order could send out a negative message to parents and reduce willingness to participate, thereby limiting the effectiveness of Parenting Orders.

It has also been held by some practitioners that Parenting Orders suffer from a lack of funding. The Magistrates' Association have claimed that Youth Offending Teams, due to insufficient resources, are very reluctant to recommend Parenting Orders to magistrates when the court is deciding whether this would help prevent repetition of anti-social behaviour. The problem of limited resources is evident when looking at relevant statistics which show that between April and December 2004 only 41 Parenting Orders were applied for by YOTs and only 13 by LEAs out of a total of 1162 made in that period.

Sections 19-22 Anti-social Behaviour Act 2003 introduced Parenting Orders and Parenting Contacts into cases of school exclusion or truancy based on the premise that parenting is often a strong influence on a child's behaviour and attendance, and that some parents need support.

Parenting Contacts are agreements between parents and their

LEA or governing body of a school setting out requirements on the parents and the support to be provided by the authorities to aid the parents in meeting those requirements. The aim of the requirement is to improve the child's behaviour or secure regular school attendance. Unlike Parenting Orders, there is no criminal sanction if the parent does not comply and the Contract is based on agreement and cooperation. However, a parent's refusal to enter into such a contact or to comply with its terms may then be used to support a subsequent application to the Magistrates' Court for a Parenting Order based on exclusion on disciplinary grounds.

ANTI-SOCIAL BEHAVIOUR ORDERS

Anti-social Behaviour Orders (ASBOs) have been available in England and Wales since April 1999, and are part of the Government's attack on 'yobbish' and anti-social behaviour. ASBOs can be made on anyone over the age of 10. A wide range of bodies can apply for an ASBO[10] including the police, British Transport police, local authorities, registered social landlords, housing action trusts and English County Councils[11]. While an ASBO can be made when a young person is convicted of a criminal offence, it may also be made by a civil court. It is not necessary to show commission of a criminal offence before an Order is made. Section 1(1) Crime and Disorder Act 1998 states that an application for an Anti-Social Behaviour Order may be made by a relevant authority, against an individual if:

'[T]he person has acted ... in an anti-social manner, that is to say, in a manner that caused or was likely to cause harassment, alarm or distress to one or more persons not of the same household as himself.'[12]

When making an ASBO the Court has the power to ban many everyday activities of the young person, including prohibiting certain behaviours and activities or banning a person from a specified geographical area, provided it believes these measures will protect the public from further anti-social acts. The Order will be in force for a minimum of two years. Although an ASBO may be imposed by the civil court where the young person has not committed a criminal offence, failure to comply with the conditions set in the Order will itself be a criminal offence and could result in imprisonment.

CASE STUDY

A, aged 14, and a large group of friends were causing havoc in their housing estate. They were noisy, abusive and generally intimidating in their behaviour and attitude. The noise continued throughout the evening and well into the night. In addition, A had a habit of following people, making derisory comments and being generally unpleasant. Children and the elderly had become frightened to go past the group of friends. The Housing Authority obtained an ASBO prohibiting A from meeting more than one friend outside the house and on the estate at any one time.

Throughout England and Wales agencies such as courts, the Crown Prosecution Service, the police, Youth Offending Teams and local authorities have established protocols that set out the agreed procedures to be followed when an agency or body are considering applying for an ASBO in the civil court (a free standing order, rather than an order made as part of a sentence when a young person is convicted of a criminal offence). When an ASBO coordinator receives notification of a possible application, a case conference will normally be convened to ensure that a valid complaint has been received and to agree an action plan to support the victims and witnesses and prevent further anti-social behaviour. The individual concerned need not be informed of the case conference. However, where the young person is informed of the conference, a youth worker may ask if he or she could attend the conference on behalf of the young person. The conference will decide whether it is appropriate to apply for an ASBO at this stage or whether mediation, an Acceptable Behaviour Contract (ABC), warnings, eviction from accommodation or criminal proceedings would be more appropriate in preventing the anti-social behaviour. If the decision of the conference is that an ASBO should be applied for, the conference will also decide whether to apply for an interim order to protect the community.

When an application is made under the civil jurisdiction (not applied for as part of sentencing for a criminal offence), the application will be heard in a Magistrates' Court rather than the Youth Court (because the Youth Court has no civil jurisdiction). Proceedings are begun by way of a complaint being laid at the Magistrates' Court, detailing incidents within the past six months. Although it is a civil action, the magistrates have to apply the criminal standard of proof to 'alleged' past anti-social acts (proof must be 'beyond reasonable doubt'). If an Order is made, it must be for a minimum of two years and, although there is no specified maximum, the Order should not be longer than is necessary to protect the community from the individual.

The Order must contain prohibitions that are necessary to protect people from further anti-social acts and must not be drafted too wide or in such a way as to make them unenforceable.

Where an ASBO is sought with respect of a young person under the age of 16, the court is also required to make a Parenting Order, if it is satisfied that such an Order would help to prevent a repetition of anti-social behaviour.

If an Order is breached it is tried in a criminal setting, i.e. youth or adult court depending on age, and it is an either way offence carrying a maximum of six months prison for adults, two years Detention and Training Order at Youth Court or five years at Crown Court. Courts are unable to impose a Conditional Discharge. Normal reporting restrictions apply for such youth breaches.

Where a court makes an ASBO in respect of a young person aged between 10 and 17 years old, it must also consider whether an Individual Support Order should also be made. Such an Order requires the young person, for a period of up to six months, to take part in specified activities, or to present him or herself to persons or places for up to two days per week or to take part in specified educational arrangements.

Requirements should, as far as practicable, avoid conflict with defendants' religious beliefs or interference with work or education. Very few Individual Support Orders are made, largely due to the failure to secure the necessary resources for the Order. Part of the problem has been the non-participation of local authorities and other agencies in anti-social behaviour strategies. If an Individual Support Order is made, and the young person fails to comply with these conditions, he or she can be convicted and if 14 or over be fined up to £1,000. For those aged under 14, the maximum fine is £250.

Reporting restrictions

Following s.49 *Children and Young Persons Act 1933*, automatic reporting restrictions apply to all matters dealt with in a youth court. This conforms to Article 40(2)(b)(vii) *United Nations Convention on the Rights of the Child 1989*, which states that young people involved in criminal proceedings should have their privacy fully respected. However, ASBOs are not applied for in the Youth Court. Where an ASBO is applied for in the Magistrates' Court, an order must be applied for under s.39 *Children and Young Persons Act 1933*, to prevent the young person being identified in the media. Such an order is made at the discretion of the Court, and is not automatic.

Despite calls for reporting restrictions from various pressure groups[13], the Home Office believes that the publicity that surrounds an ASBO is vital. The Home Office's position can be summed up by the Justice Studies Board:

> '*Enforcement of the Order will normally depend upon the general public being aware of the Order and of the identity of the person against whom it is made. Effective enforcement may require the publication of photographs of the subjects as well as their names and addresses.*'[14]

Acceptable Behaviour Contracts

Along with the ASBO has been the introduction of Acceptable Behaviour Contracts. These written voluntary agreements have no statutory basis but were originally introduced in Islington to be used as a last resort available to tackle anti-social behaviour. Acceptable Behaviour Contracts have been adopted by police forces and local authorities throughout England and Wales as yet another instrument to manage anti-social behaviour. These are voluntary agreements, usually between young people aged between 10-18 and the police or other agencies, with the aim of preventing further anti-social behaviour by the young person. The young person agrees not to carry out a series of identifiable behaviours, which have been defined as anti-social. An Acceptable Behaviour Contract is often viewed as helping the individual to address problem behaviour before applying for an ASBO. Unlike ASBOs, breach of an Acceptable Behaviour Contract is not a criminal penalty, but may be

used as evidence in a subsequent application for an ASBO. An Acceptable Behaviour Contract will also draw the young person to the attention of other statutory agencies that may provide the family with further support.

Local Child Curfews

Local Child Curfew Orders[15] were implemented in September 1998, and allowed local authorities to deal with the problem of unsupervised children on the streets late at night. Under a curfew notice a local authority or local police force can ban children under specified ages (under 10) from being in a public place during specified hours (between 9 p.m. and 6 a.m.) unless under control of a responsible adult. A local authority or police force can apply to the Home Secretary for a Local Child Curfew where a problem had been identified, for instance, with unsupervised children or young people involved in late night anti-social behaviour. If a child is thought to be contravening a ban imposed by a curfew notice, a police officer is required to return the child home and inform the local authority of the breach. No local child curfew scheme has yet been set up under these powers.

Removal of Truants to Designated Premises[16]

The local authority designates premises in a police area as premises to which children and young people of compulsory school age may be removed under s.16 *Crime and Disorder Act 1998*. The local authority notifies the chief officer of police for that area of the designation, a police officer may take a child who they believe to be truanting from school back to that school or to a local education authority '*designated place*'.

Dispersals of groups and curfew orders

Dispersal powers[17] allow the police to disperse groups within a designated area if they have reasonable grounds for believing that a group or any individual in a group have caused, or are likely to cause harassment, intimidation, alarm or distress to a member of the public. In order for an area to be subject to dispersal powers, there is no need for any individual to have acted improperly, but a police superintendent (or more senior officer) must have reasonable grounds for believing:

> '... *that any members of the public have been intimidated, harassed, alarmed or distressed as a result of the presence or behaviour of groups of two or more persons in public places in any locality in his police area*' and '*that anti-social behaviour is a significant and persistent problem in the relevant locality.*'[18]

Refusal to follow an officer's instructions to disperse is a summary offence carrying a penalty of three months imprisonment. Curfew Orders, also contained within s.30 *Anti-social Behaviour Act 2003* give the police the power to return children under the age of 16 to their homes after 9pm.

The powers contained under s.30 *Anti-social Behaviour Act 2003* have been heavily criticised for penalising young people for simply using public space. As mentioned above, there is no need to link an individual to an action before the powers can be used. It has been argued by a number of organisations[19] that

although the presence of a group of youths may be intimidating to some, this is not in itself criminal or anti-social behaviour and therefore does not necessarily justify police action[20]. Suggestions have been made that the Government should be putting more energy into creating structured activities such as youth clubs, rather than producing blanket policies that affect all children, regardless of whether they have engaged in criminal or anti-social behaviour or not.

CASE STUDY

The power of the police to return teenagers to their homes under s.30(6) *Anti-social Behaviour Act 2003*, were recently challenged by a fifteen-year-old boy who, backed by the civil rights group Liberty, claimed that the creation of two dispersal areas in his neighbourhood infringed his human rights under Article 5 (right to liberty), Article 8 (right to respect for private life), Article 11 (freedom of assembly) and Article 14 (freedom from discrimination) *European Convention on Human Rights and Fundamental Freedoms*[21]. The High Court ruled in favour of the teenager, Lord Justice Brooke holding that:

> '... *all of us have the right to walk the streets without interference from police constables or CSOs unless they possess common law or statutory powers to stop us... if Parliament considered that such a power was needed, it should have said so, and identified the circumstances in which it intended the power to be exercised*'.

Lord Justice Brooke also highlighted the practical flaws of the section 30(6) power to return unaccompanied teenagers to their home after 9pm stating that:

> '... *there is no power for a constable to require a child to give his name or address. Without it, unless the constable already knows the child's place of residence, the power, even if coercive, could not be exercised*'.

Diversionary Schemes: YISPs and YIPs

The Government's anti-social behaviour policy has been criticised for failing to concentrate on preventative strategies and instead coming down heavily on punishment and enforcement. However, the Government has implemented a number of initiatives focused on children most at risk of offending or anti-social behaviour which aim to divert young people and tackle the underlying causes of their anti-social behaviour. Youth Inclusion and Support Panels (YISPs) have been set up and are designed, according to the Youth Justice Board (YJB), to:

> '... *help the Board meet its target of putting in place, in each Youth Offending Team in England and Wales, programmes that will identify and reduce the likelihood of young people committing offences.*'[22]

YISPs are targeted at eight- to 13-year-olds most at risk of offending or anti-social behaviour and are made up of a number of representatives of different agencies, including schools, local authorities and the police. There are now 106 YISPs funded by the YJB and the Children's Fund and they aim to provide, at the earliest opportunity, support to children and their families, allowing them access to mainstream public services.

In 2000, the Youth Justice Board also established Youth Inclusion Programmes (YIPs) as part of its strategy to tackle youth crime and anti-social behaviour. YIPs are tailor-made programmes for 13- to 16-year-olds most at risk of offending in 72 of the most deprived and high crime estates in England and Wales[23]. Although participation in the programme is voluntary, programmes try to encourage those children who are identified as most at risk of offending or anti-social behaviour to participate in project activities and get help with education and careers guidance. A number of different agencies, including the police, local education authorities and local authorities, work together to identify young people at risk. The Youth Justice Board has highlighted the following three targets for each project:

- to ensure that at least 75% of the target group (the 50 most at risk young people) are engaged, and that those engaged receive at least five hours of appropriate interventions per week;
- to reduce arrest rates among the target group by 70% compared to the 12 months prior to their engagement; and
- to ensure that 90% of those in the engaged target group are in suitable full-time education or employment.

The Youth Justice Board gives an annual grant to each YIP, and YIPs are also required to find at least an equal amount in matched funding from local agencies. In many areas, programmes also obtain resources from other organisations (such as Neighbourhood Renewal).

An independent national evaluation[24] of the first three years of the programme found that YIPs had been successful in making these improvements within the youth justice system, concluding that:

- arrest rates for the 50 young people considered to be most at risk of crime in each YIP had been reduced by 65%;
- of those who had offended before joining the programme, 73% were arrested for fewer offences after engaging with a YIP; and
- of those who had not offended previously, but who were at risk, 74% did not go on to be arrested after engaging with a YIP.

Targeted diversionary and support schemes appear to have a large impact on reducing anti-social behaviour and the evaluation of YIPs carried out in 2003 show that, for those young people involved in the programmes, there has been a reduction in exclusions from school and a decrease in arrests. However, the programmes still suffer from a lack of funding. According to the Chair of the Youth Justice Board, despite the evidence pointing to the success of the schemes, there are only about 200-250 such projects in England and Wales when, 'there are possibly 1,300 difficult neighbourhoods/estates that could benefit from such schemes'[25]. The Government has

committed itself to increase the number of Youth Inclusion Programmes and Youth Inclusions and Support Panels by 50% by 2008.

FOOTNOTES:

1. See p.91.
2. s.24(4)-(7) *PACE 1984*.
3. s.25(3) *PACE 1984*.
4. s.65 *PACE 1984*.
5. A person only has a criminal record if he or she has been prosecuted through the courts and convicted of an offence.
6. s.38(6) *PACE 1984*.
7. www.ipcc.gov.uk
8. s.18 *Anti-Social Behaviour Act 2003*.
9. Memorandum submitted by Barnardos to the Select Committee on Home Affairs. 2005.
10. s.1 (3) *Crime and Disorder Act 1998*.
11. s.1 (1A) *Crime and Disorder Act 1998*, as inserted by s.61 (1)(4) *Police Reform Act 2002*.
12. It should be noted here that there is no need to prove that the individual acted in a manner that caused harassment, alarm or distress, just that the individual's actions were likely to cause harassment, alarm and distress.
13. See for instance Liberty who, using judicial review procedures, plan to challenge the decision of the police and Brent local authorities to post detailed leaflets about three youths who were given Anti-social Behaviour Orders, to every household in the area. See also Howard League for Penal Reform, Children's Society.
14. Para 3.6 *Judicial Studies Board, Reporting restrictions in the Magistrates Court*. 2002.
15. s.14-15 *Crime and Disorder Act 1998*.
16. s.16 *Crime and Disorder Act 1998*.
17. s.30 *Anti-social Behaviour Act 2003*.
18. Ibid.
19. See for instance the Howard League for Penal Reform, Liberty and JUSTICE.
20. Liberty's evidence to the Home Affairs Committee on Anti-Social Behaviour 2005.
21. *R. (on the application of W) v Commissioner of Police of the Metropolis [2005] EWHC 1586*.
22. www.youth-justice-board.gov.uk
23. The Home Office recently announced that the number of YIPs would be extended to a further 30 areas.
24. Ibid.
25. Oral evidence given by Professor Morgan in *Select Committee on Home Affairs Fifth Report 2005*, section 3, page 53.

Child witnesses

This chapter examines the role of child witnesses in the criminal process. It does not consider the role of child witnesses in the civil courts – for example, where they are asked to give evidence in a parental application for contact or residence.

A child may be asked to give evidence in a criminal court if they have witnessed a crime – either as a victim or by seeing a crime perpetrated on another person.

Regardless of the reasons for the child's involvement with the court process, where a child has to appear as a witness, it can be a daunting and frightening experience. The Government has put in place a range of special measures for child witnesses in order to alleviate some of the stress.

Youth workers may need to provide support to a young person who is due to appear in court as a witness and this chapter is designed to assist them by explaining the process such a child will experience.

Arrangements for child witnesses are set out in the *Youth Justice and Criminal Evidence Act 1999* (YJCEA) and Home Office guidance entitled *Achieving Best Evidence in Criminal Proceedings: Guidance for Vulnerable or Intimidated Witnesses, including Children* (2002 Home Office). All paragraph references relate to the Home Office Guidance.

It is important to make clear to children who are appearing as witnesses that:
- they have not done anything wrong;
- they should always tell the truth;
- they should take time in answering a question;
- they should speak as clearly as possible;
- it is OK to say '*I do not understand*' in response to a question;
- it is OK to say '*I do not remember*' or '*I do not know*' in response to a question; and
- they must not guess or make up an answer.

COMPETENCE AND CAPACITY TO GIVE SWORN EVIDENCE

Under s.53 *YJCEA*, all people, regardless of age, are competent to act as witnesses unless they cannot understand questions asked of them in court, or cannot answer them in a way that can be understood with, if necessary, the assistance of special measures (see p.104).

No witness under the age of 14 will give sworn evidence under oath. Witnesses of 14 or over are eligible to be sworn if they understand the solemnity of a criminal trial and that taking an oath places a particular responsibility on them to tell the truth. Under s.55 *YJCEA* there is a presumption that witnesses of 14 or over are to be sworn unless evidence is offered suggesting that they do not understand those two matters. Any un-sworn evidence shall be given the same weight as sworn evidence.

BEFORE THE TRIAL

There are a range of measures that can be put in place to assist a child witness in preparation for the trial. Pre-trial support is available for all witnesses from Victim Support and the Witness Service, as well as a range of other organisations. In relation to child witnesses various local arrangements exist, these may involve organisations such as the NSPCC and Barnardos.

If a youth worker provides support to a child witness pre-trial, it is important that he or she does not discuss the evidence the child is going to give, or coach the child about what to say, in any way. There are *National Standards for Young Witness Preparation* that are included in Appendix J of *Achieving Best Evidence in Criminal Proceedings: Guidance for Vulnerable or Intimidated Witnesses, including Children* (accessible via www.homeoffice.gov.uk/justice/legalprocess/witnesses).

A PRE-TRIAL VISIT TO THE COURT

It can be very useful to arrange a pre-trial visit so that the child has some idea of what the court room looks like. The child will be able to familiarise him or herself with the lay-out of the courtroom and where others, such as the defendant and judge, will sit. Crown Courts have a Child Witness Officer who can assist with arranging a pre-trial visit.

It is important to give a child the opportunity to discuss what will happen in court.

MEETING THE JUDGE

It may be possible for a child witness to meet the judge in the case prior to the hearing. Any such meeting will generally take place in the presence of the prosecution and defence lawyers.

MEASURES AT COURT

PRIOR TO GIVING EVIDENCE

In *Achieving Best Evidence in Criminal Proceedings: Guidance for Vulnerable or Intimidated Witnesses, including Children*, the Home Office makes a number of suggestions for measures that can be taken to reduce the stress caused to child witnesses who are at court waiting to give evidence:

- minimising waiting time at court;
- stand-by arrangements for witnesses who can be on call in another location nearby;
- appropriate waiting areas for the age of the child, equipped with children's toys, books etc.;
- waiting areas to which the accused's family or friends do not have access (if giving evidence for the prosecution);
- entrance to the courtroom to give evidence by a side door, or other arrangements, so as to avoid inappropriate contact with relatives or friends of the accused or of the victim; and
- the presence of a support person throughout the waiting arrangements (para 4.66).

WHAT WILL HAPPEN AT COURT?

Witnesses come into court one at a time as and when they are required to give their testimony. They cannot sit in court and listen to the case until after they have given their sworn evidence in the trial. The court usher will come and tell the witness when he or she is required. It may be a long wait before the young person is asked to give evidence.

Witnesses will be asked questions by both the side they are appearing for (i.e. the prosecution or defence) and the opposing side's solicitor or barrister.

Some witnesses may need breaks while giving their evidence, either because they are giving distressing evidence or because they have a limited concentration span (para 5.9).

SPECIAL MEASURES FOR THE GIVING OF EVIDENCE

The *YJCEA* introduced a range of measures that can be used to facilitate the giving of evidence by vulnerable witnesses. Young people under the age of 17 at the time of the trial are automatically considered vulnerable on account of their age and are, therefore, automatically eligible for consideration for special measures (para 4.17 and s.16 *YJCEA*). The special measures that are currently available under the *YJCEA* are:

1. Screening the witness from the accused (s.23 *YJCEA*)
Screens may be authorised to shield the witness from seeing the defendant. The screen is normally erected around the witness rather than the defendant. It must not prevent the judge, magistrates or jury and at least one legal representative of each party to the case (i.e. the prosecution and each defendant) seeing the witness, and the witness seeing them (Paras 5.45-5.47).

2. Giving evidence by live link (s.24 *YJCEA*)
'Live link' usually means a closed circuit television link, but also applies to any technology with the same effect. The essential element of a live link is that it enables the witness to be absent from the place where the proceedings are being held, but at the same time to see and hear, and be seen and heard by, the judge, the magistrates or jury and at least one legal representative of each party to the case. The live link will enable the witness to give evidence during the trial from outside the court through a televised link to the courtroom. The witness is usually placed in a special video room in the court building, but the video suite may be located outside the court. The witness can have a member of the Witness Support Service in the room, but the supporter is not allowed to give any help to the witness in answering questions.

If there are no live link facilities at the Magistrates' Court where the proceedings would normally be held, the proceedings may be transferred to another court where a live link is available (Paras 5.48-5.51).

3. Giving evidence in private (s.25 *YJCEA*)
The principle of open justice normally requires that evidence is given in open court – i.e. in the presence of representatives of the press and of members of the public who wish to attend. However, s.25 *YJCEA* permits the courtroom to be cleared of people who do not need to be present while a child witness gives evidence. This mostly affects those in the public gallery and the press gallery. The court has to allow at least one member of the press to remain if one has been nominated by the press.

It is often very difficult for a child witness to give details of sexual behaviour with a full courtroom and especially difficult to respond to detailed cross-examination. The court also has the power under s.37 *Children and Young Persons Act 1933* to clear the public gallery where a person under 18 gives evidence in proceedings relating to conduct which is indecent or immoral.

4. The removal of wigs and gowns (s.26 *YJCEA*)
The court can dispense with the wearing of wigs and gowns

by the judge and by legal representatives in cases where child witnesses are concerned (Para 5.58).

5. Giving evidence-in-chief by pre-recorded video tape (s.27 YJCEA)

A video-recorded interview can take the place of a witness's evidence-in-chief (which is when a young person answers questions asked by the lawyer representing the party which called them to the stand). The video may be recorded at the beginning of the investigation or at a later stage in accordance with the Guidance (*Achieving Best Evidence in Criminal Proceedings*). The video recording normally forms the whole of a witness's evidence in chief, and will be watched by the witness before cross-examination takes place. The witness will normally have had an opportunity to see the recording on a previous occasion too, in order to refresh his or her memory in preparation for the trial (Paras 5.59-5.69).

6. Video recorded cross-examination or re-examination (s.28 YJCEA)

When a court decides that a video recording can be used as a witness's main evidence. It may also decide that the witness should be cross-examined before trial, and the cross-examination and the re-examination recorded on video for use at the trial. The cross-examination is not recorded in the physical presence of the defendant, although he or she has to be able to see and hear the cross-examination and be able to communicate with his or her lawyer. The recording may or may not take place in the physical presence of a judge or magistrate and the defence and prosecution legal representatives. However, a judge or magistrate has to control the proceedings and be able to see or hear the witness being cross-examined and communicate with anyone who is in the room with the witness. Depending on age and vulnerability, young witnesses are often questioned by an intermediary who can explain the questions to them, rather than by the lawyers. Having given recorded evidence it is unlikely that the witness will be called again. Where a parent is concerned that giving evidence in court will have a serious impact on a young person, or that the time taken before the case comes to trial is having a seriously detrimental effect on the child, this is an approach that should be considered.

7. Providing aids to communication (s.30 YJCEA)

The use of communication aids, such as sign and symbol boards, may be authorised to overcome physical difficulties with understanding or answering questions, provided that the communication can be independently verified and understood by the court (Para 5.84).

Note: The YJCEA also makes provision for child witnesses to undergo pre-trial cross-examination or re-examination by videotape or to give evidence through an intermediary, but at the time of writing, neither of these provisions were in force.

COURT WITNESS SUPPORTERS

A court witness supporter can be anyone known to the witness who is not a party to the proceedings and has no detailed knowledge of the evidence in the case. It could, therefore, be a youth worker. The role of the court witness supporter is to provide emotional support and help reduce the witness's anxiety and stress by sitting near the witness in court or near them while giving evidence by live link.

MAIN CONCERNS FOR YOUNG PEOPLE

There are certain issues that are generally of concern to young people giving evidence[1].
* being sent to jail or being sent away;
* being 'got-at' by the defendant or his supporters;
* the family being angry with them;
* people shouting at them in court;
* not understanding the questions;
* not being believed;
* speaking in front of strangers;
* not understanding what they are meant to do in court;
* crying whilst giving evidence;
* needing to go to the toilet;
* being afraid to tell everything;
* having their name in the newspaper;
* the Defendant being sent to prison.

Also, children may ask questions such as:
* What will happen when they get out?
* What if they are found not guilty?

Children and young people may assume that the lawyers and others involved in the court process know the answers to the questions being asked. The young person may think that there are 'right' and 'wrong' answers and be afraid of giving the 'wrong answer'. They need to be told that except for the Defendant, people at court do not know what happened because they were not there. They need to hear what happened from witnesses who should tell them everything they remember, even little things that they might not think are important.

Young people may be afraid to disagree with adults, on the assumption that adults are more knowledgable than children. Young people should be told that it is perfectly acceptable for them to disagree and to contradict the questioner. A potential witness should be reminded he or she does not have to please the questioner.

Young people may be afraid to tell the whole truth if they think it puts them in a bad light. They may be worried that they will be asked about under-age drinking, playing truant or other similar things. Youth workers or other persons working with young witnesses should explain to them that they must tell the truth about everything, that they are not on trial themselves and the court will not punish them for such acts. Leaving out information can cast doubt on their evidence.

Young people may try to answer questions that they do not understand. They should be told that in court adults are likely to use words and questions that young people may find difficult to understand. In particular, the lawyer may use complex English and ask a number of questions all at once. The young person should be told that in such instances they will not get into trouble if they tell the court that they have not understood the question well enough. Quite often, if the young person says this, the judge or magistrate will direct the lawyer to ask the question in a more simple way.

Children may be concerned that their parents or carers will be present in court and there are things that they would not want them to hear or would not feel comfortable saying in front of them. This needs to be explored sensitively with a young person. A child must have an appropriate adult with them when giving evidence. In the Youth Court, a Witness Service volunteer can accompany a child instead of a parent, but only with the prior consent of the court. Sometimes, a court may prefer the presence of an independent supporter rather than a parent for fear that the presence of the parent will inhibit the child giving evidence.

FOOTNOTE:

1. See *Volunteers in the MCWS* Handout 16 which contains a number of helpful responses to issues that worry child witnesses, See also *Vulnerable Witnesses – A Police Service Guide* (Home Office and ACPO Guide 2001).

Index

Index cont'd

Acts and Regulations

Cases

Alfred v Nacano [1987] IRLR 292 p.3

D v D [1991] 2 All ER 648 p.2

Fowles v Bedfordshire County Council [1996] ELR 51 p.2

Fraser v Evans [1969] 1 QB 349 p.34

Gillick v West Norfolk and Wisbech Area Health Authority and the Department of Health and Social Security [1985] 3 All ER 402 p.4

Hill v Ellis [1983] 1 All ER 667 p.90

Lister and others v Hesley Hall Ltd [2001] 2 FLR 307 p.3, p.4

Mason v Essex County Council (unreported) 29 March 1988 p.3, p.4

R (on the application of B) v London Borough of Merton [2003] EWCH 1689 p.79

R (on application of J) v Caerphilly [2005] EWHC 586 (admin) [2005] All ER (D) 94 (April) per Munby J p.73

R v Rahman [1985] 81 Cr App Rep 349 p.2